Drogheda

£20.00

A NEW DAY DAWNING

A Portrait of Ireland in 1900

Dedication:
To Greta, Tara and Jason, and to my parents, Alice and Tom Mulhall

A NEW DAY DAWNING

A Portrait of Ireland in 1900

DANIEL MULHALL

The Collins Press

Published in 1999 by
The Collins Press,
West Link Park,
Doughcloyne,
Wilton,
Cork

© 1999 Daniel Mulhall

British Library Cataloguing in Publication data.

Typesetting by Red Barn Publishing, Skeagh, Skibbereen, Co. Cork

Jacket design by Upper Case Ltd., Cork

ISBN: 1-898256-65-9

Picture credits
The publishers and author would like to thank all of those who gave permission for the reproduction of the photographs in this book. With the exception of those listed below, all photographs are courtesy of The National Library of Ireland and come mainly from their Lawrence and Poole collections.
'Buckingham Street Fire Station', page 71, courtesy of Jane Lynch; 'All-Ireland Hurling Final', page 75, courtesy of The British Library, London; 'Two forms of early two-wheeled transport', page 77, courtesy of the Crerar/Chester-Walsh families, Drogheda, reproduction by Maxwell Picture Agency Ltd., Dublin; 'A Revivalist Preacher', page 130, courtesy of Michael Tutty and the Old Dublin Society; 'A young James Joyce', page 149, courtesy of Harley K. Croessmann Collection of James Joyce, Special Collections, Morris Library, Southern Illinois University of Carbondale; 'Irish regiments serving in the Boer War', page 181, courtesy of the Director, National Army Museum, London; 'Patrick Street, Cork', page 182, courtesy of *The Examiner*, Cork; 'Irish Guards regiment', pages 185–185, courtesy of Regimental Headquarters, Irish Guards, London.

Contents

ACKNOWLEDGEMENTS

PREFACE *by J.J. Lee*

CHAPTER 1

Century's End   *1*

CHAPTER 2

1900: How Ireland's Twentieth Century Began   *17*

CHAPTER 3

A Very Different Ireland: How People Lived at the Turn of the Century   *43*

CHAPTER 4

Nationalist Ireland at the Turn of the Century   *87*

CHAPTER 5

Irish Unionism at the Centuries' Crossroads   *123*

CHAPTER 6

The Dawn of Achievement for Irish Literature   *147*

CHAPTER 7

Fin de Siècle: the Turn-of-the-Century World   *175*

CHAPTER 8

Then and Now: Another Century Ends   *197*

FOOTNOTES   *215*

BIBLIOGRAPHY   *225*

INDEX   *233*

Acknowledgements

The idea of writing a book on turn-of-the-century Ireland came to me in the very early days of 1997. This was a particularly busy period for me professionally and, for a time, I wondered if I would be able to sustain the energy and dedication required to complete the project. I owe a lot to my wife, Greta, and my children, Tara and Jason, for responding with enthusiasm to the idea of my writing a book, instead of undertaking an exotic journey or organising a big party, to mark the arrival of a new millennium. They never ceased to be supportive of my efforts even when the combination of work pressures, research and writing made for an unsociable regime.

In a sense, of course, this book has been an exotic journey, one that has taken me back some twenty years to when I was a postgraduate student at University College Cork and acquired an interest in W.B. Yeats and George Russell (AE). It was not so much their writings that caught my eye, although I still read Yeats with immense pleasure, but rather the nationalist views these writers expressed during the 1890s and in the first decade of the twentieth century that drew me to them. Theirs was an expansive brand of nationalism that, as someone schooled during the 1950s and 1960s in what I now know to be the Irish Ireland tradition, I hardly recognised.

I have an early childhood memory of standing in the bitter cold on the Quay in Waterford City with my father, sometime in the early 1960s, attending the unveiling of a monument erected by the National Graves Association in memory of those who had lost their lives in the struggle for Irish freedom. The monument still stands on the spot where, as a young boy, I first saw it all those years ago. Directly across the road is the Granville Hotel, the birthplace of the Young Irelander, Thomas Francis Meagher. The lobby of the hotel contains a large Victorian clock which was presented in the 1890s to Lord Roberts, hero of those great British Imperial adventures, the Indian Mutiny, the Afghan Wars and the Boer War. Such is the diverse sweep of our complicated past.

Today, the 1960s monument looks a little forlorn, standing in a car park along the banks of the River Suir. There is something about it that must make the late twentieth-century motorists who drive past each day assume it to be a piece of devotional sculpture. One might expect the plinth to carry a figure of a pikeman, as the 1798 monuments erected around the country at the turn of the last century invariably do, or indeed of that monumental sculptor's son, Patrick Pearse. Instead, it is a statue of Christ that crowns this nationalist monument from my boyhood. If this now seems decidedly odd, it caused not a ripple in the early 1960s. In the nationalism I ingested from the Christian Brothers, religion, language and politics were deeply intertwined. It was the martyrdom of the men of 1916, the sacrifice of 'Father Murphy of old Kilcormack' and the devout 'Croppy Boy' that stilled my childish play. Catholic piety, interest in the Irish language and commitment to Gaelic Games formed the pillars of the ideal of Irish manhood to which my contemporaries and I were urged to aspire. Against these pillars, Samson-like, pushed the subversive influences of popular music and the rebellious youth culture of the 1960s. To be the subject of these competing influences was a formative experience. It was good to have a strong, if conservative, image of Ireland with which to wrestle. I now cast a kinder eye on the 'nets' of religion, nationality and language than I did when I first encountered them in the 1960s.

Yeats and AE had no place in the version of nationalism I picked up as a child. When, much later, I became familiar with their turn-of-the-century aspirations for Ireland's future, not to mention the intellectual arguments that raged about Ireland's identity, this taught me that the nationalist tradition to which I belonged was a more complex phenomenon than the orthodoxies of the 1960s, epitomised by RTE's 1966 Easter Rising drama series, *Insurrection*,

ACKNOWLEDGEMENTS

with its image of insurgents saying the rosary before entering the fray, made it out to be. The fact that both Yeats and AE grew to be deeply disenchanted with the evolution of nationalist Ireland interested me and I was keen to understand the roots and significance of this disenchantment. It was usually attributed to the poets' natural inability to accommodate themselves to the workaday realities of political life. I was left, however, with an abiding impression that there was something special about turn-of-the-century Ireland which was lost almost as soon as the new century found its feet. In a sense, therefore, this book has been gestating for more than 20 years. It has taken a millennium to release it from captivity.

There is another way in which this book has been a journey back in time. I had not been inside the National Library of Ireland since I was a postgraduate student. Over the last two years, this wonderful institution became my haunt on Saturday mornings and on the odd weekday evening when competing commitments permitted. Many thanks are due to Brendan O'Donoghue and his staff at the Library, particularly Gráinne McLoughlin who helped Greta with the photographic research. I also made use of the resources of the National Archives of Ireland and of the Public Library at Dean's Grange, whose staff were helpful and courteous.

Pádraic MacKernan, Noel Fahey, Niall Mac-Monagle, Rory Montgomery, and Owen Dudley-Edwards read and commented on drafts and gave me the confidence to believe I was on the right track and ought to continue. My longtime friend, Pat Cooke, who has an impressive knowledge of this period of Irish history, and of much else besides, deserves special mention for his willingness to discuss my work, even when we were out on a golf course together. Ciaran MacAnally gave me access to his impressive collection of little known books from the turn of the

century. Bobby MacDonagh drew my attention to Percy French's poem about Queen Victoria's 1900 visit to Ireland, which is quoted liberally in Chapter 2. Professor J.J. Lee was unfailingly helpful and full of characteristic wisdom and encouragement when I approached him for advice. Bill Nolan, Paul Murray, Michael Lonergan, Jennifer Laurie and Breda Young assisted me in different ways.

My wife, Greta, proofread every word I wrote with an eagle eye for stylistic frailty and verbal obscurity. She also laboured, with characteristic diligence, to compile the photographs that illustrate this book. Patricia McHugh and Kari Stephenson drew her attention to some useful photographic sources. Michael Tutty went to great trouble to track down a photograph belonging to his late father. Our friend from our days in New Delhi, Colin Partridge, helped with photographic research in London.

I am always amused by the author's standard, and it seems to me unnecessary, statement that those who have helped are not responsible for errors of fact or omission, as if anyone could ever reasonably be deemed culpable in such circumstances. Nonetheless, in case such a disclaimer might somehow prove necessary, I make it now.

A final word of thanks is due to W.B. Yeats and James Joyce for writing the words that drew my attention to the turn of the century, a period whose appeal for me continued to grow the more deeply I explored it. Our two greatest twentieth century writers have also been a fruitful source of apt quotation. It will be a loss for me when, millennium bug permitting, they become, on New Year's Day 2000, writers from 'the last century'.

DANIEL MULHALL
EDINBURGH, AUGUST 1999

Preface

PROFESSOR J.J. LEE

The end of the century naturally fosters reflection on what life was like at the turn of the last century, and to what extent it has changed since then. Into what sort of Ireland were our grandfathers and grandmothers, or even, for some of us, our fathers and mothers, born? How different was life for them then? Would they feel at home in our world, or aliens in it? And how would we have felt in theirs?

That last question can probably never be fully answered, because we would have to shed so many of our assumptions about the nature and meaning of life to enter completely into earlier mindsets. But it is part of the charm of history to inspire us to make the imaginative leap to feel as far as humanly possible what it must have been like to be alive in another time. It takes no common historian, however, to recapture the ethos of a bygone age. It is, if anything, even harder to recreate an age still reasonably close to us, compared with one further away, because so much of it seems so familiar that we don't realise how different it really was. The half familiar is often more difficult to understand than the totally different. It was therefore a happy conjuncture that Daniel Mulhall should have decided to devote time to such an enterprise, bringing to it not only the training of an historian, but the discerning eye of a professional diplomat, experienced in the ways of the wider world, and a deep love of literature, which provides a window into the soul of the Ireland of a century ago. This potent blend of qualities has enabled him to compose an enthralling account of the Ireland of 1900.

The visit of Queen Victoria in April 1900, the first opportunity her Hibernian subjects had of feasting their eyes upon their monarch for a generation, provides Mulhall with the opportunity, which he seizes with relish, for a sardonic survey of the propaganda techniques of both British and Irish nationalists competing for popular support in Ireland, and for observation of the fawning skills among the goodly flock of the social climbers of their day. The visit was ostensibly to celebrate the Act of Union of a century before, in the course of which the official mind managed to persuade itself that Ireland had flourished as never before, but in reality it was a manoeuvre to counter a wave of anti-British feeling provoked by the Boer War, and to promote recruitment for military service under South African skies among potential Irish cannon-fodder.

It is one of the many strengths of Mulhall's approach that he pays due attention to the role of the army in Ireland, so often neglected, including the activities of the recruiting officer and, in this case, of the anti-recruiting officer, incarnated in the persona of none other than Maud Gonne MacBride herself. The spectacular public profile of Maud Gonne, now in the noon-day glory of that translucent beauty that transfixed Yeats among a host of others, itself sufficed to ensure high publicity for her anti-war activities.

There were at the time 27,000 soldiers stationed in Ireland, in addition to 12,000 armed members of the Royal Irish Constabulary, leaving Ireland much the most densely militarised area in the British Empire in peacetime. The Intelligence Reports of the R.I.C. are an endless source of fascination for students of the intestinal intricacies and inanities of daily life. There is scarcely a comparable source in the rest of western Europe, one of the manifold blessings of the Pax Britannica being a police force that kept every politically deviant activity in the country under surveillance, as if subversion were simmering behind every hedge, bestowing to posterity a rich chronicle of the activities of the politically incorrect of the time, which the author uses to great effect. And the incongruities are memorably caught in the marvellous vignette of Kerry recruits to the British army cheering for the Boers as they marched off to fight them!

Mulhall's treatment of crime, another subject much neglected in conventional accounts, helps remind us that the R.I.C. was essentially a para-military organisation, for ordinary crime was on a scale inconceivably minuscule by today's standards. The entire prison population in 1899 amounted to 322, only 19 of them women. It is indeed a vanished world.

The Catholic Church exerted much more influence than today. Or did it? Those who take the view that the Church could lead only where its flock wished to go will find some supporting evidence here. The Lenten Pastorals of 1900, for instance, fulminated against the evils of drink. Despite the remarkable work of the Pioneer Total Abstinence Association, the evils of drink would continue to sustain a redoubtable resistance against the clerical assailants. If Church influence were to be measured by the success of its campaign against alcohol, its hold on the country's convictions might seem fragile indeed!

Rummaging with an eye for a challenging quotation through a wide variety of sources, from landlord memoirs to hotel menus, from Joyce to journalists, Mulhall evokes the striking mixture of wealth and poverty, of credulity and cynicism, that constituted turn-of-the-century Ireland. Wages and salaries, housing conditions, transport conditions – it could be quicker to get through Dublin then than now – school conditions, and the role of the pawn-shop, all come under his roving and probing gaze.

The reader will note the extent to which, despite the extent of resistance to English power among many of the Irish, that resistance occurred almost wholly within English terms of intellectual reference, except for the language and sporting revivals. This was probably inevitable in the circumstances. One will be naturally tempted to ask, how much change did Independence bring? Mulhall does not shirk the challenge of asking the question, sketching the Ireland of today, as he sees it, to identify degrees of continuity and of change between the Ireland of a century ago and our Ireland. Recent change has been so rapid that it moves him to ask what is Irish in today's world? Have we now become 'Europeans' since our entry to the European Economic Community in 1973? If so, how?

Will the historian a century hence, looking back at the turn of the millennium, detect equally striking changes over the intervening century? What are such changes likely to be?

If there is one lesson to be learned from contemplating the condition of Ireland in 1900, as so graphically portrayed by Mulhall's vivid strokes and delicate touches, it is that nothing is written in stone. Anyone accurately sketching in 1900 a portrait of Ireland a century later, to say nothing of the intervening vicissitudes, would have probably been mocked for their pains. There is no final condition, unless we are the last generation on earth. We cannot know what changes the future will bring. All we can surmise with reasonable confidence is that it will bring change.

A New Day Dawning prompts us to wonder how much of that change will lie within our own grasp to shape and mould, or how much of it is 'inevitable' – and if so, why? How much will be generated internally, how much imported? If it is imported, from where? Will the Ireland of a century hence exist as anything more than a geographical expression? How far will it be able to say 'We did it our way'? How far will it say 'We made our own history', or will it have to say 'History happened to us'?

One thing is clear. The historian of 2100 will be immensely grateful to Dan Mulhall for providing such a guide to Ireland at both the beginning and the end of the twentieth century. But he, or more likely she, will be hard put to match the breadth of knowledge, the range of interests, and the expository skills that go into making this a splendid survey that deserves a wide and reflective readership.

CHAPTER I

Century's End

And yet, unless my senses deceive me, the old centuries had, and have, powers of their own which mere 'modernity' cannot kill.

From Bram Stoker's *Dracula* which scored a great popular success when it was published in paperback in 1900.

I preferred to think that the sudden emotion that now came to me, the sudden certainty that Ireland was to be like soft wax for years to come, was a moment of supernatural insight.

W.B. Yeats, 'Ireland after Parnell'.[1]

This period, and indeed the decade of years which followed the political reunion, saw the sowing of ideas out of which an entirely different Ireland came into being ... the effect of the movement was to heighten, deepen and make still more acute, the national consciousness of the separate and distinct individuality of Ireland, and its inevitable tendency was to seek for the determination of the spirit it aroused in the completest form of independent government.

A contemporary's view of Ireland's transformation at the turn of the century.[2]

It is a dark, moonless night in late December. Rain is falling heavily outside and the wind gusts noisily through the winter trees. It has turned cold and the weather forecast suggests that there may be snow on the way. This could even be the first white millennium in ages. The date is 31 December 1999 and the world is full of mixed emotions, torn between nostalgia and the enthusiasm that new departures bring. All is set for the biggest departure anyone can recall. Tomorrow begins another year. It opens a new century. The long-anticipated third Christian millennium is about to get underway. Inside, the New Year's Eve celebrations are in full swing, the house is warm, the food and drink are plentiful. A typical late twentieth-century scene unfolds. Upstairs, the family computer is nonchalantly doing what it always does, playing screen savers, its clock quietly counting out the year's remaining hours, minutes and seconds. At a minute to midnight, its electronic forward planner begins to panic as it wonders what year comes next. 00 is what the dashboard says, but that cannot be right, or is it? The millennium bug has bitten. The remedial software which tells the machine that there is a future after 99 has not been properly installed. We're braced for the kind of time travel adventure that even Jules Verne, that late nineteenth-century creator of science fiction, could scarcely have imagined.

As far as the computer is concerned, it must be 1900, and it is! Painless time travel brings us back one hundred years in the space of a millisecond. Now that we have arrived in 1900, what kind of world greets us and how stands Ireland in this, the last year of the nineteenth century, or is it the first year of the twentieth century? The chapters that follow set out to tell this tale, but as a popular history rather than a work of science fiction. They provide a snapshot of Ireland the last time a century came to a close, touching on those things that delineate any slice of time – the country's politics; its economic circumstances; its way of life; its cultural and literary achievements; its sports and pastimes; the crimes that were committed. The aim is to afford late twentieth-century readers, and their successors in the new millennium, a clearer picture of what life was like for those Irish people who experienced the birth of the twentieth century, wedged, as we are, between the achievements of one century and the expectations of another.

1

The time traveller bound for New Year's Day 1900 arrives on a Monday. The streets of Dublin are unusually quiet. The traditional Lord Mayor's Parade does not take place this year as the nationalist-controlled Dublin Corporation has decided to transfer the festivities to St Patrick's Day, thus inaugurating a modern Irish tradition. In 1900, there is little turn-of-the-century enthusiasm. There is much dispute over when centuries end and new ones begin. People seem reluctant to let go of the nineteenth century which has been a good one for those who think in centuries. Europe has enjoyed a largely peaceful century. After Napoleon had been dispatched from Waterloo in 1815 to his exile on St Helena, the continent settled down to a long period of relative calm, punctuated by sporadic outbreaks of revolution accompanying the slow advance of liberal democratic ideas and steady economic progress founded on increasing industrialisation. By the end of the nineteenth century, Europe had successfully spread itself across Africa and Asia as an imperial colossus, even if it had lost its old Empire in the Americas, where Spain's defeat

O'Connell Bridge, Dublin. At the turn of the century the city had an extensive tramways network. The system was fully electrified by 1901.

*Grafton Street, Dublin. Around 1900, Trinity
College, seen here on the right, was the scene
of periodic clashes between Unionist students
celebrating British victories in the Boer War
and local Nationalist residents.*

in the Spanish-American War of 1898 foreshadowed a twentieth-century future dominated by the economic and military might of the United States.

By the turn of the century, Europe's imperial powers were beginning to try each other's patience. England and France, who would become allies in the new century's wars, were big rivals as the 1800s gave way to the 1900s. Imperial Germany, still a young state just thirty years after its unification, was a restive power, dissatisfied with its share of the spoils and eager to make up for lost time as a world force. Its ambitious Emperor, Wilhelm II, had high hopes for himself and his country in the new century. The naval bill passed by the Reichstag in 1900 turned out to be a foretaste of things to come. How to cope with Germany's new-found might would become one of the twentieth-century's great conundrums, the working out of which was to cost many millions of lives.

While late Victorians drew great pride from the accomplishments of nineteenth-century civilisation, the turn-of-the-century world now comes across as a strangely deprived and backward place. Material conditions and attitudes have altered out of all recognition in the interim. Any late Victorian carried forward ten decades by the millennium bug would no doubt be astounded to discover a world of jet travel, computer technology and worldwide communications. Though perhaps acquainted with the wonders of the infant cinema, our turn-of-the-century time traveller would be dazzled by the phenomenon of moving pictures in every family home and by the wealth of household appliances found in late twentieth-century homes. There would be equal amazement at the advances registered in medical science, which

has conquered a range of previously life-threatening illnesses and relieved the discomforts of the plethora of lesser ailments that infest the pages of so many nineteenth-century letters and diaries.

Set apart from the European mainstream, Ireland had endured a miserable nineteenth century. The Great Famine had caused the country's population to plummet alarmingly. This dramatic depopulation was still in train at the turn of the century, even if the rate of decline had, mercifully, been checked. Ireland as a whole had failed to benefit from the industrial revolution whose full impact was felt only in the northeastern counties of Antrim and Down. Agriculture suffered from periodic crop failures which were potentially disastrous for the large numbers engaged in near-subsistence farming. In 1900, the country's economy remained stubbornly stagnant. There were all too many Irishmen and women firmly stuck on the bread line from which emigration appeared to offer the only prospect of release.

Politically, Ireland's nineteenth century had also been a mess. The country's quasi-independent status had been lost with the passage of the Act of Union in 1800. Throughout the nineteenth century, Irish nationalists mounted a number of imposing constitutional challenges to the political *status quo* – in addition to a few fairly feeble insurrectionary ones – aimed at restoring what had been taken away in 1800. Nationalist claims were rebuffed by successive British Governments with the aid of those in Ireland who were committed to the continuation of the country's constitutional link with Britain. The most sustained, and effective, Irish political campaign of the nineteenth century, orchestrated by the charismatic Charles Stewart

Main Street, Gorey, Co. Wexford. A typical market town of the period, totally free of traffic congestion.

Listowel, Co. Kerry. A cattle fair in the main square.

Parnell in the 1880s, scored a major break-through when, under Gladstone's leadership, the Liberals, one of Britain's two great political parties, gave their backing to Home Rule.

There are strong arguments for regarding the death of Parnell in 1891, this tragic tale of a life ended early in personal heartbreak and political disappointment, as the true terminus of Ireland's nineteenth century. The achievement of Parnell's movement, which represented a culmination of the patterns of political life that characterised nineteenth-century Ireland, had been to bind together various elements – parliamentary agitation, popular discontent, agrarian upheaval and radical separatist sentiment – into an effective whole. At the height of his powers, Parnell appealed to, and utilised, these strands but, great though his appeal was, his legacy turned out to be one of profound division. Parnell's Party splintered rancorously as a result of the scandals surrounding his affair with a married woman. His followers banded into irreconcilable factions, squabbling relentlessly in the wreckage of parliamentary nationalism, thereby frittering away the political influence they had wielded during the 1880s. The upshot of all of this was that the 1890s were traumatic years for Irish nationalists. The Home Rule Bill was blocked by the conservative-controlled House of Lords when it eventually passed through the Commons in 1893. This left the Irish parliamentarians in disarray. Their Liberal allies were divided and then succumbed to a crushing electoral defeat in 1895, which saw a Government hostile to nationalists securely installed in power in London.

The period between 1891 and 1912 comes across as something of an interregnum between Ireland's nineteenth and twentieth centuries, but what an interregnum! It was an era that bred the people who conducted the Easter Rising and the War of Independence which transformed Ireland. This period was equally fruitful on the creative front, producing some of the most highly-regarded writers of the twentieth century. By 1900, there were strong signs of national revival in the air, but parliamentary nationalism was no longer alone at the helm. The rifts within the Irish Party, which stubbornly refused to heal, severely retarded the cause of Home Rule and permitted alternative forms of political activity to assert themselves. Fanned by the outbreak of the Boer War, a more restless brand of nationalism was making its presence felt. The new nationalism of the period had more of an urban face and was based primarily on concerns about Ireland's cultural identity rather than on a strict sense of economic and political grievance. The Gaelic Athletic Association, the Gaelic League, with its crusade to revive the Irish language, and the Irish literary movement all contributed to this potent idea of a culturally-distinctive Irishness. While not at first overtly political, this image of Ireland as a cultural nation would not easily be reconciled with provincial status within an English-dominated constitutional union.

From 1895 onwards, the London Government was in the hands of conservatives deeply wedded to the Union and instinctively hostile to the aspirations of Irish nationalism. Paradoxically, this combination of conservatism and unionism created a reform-minded strategy which produced a land act in 1896, fundamental reform of local government in 1898 and a new Department of Agriculture and Technical Instruction armed with what was, for its time, an impressively interventionist mandate. Conservative-inspired reform, with its designs on 'killing Home Rule with kindness', alarmed

Irish nationalists, who were not prepared to see Home Rule lie down and die just yet.

For many Irish people, the New Year of 1900 was notable for having been declared a Holy Year by the reigning pontiff, Pope Leo the Thirteenth. The Roman Catholic Church had been the great winner from Ireland's nineteenth-century ordeal. Its position had improved steadily throughout the century with Catholic emancipation in 1829, the disestablishment of the Church of Ireland in 1869, a series of concessions to Catholic thinking on education and a relentless rise in the Church's prestige, influence and social standing. It had seen off the threat of revolutionary politics and successfully turned its back on a scandal-ridden Parnell at the height of his power. At the turn of the century, the Irish bishops were comfortable with parliamentary nationalism and satisfied with their capacity to wield significant influence at the heart of Britain's worldwide Empire.

Father Tom Laverty had a motto for the twentieth century which read:

' 'Twill be all the same in a hundred years.'[3]

Inscribed in large Gothic letters, the priest's legend hung above the mantlepiece at his home in Kilronan, a fictional village in the west of Ireland. A character in the novel, *My New Curate,* which appeared on the threshold of the new century, Father Laverty, like other clerical figures in the works of Canon Sheehan, epitomised the conservative ethos of the Irish Catholic Church. The evidence of the last hundred years has dashed the priest's confidence in an unchanging society. One hundred years on, there is relatively little that has stayed the same, in Ireland or in the wider world. It is, to say the least, unlikely that any late twentieth-century cleric, or laymen, in fact or in fiction, would dare to make a prediction about the first century of the third millennium akin to Father Laverty's century-old motto.

The years around 1900 were ones when the conservative and deferential Ireland depicted in Canon Sheehan's novels was – Father Laverty's motto notwithstanding – already coming under threat of change. While 'the bishops and the party' propagated an essentially conservative philosophy, there were also plenty of proponents of change on the loose. Horace Plunkett and his followers in the cooperative movement were determined to engineer social and economic progress. Their efforts met with much scepticism, and even resistance, from clerical and parliamentary quarters where there was a strong stake in the established social and economic order that the cooperative movement sought to change. Advanced nationalists, impatient with the relative quiescence of parliamentary nationalism, were eager to create a new Ireland in the new century. The Gaelic League fed the idealism of a new generation of activists weary of what they saw as the jaded actualities of late Victorian Ireland. Meanwhile, the nascent labour movement drew inspiration from outside of Ireland for its challenge to existing economic inequalities. In rural Ireland, the unfinished business of the land war retained the potential for a radical confrontation between tenant and landlord interests. Even within Unionist Ireland, which inevitably possessed a deeper affinity with the *status quo*, the impact of economic and social change was capable of cracking the conservative façade presented by mainstream Unionist politicians.

2

The approach of a new millennium will inevitably make many people want to look back

9

GRAND PARADE, CORK. 5252 W.L.

*Grand Parade, Cork. A Temperance Rally,
which attracted a huge crowd. Temperance was
a major issue for both sides of the political
divide in Ireland. Temperance candidates
scored some successes in the local elections of
1899. The Pioneer Total Abstinence
Association was founded in the same year.*

and reflect on the passage of historical time and its significance. The period around the year 1900 is an appealing one in which to anchor such a retrospective for, millennium fever notwithstanding, centuries are a more compelling historical phenomenon. To go back to the year 1000 would involve returning to a world so radically different from our own as to undermine the value of comparison. The sweep of time represented by a millennium is too vast to be meaningful or manageable. Although more than an average lifetime away, 1900 is not so remote from our experience. There will be a number of people capable of reading this book who were already born in the year 1900. The parents of older readers may well have been born in the last century and many others living today will have memories of grandparents or great-grandparents who had nineteenth-century birth certificates.

The second reason for choosing to probe the period around 1900 is its pertinence in an Irish context. While the country had all of two decades to go before its achievement of independence, 1900 may be seen as a time when today's Ireland was being born, a time when the seeds of its subsequent development, and divisions, were being sown. In subjecting this particular time to such special scrutiny, this work seeks an understanding of the realities of Irish life a generation before the achievement of independence. Politically, at the turn of the century, there were three separate Irelands. First, there was the official Ireland, centred around the British administration in Dublin Castle and British interests in Ireland. Second, there was Unionist Ireland. For a variety of reasons, Irish Unionists viewed a continuation of the Union between Britain and Ireland as an imperative, and were alarmed at any prospect of having to

live in a self-governing state with an inevitable Catholic majority. Though closely associated with, and politically dependent on, the British presence in Ireland, Irish Unionists had interests of their own which did not always coincide with, and could even oppose, those of London. Nationalist Ireland comprised the great majority of the island's population which defined itself in terms of its opposition to the political and economic ascendancy of the Protestant and British-orientated minority that had prevailed in Ireland for over two hundred years.

Ireland in 1900 stood at something of a crossroads where different political tendencies thrown up during the 1890s converged and clashed. At the turn of the century, this intersection was crowded with the competing claims of parliamentary nationalism, the cultural revival and advanced nationalism on one side of the constitutional divide, with liberal unionism and conservative unionism occupying the other side. For its part, Ulster was marked by very different circumstances and their related tensions. The working out of these competing forces, which went on well beyond 1900, proceeded to shape twentieth-century Ireland. While the defining years in modern Irish history were still more than a decade in the future, the battle lines of the revolutionary upheaval were already discernible as the century began.

This book looks into the heart of an Ireland peopled by many memorable characters. Some of the central figures in the drama that was 1900 have fallen into obscurity as later developments buried the preoccupations that made them prominent at the height of their renown. A number of the leading Irish parliamentarians of the period fall into this category – Tim Harrington, William O'Brien and John Dillon to name a few. The reputations of other turn-of-the-century parliamentarians have fared better; John Redmond[4] because of the prominence he enjoys within the modern, 'revisionist'[5] view of Irish history as the last leader of the Home Rule movement, and Tim Healy as a vivid character in the compelling and enduring drama of Parnell's fall.[6]

This turn-of-the-century story also has its fair share of characters to whom the twentieth century has been kind. In 1900, W.B. Yeats and Maud Gonne already enjoyed considerable renown, and this has deepened as their images have seeped into the collective memory of the twentieth century, through the medium of Yeats' poems. There were others, James Joyce and Patrick Pearse are examples, who, though quite obscure when the century began, gained rich reputations as its years unfolded. As with every year, however, the bulk of its *dramatis personae,* those who lived their lives beyond the realm of public attention, can scarcely be retrieved from the obscurity to which the lack of surviving testimony about their trials and achievements condemns them.

3

With the twentieth century soon to slip away into the past, it will cease to be talked about in the present tense, and will join the parade of centuries that make up our history. The arrival of a new millennium is bound to alter the way in which we view the past. Perspectives will shift and slices of time will come to be viewed differently. As the twentieth century becomes the preserve of memory and archive, current perceptions of the nineteenth century will undergo a corresponding change. It will seem far more remote than it is today. No longer will

it be 'the last century', but a less accessible page in the catalogue of human experience, lacking any direct chronological connection with the contemporary world. Its influence on the modern world will remain, but it is destined to seem less relevant to those whose experience will increasingly be a twenty-first-century one.

There are those who will question an arbitrary focus on what was, in one sense, just an ordinary year like any other. Why, it may be asked, should the point of transition from one century to another be regarded as having any special significance? It may be pointed out that the very concept of a century is a relatively modern creation[7] and that, in practice, nothing of substance changes between the last year of one century and the first year of the next! And yet, we do measure time in years, decades and centuries. While the year is the key unit of measurement of our individual lives, centuries are crucial to the way we process the past. For non-historians, the century is a vital tool in situating events. Many people, with little facility for recalling precise dates, would know that Saint Patrick came to Ireland in the fifth century, that the Viking incursions occurred in the eighth and ninth, that the Normans came in the twelfth, and Cromwell in the seventeenth. The Penal Laws are indelibly associated with the eighteenth century and the Great Famine dominates the nineteenth. In the wider European context, the renaissance is seen as a fifteenth- and sixteenth-century phenomenon and the enlightenment an eighteenth-century one.

Some may question the wisdom of devoting an entire book to such a short period of time. There are various ways of coming to terms with the past. In opting for a tight chronological focus, I have drawn inspiration from Norman

Davies' *Europe: a history* in which he observes that 'history can be written at any magnification. One can write the history of the universe on a single page or the life cycle of a mayfly in forty volumes'.[8] At the end of each chapter, Davies includes short time capsules which help to make sense of the vast sweep of time being covered. The pages that follow utilise a turn-of-the-century time capsule as a means of understanding a seminal period in modern Irish history between the death of Parnell and the start of the revolutionary decade in 1912.

While a year may seem like an insignificant mark on the vast canvas of decades, centuries and millennia, in fact it confronts us with a sizeable chunk of evidence, too great indeed to be digested in full. To read all of the primary material that exists from the year 1900 would be a well-nigh impossible task and this enforces rigorous selectivity. The existence in 1900 of at least nine Irish daily newspapers, each with its own peculiar window on the world, testifies to the Everest of evidence waiting to be climbed for the sake of the view to be had from the right lookout point.

4

There is, of course, a sense in which the choice of the year 1900 may be seen as an arbitrary one. In the maelstrom of events that comprise our history, centuries do not necessarily begin on the dates dictated by the calendar's convenience. It is the historians of the future who will determine which significant date is to mark the true beginning of the epoch to be called the twenty-first century. With good reason, European historians tend to think of the nineteenth century as having begun with the outbreak of the French Revolution in 1789. Events in revolutionary Paris ushered in new political concepts that were to work themselves out during the nineteenth century, making it a radically different era from that which came before 1789. The nineteenth century is commonly perceived to have ended in 1914 with the commencement of hostilities in the Great War. If the nineteenth century, with no end-of-term event to bring it to a close before 1914, was thus a long century, the twentieth century may well be seen as having been a short, if decidedly complicated, one. Eric Hobsbawm's masterly survey of twentieth-century history[9] has it lasting a mere 77 years until the end of the Soviet Union's 45-year domination of Eastern Europe in 1991.

Chronological patterns vary in different places. Ireland's eighteenth century can reasonably be said to have ended conveniently in 1800 with the passage of the Act of Union, although its most obvious starting point was the Battle of the Boyne in 1690 rather than 1700. In the case of the nineteenth/twentieth centuries, the most logical breakwater is the 1916 Rising, although there are competing possibilities. The fall of Parnell, which brought an end to the most potent nineteenth-century effort to unravel the Act of Union, is an early alternative. The passage of the Third Home Rule Bill in 1912, and the reaction it provoked in Ulster with the establishment of the Ulster Volunteers, has claims to being considered the true harbinger of Ireland's twentieth century. 1920, with the passage of the Government of Ireland Act, and 1921, with the negotiation of the Anglo-Irish Treaty, are plausible alternatives viewed respectively from northern and southern perspectives.

As a contender for attention, the year 1900 is nowhere in sight. Even students of Irish history might well be hard pressed to cite a significant event from that year. Viewed through the prism of twentieth-century Irish history dominated by the events of the revolutionary decade between 1912 and 1922, 1900 seems a tame starting point, marked principally by developments within the subsequently overshadowed parliamentary tradition with its demand for Home Rule rather than outright independence. Only one of the recent crop of histories of Ireland in the twentieth century chooses 1900 as its starting date.[10] As a result, the first decade and a half of Ireland's twentieth century tends to be passed over in relative silence as a dull prelude to subsequent excitements.

While the year 1900 may have lacked the cataclysmic events associated with subsequent dates, it was, nonetheless, an eventful one. 1900 saw the end of the decade-long split in the Irish Party at Westminster, an event that gave a considerable fillip to parliamentary nationalism. It was also the year when the United Irish League, the last national mass movement in the tradition of Daniel O'Connell's Catholic Association and Parnell's National League, came into its own under the pugnacious leadership of William O'Brien. During 1900, the organisation that later became Sinn Féin was founded. The Irish literary and language movements were growing in influence and achievement, helping to mould a new national consciousness. 1900 saw the appearance of *The Leader* magazine as a mouthpiece of an Irish-Ireland ethos that would go on to dominate popular perceptions of Irish identity for much of the twentieth century. Within unionism, the tradition of constructive unionism, whose reform agenda had the potential to sap the vitality of the demand for Home Rule, began to come under serious fire from more conservative forces within the Irish Unionist community. In 1900, W.B. Yeats believed that 'a new period of political activity' was on the way in Ireland fuelled by urban as opposed to rural discontent.[11] This turned out to be an astute observation. A study of 1900 affords scope for coming to terms with Irish affairs in the late nineteenth and early twentieth centuries without the distractions of dramatic developments that marked such fateful years as 1891, 1913, 1916 or 1921.

Ireland's twentieth century may not end in 1999. Some momentous event lurking in the undergrowth of the early twenty-first century may persuade future historians to fix its starting point in 2005 or 2010. Until then, the year 2000 will retain its symbolic power as a moment of passage, just as the year 1900 did for those who saw it as marking the birth of a new century.

Although this was not obvious to contemporaries, the years around 1900 turned out to be the dawn of a new era in Irish history. Within the space of just over two decades, a political pattern of English domination of Ireland established for more than seven centuries would be successfully reversed. The Irish Ireland that suffered a series of crushing defeats in the seventeenth century would be reborn in the shape of, constitutional niceties aside, an essentially independent Irish State. It was to be a State vastly different, of course, from what might have come into being had Home Rule been granted during the latter part of the nineteenth century. The cultural ferment of turn-of-the-century Ireland made the vital difference. The new day that dawned for Ireland in the twentieth century carried a distinctive turn-of-the-century hallmark whose design is explored in the pages that follow.

15

CHAPTER 2

1900: How Ireland's Twentieth Century Began

Then in 1900, everybody got down off his stilts; henceforth no one went mad; nobody committed suicide; nobody joined the Catholic Church, or if they did I have forgotten. Victorianism had been defeated.

W.B. Yeats[1]

. . . Maud Gonne marches forty thousand children through the streets of Dublin, and in a field beyond Drumcondra, and in the presence of a priest of their church, they swear to cherish towards England until the freedom of Ireland has been won, an undying enmity. How many of these children will carry bomb or rifle when a little under or a little over thirty?

W.B. Yeats

The year 1900 began on a Monday. In Dublin, the weather was bright, sunny and cold. There was little excitement at the idea of a new era getting under way. The newspapers, which sold for one penny, carried no front page headlines marking a momentous date on the calendar. In fact, there were no front page headlines of any description. A century ago, the daily papers were paragons of understatement, their front pages devoted to advertising and devoid of news reports.

This lack of any sense of occasion could be attributed to the fact that the year's significance was disputed. The question of whether 1900 was the last year of the nineteenth century or the first year of the twentieth generated considerable debate.[2] The majority view was that the new century would commence in 1901. John Maynard Keynes, the twentieth-century's most influential economist, then a pupil at Eton, took the alternative view, recording in his diary on the first day of 1900 that 'sentimentally there is much to be said in favour of to-day' as the beginning of the century. Confiding to her private diary on the first day of the year, Queen Victoria recognised 1900 as the beginning of a new century which, no doubt with the Boer War and her own declining health in mind, she approached 'full of anxiety and fear of what may be before us'.[3]

One Irish newspaper wrote of 'the Battle of the Centuries' while another concluded that the debate hinged on whether the early Christians considered Christ to have been born in December of the year 1 A.D. or in the preceding year. *The Dublin Daily Express* concluded that 'custom puts us in the twentieth century while science pens us, not altogether reluctant, in the nineteenth'. In a haughty article published on the second day of the year, *The Irish Times* poked fun at the German Emperor for 'hilariously but unscientifically' declaring 1900 to be the first year of the century. It seems that Germany could hardly wait for the new century to start, while imperial Britain did not want its century of greatness to end.

1. A Royal Visit

Perched on top of Killiney Hill overlooking Dublin Bay, there is an eighteenth-century obelisk that is visible from many of the southern suburbs of Dublin. This stark monument, erected in 1742 as part of a famine relief scheme, stands at the highest point of a public park that carries in its name a reminder of Ireland as it was the last time a century came to a close. In 1900 this amenity was known as Victoria Park and this was the year when Queen Victoria made only the third visit to Ireland of her very long reign. Victoria Park had been acquired in 1887 by the Queen's Jubilee Memorials Association to commemorate the 50th year of her reign. In April 1900, as the recently-commissioned royal yacht, *Victoria and Albert*, sailed into Dublin Bay for the start of the Queen's three-week stay in Ireland, the obelisk in Victoria Park could be seen from the deck of the monarch's vessel. Someone in her party may well have pointed the monument out to the ageing monarch, and recalled its connection with her. There was a fireworks display on Killiney Hill on the evening of her arrival while the Queen was still on board the vessel docked at Kingstown.

For many in turn-of-the-century Ireland, this rare Royal visit was a huge highlight, the year's undoubted centrepiece. For others, the aged Queen's presence in Dublin served as an uncomfortable reminder of the painful calamities that had befallen the Irish people during her reign. It was essential for the British establishment to tread warily between the competing forces of nationalism and unionism. In a burst of doggerel, the popular poet, Percy French, imagines the Queen's after-dinner speech as overheard by Jamesy Murphy, the fictional Deputy-Assistant-Waiter at the Vice-Regal Lodge. The Queen recalls advice she received not to travel to Ireland:

'They was greatly in dread,' sez she,
'I'd be murthered or shot,' sez she,
'As like as not,' sez she.[4]

French's lines manage to conjure up the atmosphere of the period and the political squabbles generated by the Queen's Irish sojourn. He visualises the advice she might have given Lord Zetland before they set out for Ireland:

'Remember and steer,' sez she,
'Uncommonly clear,' sez she.
'I know what you mean,' sez he.
'Up wid the green,' sez he,
'And "God Save the Queen",' sez he.[5]

Throughout Britain, the closing years of the nineteenth century were ones of regal celebration and thanksgiving for the impressive political and economic advances recorded during the Queen's years on the throne. The Queen's jubilees in 1887 and 1897 were marked with displays of patriotic fervour and imperial pomp. Royal appearances in Britain, which were comparatively uncommon by late twentieth-century standards, drew large and enthusiastic crowds. The jubilees gave Irish unionists a pretext for conspicuous displays of loyalty which irked nationalists. One observer described their changed attitude:

With the Queen's jubilee came a change. The city was beflagged with Union Jacks; the fashionable shops, known to enjoy viceregal patronage by the royal arms displayed on their fronts, had special decorations with monograms and mottoes conspicuously mounted, and at night all were brilliantly illuminated. Special trains brought every loyalist in the country up to see the city lights, and the crowds which filled the streets were plain evidence to *The Times, The Irish Times* and *The Daily Express* that the loyalty of the Irish people to the crown had been grossly misrepresented.[6]

Clashes between ebulliently loyal Trinity students and groups of Dublin nationalists became commonplace. Trinity students sometimes forayed to the Mansion House, a bastion of nationalism on Dawson Street, to replace the civic flag with a Union Jack. This invariably sparked a reaction from nationalist elements who were only too glad of the chance to teach the Trinity boys a lesson in street skirmishing. Hot on the heels of the 1897 jubilee came the centenary of the 1798 rebellion which gave nationalists an excuse to flaunt their own political allegiances.

The Royal visit's immediate political purpose was to stem the tide of anti-British feeling generated by the outbreak of the Boer War. As the Marquis of Salisbury remarked, 'no one can suppose that she goes to Ireland for pleasure'.[7] Cadogan, the Lord Lieutenant, assured the Queen, who was known to have had no great warmth of feeling for Ireland, that she would be greeted 'with unbounded loyalty and pleasure',

Royal Carriage passing through the Phoenix Park, Dublin. In April 1900 Queen Victoria paid her third visit to Ireland, as part of an effort to promote army recruitment for the Boer War.

but this reassuring simplification was not the full story.[8]

In nationalist circles, Dublin Corporation's decision, taken by 30 votes to 22 despite the body's nationalist majority, to deliver a 'loyal address' to the visiting sovereign, caused a considerable stir. The prime mover behind the decision was the Lord Mayor of Dublin, Sir Thomas Devereux Pile. Elected as a home ruler, and having been a member of the Wolfe Tone and '98 Martyrs Memorial Committee, Mayor Pile, an English-born fish merchant about whose political views Dublin Castle initially had strong misgivings on account of his association with Fred Allen, a Lancashire man with a Fenian background,[9] had already broken the conventions of nationalist politics by making an official call on the Lord Lieutenant and by failing to keep himself sufficiently aloof from the British administration.

Pile's unpopularity marred Dublin's first ever St Patrick's Day Parade which was 'favoured with charming weather'. The Mayor was hissed by sections of the crowd and had stones thrown at his carriage. There were pro-Boer cheers from sections of the crowd and when a Boer flag was flown it was seized by a mounted policeman and the crowd was baton charged.[10] On the eve of the Queen's arrival, dissenting members of the Corporation provoked renewed political debate, this time about the Act of Union, whose centenary was the ostensible rationale for the visit. They declared that the Union had been 'obtained by fraud and shameful corruption', and that there would be 'neither contentment nor loyalty in this country until our national parliament is restored'.[11] The public gallery was crowded for the debate and those who condemned the Act of Union were loudly cheered.

After heated exchanges, the nationalist motion was carried by 42 votes to nine. Taunts of 'flunkeyism' were levelled at the motion's opponents who complained of its extreme language. As a result, the Royal Visit, though meant as an opportunity to acknowledge Ireland's English connection, was turned into an occasion for underlining nationalist Ireland's undying opposition to the Union between the two islands. Local authorities had become an important new arena within which nationalists could air their political grievances and vaunt their identity. Later in the year, Dublin Corporation moved to confer the freedom of the City on the Boer leader, President Kruger, who was then in exile in Paris. While this bid was ruled out of order on procedural grounds, it further highlighted the Corporation's anti-establishment credentials. Other local authorities did succeed in honouring Kruger. There were frequent disputes because of decisions by local authorities to fly nationalist flags on public buildings in defiance of local unionist opinion.

The Royal visit posed a dilemma for nationalist parliamentarians who could hardly warm to it. At the same time, they had no desire to give offence to the aged monarch. To mark the visit, there were a number of Royal pronouncements designed to please Irish opinion, including the creation of a new regiment, the Irish Guards, to be based at Buckingham Palace. After consulting with Tim Healy, John Redmond decided to adopt a conciliatory line. Alluding to another recently-announced Royal gesture, he predicted that the Irish people:

would receive with gratification the announcement that Her Majesty has directed that for the future the shamrock shall be worn by Irish regiments on March 17th to commemorate the gallantry of Irish soldiers in South Africa.

Parnell's sister, Anna, was decidedly unimpressed by the Queen's 'cruel little insult' to the shamrock, and wrote that:

> those who cannot refrain from wearing the shamrock should dip it in ink until its dishonour has been wiped out either by the final triumph of the Boers or in some other way.[12]

The issue divided the Parnell family. Her brother, John, distanced himself from his sister's defence of the shamrock's honour and took part in the ceremonies marking the Queen's arrival in Dublin. On St Patrick's Day 1900, many English people took their cue from the Queen and decided to wear the shamrock. On arrival at Kingstown, the Queen was careful to display the emblem prominently on her lapel.

Redmond's conciliatory sentiments on the Royal visit were inevitably criticised by the more advanced nationalists, but even some of his own parliamentary colleagues were appalled by what they saw as his tame acquiescence. His political ally, William O'Brien, described the Queen as typifying 'all that is most hateful in English rule'.[13] John Dillon remarked sternly that those 'who crawl or sprawl before the Queen when she comes to Ireland, are the enemies of Ireland and of the national cause'.[14] On the eve of the visit, the parliamentarians passed a resolution drafted by the poet, W.B. Yeats, which made clear that their failure to oppose the visit did not imply any acceptance of the Union which rested 'on no moral basis' and was 'absolutely inconsistent with real peace or real loyalty in Ireland'.[15] There were well-publicised objections to the visit. In a letter published in March 1900, Yeats accused the Queen's advisers of 'hatred of our individual national life'[16] and felt the event was inspired by 'the necessities of Empire'. The poet thought it incumbent on those who 'believe that Ireland has an individual national life to protest with as much courtesy as is compatible with vigour'.[17] He observed that the Queen's presence in the country had 'commonly foreshadowed a fierce and sudden shaking of English power in Ireland'.[18] Percy French penned the Queen a sharp riposte:

> 'And I think there's a slate,' sez she,
> 'Off Willie Yeats,' sez she.
> 'He should be at home,' sez she,
> 'French polishin' a pome,' sez she,
> 'An not writin' letters,' sez she,
> 'About his betters,' sez she,
> 'Paradin' me crimes,' sez she,
> 'In the "Irish Times",' sez she.

The Queen's three-week visit began on 3 April when the new royal yacht, *Victoria and Albert*, sailed into Kingstown Harbour and berthed at Victoria Wharf several hours earlier than expected, as fears about the weather on the Irish Sea had prompted a premature departure from Holyhead. Anxieties about the crossing may have been well-founded for the royal yacht had been commissioned in inauspicious circumstances in January 1900 when it had capsized as soon as it was put into the water in Southampton. The arrival of the British fleet in Dublin Bay excited great interest and there were many who made the trip to Kingstown to witness the spectacle of the fleet's nightly illuminations.

It was not until the following morning that the Queen, with her retinue of 100 attendants, stepped ashore in Ireland for the first time in 39 years. Considering the fears expressed for her safety, it was ironic that on the day the Queen set foot on Irish soil her son, the Prince of Wales and future King Edward the Seventh, survived an assassination attempt when a 16 year-old Belgian anarchist, Jean-Baptiste Sipido, shot at him in a Brussels railway station.

> ''Tis them Belgiums,' sez she,
> 'That's throwin' bombs,' sez she,
> 'And scarin' the life,' sez she,
> 'Out o' me son and the wife,' sez she.

Victorian Ireland put on its best face for its Royal visitor, who had agreed to forego her annual visit to the south of France to travel to Dublin. Despite this air of celebration, however, the visit took place at a time when Ireland's political climate was becoming more heated following a period of relative calm. For unionists, the visit provided an opportunity to celebrate the country's position within the Union and the Empire. The unionist press wallowed in royal fervour, but nationalist newspapers also gave the event substantial coverage. While nationalist newspapers described the public attitude as a mixture of 'enthusiasm and moderation'[19] and declared that the majority of Irish people would 'be just as glad if she had never set foot on Irish soil', there was no desire among constitutional nationalists that she be met 'with any manifestation of disrespect'.[20] Even if the popular reception was not always 'particularly imposing',[21] large crowds did line the route from Kingstown. Pupils at the well-known Catholic school, Blackrock College, which lay along the route of the Queen's entry

Leeson Street Bridge, Dublin. A ceremonial arch, the replica of an ancient castle, was erected on Leeson Street Bridge for Queen Victoria's formal entry into Dublin City, following her arrival at Kingstown Harbour.

24

into Dublin, were instructed to go outside to cheer and raise their hats as the Queen's carriage passed. Alfred O'Rahilly, then a young Blackrock student and already a budding nationalist who was to leave his mark on twentieth-century Ireland as an educator and controversialist, claimed later that he had refused to toe the line and kept his hat firmly on his head.[22]

At Leeson Street Bridge, a replica of the old Baggotrath Castle had been erected for a ceremonial opening of city gates to admit the Queen. There, the keys of the City were presented by the City Steward, Charles Stewart Parnell's brother, John, although, tellingly, about half of the Corporation's members absented themselves from the ceremony. In the absence of the Corporation's Sword Bearer, James Egan, the City Sword was handed over by his Deputy. Egan, a supporter of the pro-Boer fighter, Major John MacBride, in the South Mayo by-election held in February 1900, snubbed the welcoming ceremony for political reasons, having spent five years in an English jail. Even he was careful to stress his respect for the Queen's person.[23] The 'loyal address', delivered by the Mayor, maintained that the Queen had come to Ireland 'above and apart from all political questions'.

> 'An' was welcomed in style,' sez she,
> 'By the beautiful smile,' sez she,
> 'Of me Lord Mayor Pile,' sez she,
> '(Faith, if I done right,' sez she,
> 'I'd make him a knight,' sez she).

In response, the Queen referred to the pleasure she felt at being in the motherland of those:

> brave sons who have recently borne themselves in defence of my Crown and Empire

with a cheerful valour as conspicuous now as ever in their glorious past.[24]

There were no overt protests along a route that was heavily policed, but many spectators wore miniature Boer flags and buttons with portraits of Boer leaders. The very different attitude to the War within unionist Ireland was illustrated by a banner hung on the Queen's route through Monkstown which carried the words 'our Bobs; God bless him', a reference to General Roberts who was by then successfully turning the military tide against the Boers in South Africa. Nationalists were not without respect for Roberts. Earlier in the year, Waterford County Council had unanimously approved a message of sympathy to Roberts and his wife on a family bereavement while, almost in the same breath, happily condemning the immorality of the Boer War with which Roberts' name was already strongly identified.[25]

Percy French conjures up the Queen's appreciation of her reception in Dublin:

> 'They have warrum hearts,' sez she,
> 'And they like me well,' sez she,
> 'Barrin' Anna Parnell,' sez she,
> 'I dunno, Earl,' sez she,
> 'What's come to the girl,' sez she,
> 'And that other wan,' sez she,
> 'That Maud Gonne,' sez she,
> 'Dhressin' in black,' sez she,
> 'To welcome me back,' sez she,
> 'Though I don't care,' sez she,
> 'What they wear,' sez she,
> 'An' all that gammon,' sez she,
> 'About me bringin' famine,' sez she.
> 'Now Maud Gonne will write,' sez she,
> 'That I brought the blight,' sez she,

26

'Or altered the saysons,' sez she,
'For some private raysins,' sez she.

The Transvaal Committee, founded some months before to rally support for the Boer cause, organised a protest meeting which passed a motion, seconded by the socialist, James Connolly, later one of the leaders of the 1916 Rising, making the point that the Queen's reception 'in no wise reflects the sentiments of the people of Dublin'. Attempts at torchlight protests were foiled by a large contingent of police who seized the torches and scattered the would-be marchers. The Committee maintained that Dublin was virtually in the grip of martial law in a bid to stave off demonstrations against the visit. Inspector Hourahane of the Dublin Metropolitan Police confiscated a tricolour from a 'Digger' Farrell in Francis Street. Years later, Farrell took part in the 1916 Rising as a member of the 4th Battalion of the Irish Volunteers.[26] It was said that an ass and cart with a coffin labelled 'the famine Queen' made fleeting appearances on the streets of Dublin.[27] In places, black flags were hung from windows as a sign of protest although these were quickly confiscated by the police.

It was estimated that up to 500,000 people took to the streets to witness the Queen's procession through the city.[28] Pickpockets and burglars flocked to Dublin for the occasion, and police arrested English thieves who may have been responsible for a spate of burglaries in prosperous Rathmines where goods worth £400 were stolen in break-ins on the morning of the Queen's arrival.[29] The evening saw minor clashes between loyalists and nationalists in Sackville Street, or O'Connell Street as it was already commonly known amongst nationalists. Large crowds gathered in Grafton Street to view the giant cinema screen erected to show images of the Queen and her generals in South Africa.[30] For the remainder of her stay, the Queen took daily carriage rides through various part of Dublin, always accompanied by her two Scottish servants, Rankin and Brown. Evenings were spent dining with small groups of invited guests at the Vice-Regal Lodge.

The attitude to the visit of the Catholic hierarchy was lukewarm. Dublin's Archbishop Walsh later described it as 'an act of sadly mistaken policy on the part of those who advised it'.[31] While the Queen was in Ireland, the prelate had refrained from any public expression of dissent, having conveniently arranged to be out of the country on a journey to Rome. Evidently taking a different view, Armagh's Cardinal Logue was present at a number of events on the Queen's itinerary which included visits to hospitals and Catholic-run schools.

An edition of Arthur Griffith's weekly journal, *The United Irishman,* a recently-founded mouthpiece for advanced nationalism, was banned and copies were seized because it contained a fiery broadside, penned by Maud Gonne, condemning the Famine Queen's record in Ireland.[32] Controversy persisted when Arthur Griffith physically assaulted Ramsay Colles, the editor of a conservative publication, *The Irish Figaro,* because he was incensed by the journal's treatment of Maud Gonne. Griffith ended up serving a two-week jail sentence in Mountjoy, where Maud Gonne found him in good spirits despite 'wearing prison dress of an extraordinarily ugly description'.[33] Gonne mounted a libel action against Colles which concluded when he apologised for having suggested that she was hypocritical by being anti-English while in receipt of a British Government pension on foot of her father's service as an Army officer.[34] Colles later revealed that he had learned of Maud Gonne's £300-a-year pension from Ireland's most celebrated late-Victorian policeman, Assistant Commissioner John Mallon, but felt unable to name his source in court.[35] Although a Catholic and a nationalist, Mallon had made a name for himself investigating the Phoenix Park murders of a former Lord Lieutenant, Lord Cavendish, and his secretary. Mallon had risen to the very highest ranks of the Irish police.[36] During the libel trial, Maud Gonne did not hide the intensity of her nationalist views. Asked by the judge if she would approve of Irish soldiers in the British Army shooting their officers in the back, she replied, 'I would'.[37] Although Ramsay Colles suffered a legal setback at Maud Gonne's hands, and detested her politics, he did not bear a grudge against her. In his memoirs, he generously enthused about her good looks:

> if Joan of Arc was half as beautiful as Miss Maud Gonne, no man could possibly have been found willing to burn her.[38]

Advanced nationalists were especially irked by an event in the Phoenix Park when children from all over the country were assembled to greet the Queen with a display of youthful loyalty. It was claimed that children had been dragooned from workhouses with little choice but to attend the event. This spurred Maud Gonne, who would later wed Major John MacBride following his return from the Boer War, into organising a patriotic riposte to the Royal Visit. The Patriotic Childrens' Treat drew 30,000 children when it took place in early July. It was described at the time as 'one of the most remarkable nationalist demonstrations ever held in Dublin'.[39] The children came from Catholic schools which had boycotted the royal festivities. Among other things, the children consumed 50,000 buns, 300 dozen bottles of minerals and 80 casks of ginger beer. They were also treated to rousing patriotic speeches with Maud Gonne, herself the daughter of a British army officer, decrying the evils of army enlistment to an audience whose members were mostly far too young to take 'the Saxon shilling'.

As an effort to counter pro-Boer sympathies, the Queen's visit was not a notable success. Her mixed reception aptly echoed the condition of Irish opinion at the time and, in fact, prompted pro-Boer elements to mobilise against the Government's recruiting effort. From the time the war broke out, nationalists saw resistance to army enlistment as a means of stymieing the Imperial war effort and galvanising anti-British sentiment. Throughout 1900, Maud Gonne and her cohorts were a thorn in the side of British Army recruitment efforts, distributing leaflets cautioning girls against dating soldiers, badgering recruiting officers and provoking fights with British soldiers in the streets of Dublin.[40] These moves were aimed at convincing the public that 'enlisting in the English army is treason to Ireland'.[41] Contemporary police reports reveal that Dublin Castle took seriously the political threat posed by this group and felt that they were curtailing the numbers signing up for service. The police watched Maud Gonne's movements and were aware of her visit to the continent in the company of W.B. Yeats. They may even have had knowledge of the meeting she had with the Boer representative in Brussels, Dr Leyds, from whom she sought financial support for an audacious scheme to sabotage troopships by smuggling explosives on board.

Nationalists had good reason to fear the wiles of recruiting officers. With the Boer War as its spur, recruitment into the British Army was on the rise at the turn of the century. Over 8,000 new recruits had enlisted in the regiments and the militia during 1899. Dublin, Belfast and, curiously, Tralee (where there had been a particularly energetic recruiting effort) were the most prolific sources of recruits. Towards the end of the nineteenth century, Ireland contributed over 26,000 men to the British army, representing around 12.9% of the army's total strength. This percentage had dropped in the course of the century in line with Ireland's population decline. In 1830, it had stood at 42%. [42] At the century's end there were 25,000 to 30,000 British troops stationed in Ireland. Army recruitment was not the only front on which the lure of gainful government employment attracted Irish people. This was a time when the British Civil Service was undergoing rapid expansion, and the significance of Civil Service recruitment was reflected in the attention devoted by the nationalist press to helping prepare their readers for the competitive entrance examinations.

Overall, the Queen seems to have been well received in Dublin, with curiosity about the famous visitor and a desire to avoid insulting the aged monarch evidently outweighing any political reservations. A visitor to Dublin remarked that the city was in 'a state of complete dementia over the presence of the greatest Queen in the world' and noted the surging masses of enthusiastic onlookers that turned out to greet the Queen.[43] Another contemporary source adjudged that she had been received with a 'hearty welcome and even with fervour.'[44] Her biographer, Lytton Strachey, thought the visit had been 'a complete success' although while in Ireland

she began 'for the first time, to show signs of the fatigue of age'.[45] Reflecting on the visit, a contemporary unionist publication noted that:

> our highest hopes were satisfied, our anxieties dispersed to nothingness by the Queen's entry into Dublin. Weather, decorations and people all behaved splendidly

and remarked approvingly on 'the order and enthusiasm of the vast throngs that welcomed the Queen'.[46] Looking back on the visit, a Home Rule nationalist observed that the Queen was 'on the whole well received, driving unescorted through the streets'.[47] Another less charitable assessment was that:

> her appearance here aroused more pity than dislike – a sullen, drowsy, hardly conscious figure, mechanically tilted in her carriage seat, as we understood, to acknowledge what salutations greeted her.[48]

The Queen's personal journal records her impressions of 'a wildly enthusiastic greeting' even in 'the poorer parts' of the city and claims that nationalists who gathered outside City Hall 'seemed to forget their politics and cheered and waved their hats'.[49]

> 'Well I needn't repeat,' sez she,
> 'How they cheered in each street,' sez she.

Inevitably, the fact that the Queen received a reasonable welcome was interpreted by unionist commentators as a sign that nationalist truculence was a minority interest. With their imposing intelligence network throughout the country, however, the police, and through them

Dublin Castle, were well aware of the depth of animosity that confronted the *status quo*, even if, war in South Africa notwithstanding, there was, as yet, no direct threat to British interests in Ireland. The Queen's visit brought into sharp relief some of the political tensions that were ripening at the turn of the century. It drew attention to an irreconcilable element in the Irish body politic that was not Fenian in the traditional sense, but whose political ambitions went well beyond the desire for land reform and a Home Rule parliament that was the *raison d'etre* of the Irish Party at Westminster. This new turn-of-the-century spirit was typified by Arthur Griffith and his friend, William Rooney. Their outlook was a casserole of influences – cultural, separatist, and Irish Ireland – which produced a demand for an Irish State governed by Irishmen in the interests of the Irish people. Their publication, *The United Irishman*, unleashed the most unabashed criticisms of the Royal Visit. In the controversies surrounding the Royal Visit and the Boer War, sponsors of this publication spawned two new political organisations, *Cumann na nGaedhael* and *Ighninidhe na hEireann* which, though relatively obscure and insignificant in their own right, tested out ideas and blooded personnel for future political struggles.

2. Crime and Punishment

A look at some of the crimes that attracted attention in 1900 gives an idea of what life was like at the bottom of the social ladder among those misfortunate enough to have had their lives touched by violent crime. It is among the more impoverished groups in society that the contrast between late nineteenth- and late twentieth-century circumstances comes across most starkly. A report on policing published in 1902 declared that, while political agitation kept the Irish police on their toes, 'there is practically no criminal class' in Ireland.[50] Nonetheless, turn-of-the-century Ireland was no crime-free idyll. Although crime rates had declined throughout the nineteenth century, murder was still a relatively common occurrence at the century's end and, in proportion to its population, there were three such crimes in Ireland for every two committed in England.[51] Public reluctance to co-operate with the RIC multiplied the difficulties involved in solving crimes. Appearing before a Committee of Inquiry in 1901, Denis Horan outlined the problem and a favoured solution:

> The people, if they do not assist the prisoner, remain passive . . . If you want to look for information in Ireland, it is by the greatest engineering that you will get anything out . . . many a good case falls to the ground for want of funds with which to purchase information.[52]

Much crime in small towns was of a minor variety, petty larcenies and offences connected with drunkenness. In 1900, however, violent crime made its presence felt in both urban and rural areas. In Tubbercurry, an 80 year-old man was killed by a cousin of his, who hit him over the head in a dispute about a trespassing cow before throwing him into a bog hole.[53] In a move resembling the flight of Christy Mahon in Synge's *Playboy of the Western World*, the attacker fled the scene of the crime, this time to Liverpool, but was apprehended in Dublin before he set foot on the boat for England. Since the 1870s, the RIC had maintained a presence at Holyhead to deal with wrongdoers absconding from Ireland.

In Tallaght, Co. Dublin, an elderly man was beaten to death by an assailant who was after his money. The princely sum of four-and-a-half sovereigns was stolen from the dead man's home. In County Antrim, a man in his late twenties fatally injured his mother in a fit of rage provoked by the late arrival of his evening meal and then, filled with remorse for what he had done, blew his brains out with a shotgun.[54] Elsewhere, a 70 year-old man, Jeremiah Harrington, was charged with the murder of his 82 year-old brother, Daniel.[55]

At the turn of the century, 'the keeping or not keeping of domestic servants' was what distinguished the higher social classes from the working classes.[56] Students at Trinity College commonly had their own manservants. The 1901 Census shows a Tipperary national school teacher employing a domestic servant as well as a governess for his children.[57] Domestic servants were mostly young women aged between 15 and 24.[58] By 1914, up to seven per cent of the population of Europe's leading cities were migrants from the countryside employed as domestic servants, the product of decades when people shifted from rural to urban areas in search of economic advancement and emancipation from the conservative bonds of family and society.[59]

At the turn of the century, because of the lack of viable alternative employment outlets, Ireland had a higher proportion of domestic servants than England and Wales.[60] Although there was said to be a scarcity of servants at the time, the 1901 Census counted 193,300 women engaged in domestic service throughout the country, which accounted for one in every three women in employment. In 1891, there were 23,726 female servants working in Dublin city and its increasingly prosperous suburbs.[61]

Dublin's domestic servants, who were usually accommodated by their employers, earned miserably low rates of pay, as little as £10 to £12 a year in 1901.[62] In September 1900, a domestic servant in Dublin was charged with stealing £1 from her employer and, when convicted, was sentenced to fourteen days in jail.[63] In 1900, two of Dublin's domestic servants, Bridget Gannon and Hannah Kavanagh, were linked to criminal trials, one as a victim, the other as an accused. Their stories offer an insight into some of the harsher realities of the time.

What came to be known as 'the Dodder Mystery' was a tangled tale, peopled by policemen, domestic servants and women of what was referred to as the 'unfortunate class'. It was a mystery that was never satisfactorily resolved and, impinging as it did on the conduct and probity of the Dublin Metropolitan Police, had a special resonance in a country where, for broadly political reasons, the police perennially bore the brunt of public suspicion and disapproval. 30 year-old Bridget Gannon worked as a parlour maid at the home of a Dublin solicitor in Lower Baggot Street. In August 1900, her body was discovered in the Dodder River near Londonbridge Road. The mystery centred on whether she had fallen in by accident or had been pushed and, if so, by whom.

Unfolding evidence about the circumstances of Bridget Gannon's death fascinated contemporaries and the case, in which there were three separate inquests, attracted full houses each time it came to court. According to a friend of hers, Margaret Clowry, who was also a domestic servant, Bridget Gannon had met a member of the Dublin Metropolitan Police, Constable Henry Flower, on the eve of her death. Constable Flower was among a group of policemen who retrieved Bridget Gannon's body from the river although he did not, at the time, admit any acquaintance with the deceased woman. Flower accompanied the body to the morgue and was said by the cart driver to have behaved strangely on the way there, gazing repeatedly at the corpse and muttering inaudibly at it.

Following the first inquest, Bridget Gannon was buried at Glasnevin Cemetery as an unidentified woman who had died from drowning. When her identity, and the facts of her relationship with Henry Flower, became known, the coroner ordered her body to be exhumed for a second inquest, but this was halted when its legality was challenged by Flower's barrister, Tim Harrington, who succeeded in having the issue referred to the High Court for a ruling. In 1900, Harrington was an Irish Party M.P. of 20-years' standing. A member of the faction that had stuck by Parnell, Harrington had been a prominent player in the protracted political drama stemming from Parnell's demise. In January 1900, he had chaired a crucial meeting of parliamentarians which brought an end to the split in the Irish Party and had important consequences for the country's political fortunes at the start of the new century. By way of a pro-Boer gesture, W.B. Yeats had tried to persuade Harrington, who was considered by some to be a potential party leader, to relinquish his Westminster seat to Major John MacBride, but to no avail. In 1901, Harrington was elected as Dublin's Lord Mayor. Outside of politics, Harrington had an interesting legal pedigree. It was he who, in a series of newspaper articles in 1884, had cut holes in the State's case against those convicted of the brutal murder of five members of the family of John Joyce of Maamtrasna near Lough Mask in August 1882. Seven men were

arrested, two of whom turned prosecution witnesses while two others, Pat Joyce and Pat Casey, were executed.[64] Harrington had been a member of Parnell's defence team during the celebrated court hearings of the Special Commission on 'Parnellism and Crime'.[65]

Once the legal arguments were out of the way, Bridget Gannon's body was exhumed for a second time in the presence of a jury, whose members were ferried to Clonsilla Cemetery where, in a scene that might have appealed to Bram Stoker's gothic imagination, they were sworn in again beside the open grave in the presence of the corpse. It was reported that this 'impressive and unusual ceremony' drew a local crowd who 'watched in awe-stricken manner the opening of the grave and the uncovering of the face of the deceased'.[66] Testimony given at this final inquest pointed the finger of suspicion firmly at Henry Flower. According to Margaret Clowry, Bridget Gannon had been last seen alive in the company of the constable. She told the Court how, when the three were out walking on the night of the drowning, Flower had pointedly sent her away, leaving him alone with Bridget Gannon. A colleague of Flower's, Constable Dockery, who acknowledged a six-year-long intimate relationship with Margaret Clowry, confirmed her testimony. Dockery had known the deceased servant for three or four years and claimed that she had also been friendly with a Constable McManus, but did not know 'if she ever walked with him'. In spite of the weight of evidence to the contrary, Flower adamantly denied ever having known the dead servant who was described in court as a respectable girl, some of whose relatives were members of the police force.

As the inquest wore on, the plot appeared to thicken. A railway watchman had seen Constable

Dockery walking towards the Dodder with an unidentified woman on the night of Bridget Gannon's death. This raised the possibility that Dockery rather than Flower could have been the culprit. Dockery insisted that the woman he was with had been Lizzie Kavanagh whose exchanges with the coroner throw further light on the seamier side of life in the Ireland of the Celtic revival:

> I am sorry to have to ask you the question, but are you a respectable girl? Yes, I assume so. Are you of the unfortunate class? No, sir: I don't think so anyway.[67]

She had previously been arrested twice in the company of women of 'the unfortunate class' and fined 10 shillings each time for 'soliciting'. When described in court as 'a night walker', she replied 'I do not consider myself common', and denied any connection with Dockery who, she alleged, had tried to coerce her into backing up his story. The coroner remarked that the jury would have little doubt about the character of a girl who had been fined twice for an offence which, he said, would repel any respectable girl.

Flower was brought to court for a preliminary hearing. In his defence, Tim Harrington argued that there was no proof of any violence against the victim and suggested that she may have slipped and fallen into the river while taking a short cut home. Visiting the scene a few days after the drowning, Margaret Clowry found a flower on the river bank that Bridget Gannon had been wearing on the evening of her death, but which had been overlooked by the police investigating the incident. This implied that some kind of struggle had taken place before she had entered the water. One witness testified to

seeing an unidentified couple lying on the river bank and hearing the woman cry out 'don't' as he passed by. At the time, the Dodder was an area much visited by amorous couples with nowhere else to go. A Dublin wit later quipped that 'the trees along the Dodder were more sinned against than sinning'.[68] A scream was heard from the vicinity of the Dodder at about 3 a.m., but Flower insisted that he was back at the station well before then, and had a police officer to confirm his story.[69]

The case took a further strange twist when a Sergeant Hanily, one of the policemen who had retrieved Bridget Gannon's body from the Dodder, died after cutting his throat at Islandbridge Police Station. Reporting on Hanily's suicide, the coroner found that the Dodder case had had no bearing on it and that the sergeant's history of chronic illness had unbalanced his mind. The Dodder was evidently a dangerous place in 1900, for a local fisherman, Samuel Rowden, drowned there after a bout of drinking, while the hearings connected with the Dodder mystery were still going on.

Asked whether there was sufficient evidence to commit Flower to trial for murder, the jury accepted that he had been the last person to see her alive, but acquitted him for lack of proof that he had been responsible for her death. In his summing up, the Judge concluded that the drowning had probably occurred when Bridget Gannon fell into the river as a result of Flower 'taking liberties or larking with her'. He condemned Flower for having 'with inconceivable baseness allowed her to perish'.[70] There was much nervousness about the damage the case was capable of inflicting on the standing of the Dublin Metropolitan Police which announced an immediate inquiry into the conduct of those involved. It found that the 'greatest laxity and looseness' had been allowed to prevail at Irishtown police station and this resulted in transfers, censure, fines and demotions. Flower resigned from the force and emigrated, reputedly to Australia. His misfortunes evidently caught the eye of the young James Joyce who used Henry Flower as the pen name employed by Leopold Bloom in *Ulysses* when he was conducting a secret affair with a woman in Mullingar.[71] Flower's barrister, Tim Harrington, would later play a modest supportive part in Joyce's life when he supplied the young writer with a character reference as Joyce ventured forth to France for the first time in 1904. Joyce later repaid him by inscribing Harrington's initials in *Finnegan's Wake*.[72] Written while he was in Trieste in 1905, Joyce's short story, *Two Gallants*, tells of a 'relationship' between 'a slavey in a house in Baggot Street', the area where Bridget Gannon worked, and a young Dublin Lothario who believed that, in terms of willing sexuality, there was 'nothing to touch a slavey'.

While the saga surrounding the inquest on Bridget Gannon was still unfolding, another young woman drowned in Dublin's Royal Canal. Margaret Cowley was just nineteen and her unfortunate tale is a sadly revealing one. According to a witness at her inquest, she had been in trouble for 'keeping company with a married man' and had been turned out of home by her father after he had spotted her one evening meeting a man from a 'dancing academy'. As it happened, this man, John Daly, was in the Court and, having been pointed out by the deceased's father, took the witness stand to defend himself, insisting that there had never been anything improper between the two of them.[73] The judge concluded that Margaret Cowley had died while of unsound mind.

Margaret Hayden was a charwoman aged 40 when her body was recovered from a quarry in Kimmage. A surprisingly substantial sum of money, over £12, was discovered in her clothing. Testimony at the inquest revealed that she had been married 20 years before, but shortly after the marriage was abandoned by her husband and lived with her brother. A man named McNaughton told of how he had met a woman of her description for the first time at 11 p.m. on a Saturday night on Clanbrassil Street. They had walked towards Kimmage and entered a field where they sat on the grass. According to his story, she had asked him for two shillings and he gave her an evasive answer. McNaughton alleged that he had been attacked by a group of men looking for money, had been thrown into a quarry pool and never again laid eyes on Margaret Hayden. The coroner returned a verdict of death by drowning and referred the case to the police for any action they might wish to take.[74]

The plight of single women in turn-of-the-century Ireland is further illustrated by the experience of Kate Barry. A cook at Foley's Hotel in Wicklow Street, Kate Barry gave birth to a child in a lavatory at the hotel. The child suffocated in a box with a towel in its mouth and was found dead the next day.[75] Nora Barnacle worked in a similar city centre hotel, Finn's of Leinster Street, after she moved from Galway to Dublin and before she eloped with James Joyce.[76] In County Louth, the body of a three month-old child was found in a box that had been left in a stream. The infant had evidently died of starvation.[77]

Turn-of-the-century Ireland was unforgiving of illegitimate pregnancies, confinement in a workhouse being a common experience for working class women in this situation. In the early years of the new century, the Poor Law

Reform Commission described the prevailing attitude towards illegitimacy:

> . . . in one case we were shown in the same workhouse a baby, its mother, its grandmother and its great-grandmother, or four illegitimate generations in the female line. The lapsing into confirmed immorality seems to be a tendency in Irish workhouses, because when a girl falls from virtue she is rarely able in Ireland to return to her home owing to the sentiment of aversion from immorality which is too strong in most parts of the country to permit her to face that feeling and to return with her baby to her relatives, even if they would receive her.[78]

A domestic servant from Ballymena, Ellen Kirk, was prosecuted for infanticide after her six month-old infant died from apparent neglect. They had recently come out of the Ballymena workhouse where she had been confined with fever. Two of her other children had died young from 'consumption' and bronchitis. It was revealed that Ellen Kirk, her mother and children, lived together on an income of eight pence a week, plus whatever her brother managed to send back from Glasgow. They were unable to afford milk or medical attention for the children.[79]

Hannah Kavanagh was a domestic servant from Tipperary. In October, she was sentenced to death for killing her infant son. In circumstances that must have had many parallels in rural Ireland at the time, she had come to work in Dublin the previous year at the behest of her boyfriend. While in Dublin, she became pregnant and was promised marriage 'after Lent'. Having supported her boyfriend financially for some time, Hannah Kavanagh found herself deserted by him and had to arrange for the child to be looked after by a nurse for whose services she paid 2s 6d a week.

Born in June, Hannah Kavanagh's child was found drowned in September. Her defence told of a dismal family history – an aunt in a lunatic asylum, two sisters who were imbeciles – and of the pressure she came under from her family to send part of her earnings home for their support.[80] This left her unable to afford the upkeep of her child. Found guilty, she was sentenced to hang in November, although the judge expressed the hope that mercy would be exercised in her favour. She was led away 'apparently unable to realise her terrible position'. The Lord Lieutenant subsequently commuted her sentence to penal servitude for life.[81] In 1901, she was listed among those in prison, but subsequently disappears without trace from one of the few pages of history inscribed with her name.

Executions were still an integral part of the Irish penal system in 1900. In the month of April, an executioner from Halifax was in Waterford Jail where Patrick Dunphy awaited his fate. A large crowd gathered outside the jail at the early hour of 8 a.m. to see the hoisting of the black flag which confirmed that the sentence had been carried out. Dunphy had been convicted of poisoning his two children with strychnine. Such violence within the family was by no means an isolated occurrence.

In July 1900, Michael Kiernan, a labourer from County Westmeath, shot his wife with a double-barrelled gun and tried to dispatch himself with a knife wound to the throat. These events followed a domestic row in which 'heated language' had been used. Remarkably, Mrs Kiernan, who had only been married for eight months, escaped with a wound to her shoulder while her husband botched his suicide attempt. Echoing the kind of sentiments that feature in crime reporting to this day, the couple were described by locals as 'very popular' while Michael had the reputation of being 'a quiet, inoffensive person'.[82]

Then, as now, economic difficulties lay behind much recorded crime. Overcrowded accommodation was commonplace. In December, a man who had paid one shilling to sleep in a house in the Coombe, murdered his female companion in the presence of the other four occupants of a room in this unregulated boarding house.[83] In County Limerick, a Protestant rector, Reverend Hudson, was shot and killed by one of his parishioners, Thomas Smith, who had a record of eccentric behaviour brought on by excessive drinking and ensuing financial difficulties. A tenant of Lord Clarina, Smith had run up debts of £382 and was in default of his annual rent of £65. On one earlier occasion, Smith was reported to have consumed a bottle of brandy, brandished a revolver while singing *The Boys of Wexford*, and claimed his mother had been a Catholic and that he was 'a Hillside man and one of the old brigade'. Mr Hudson, who had been on good terms with his killer, was shot after he had gone to Smith's house to encourage him to seek a settlement with the landlord's agent. Smith claimed that the killing had been accidental, but the jury found him guilty while insane. The judge expressed concern about the disorderly climate in the area of the crime, which in three months had seen four cases of arson and three cases of killing or maiming of animals![84]

The Catholic Church's perennial fear of a deteriorating moral climate is reflected in the Pastoral Letters issued during 1900 in which drunkenness came in for special targeting. In the eyes of the bishops, drunkenness carried a grave social and moral threat. The vice of intemperance was seen as wreaking 'dreadful havoc' and as 'the chief cause of poverty, and sin, and crime in our country'.[85] When crime statistics were published, these gave scant support to the bishops' fears, although 'offences against morals' were shown to have registered a slight increase in Kildare, Carlow, Antrim, Dublin, Wicklow and King's County.[86] The country's prison population was actually in decline. In 1899, only 89 people were convicted to serve prison sentences and the prison population had declined to just 322 compared with 1,031 twenty years earlier. The century opened with only 19 women in prison, which was less than 10% of the comparable figure in 1880.[87]

The Catholic hierarchy was not alone in worrying about the evils of drunkenness. The Irish Temperance League was active in trying to limit the number of public-house licences granted and to curb their opening hours. A number of temperance candidates had been successful in the 1899 local elections. Each year, the Dublin Metropolitan Police made many thousands of visits to public houses to check for breaches of the licensing laws. The President of the Dublin United Trades Council, George Leahy, was convinced that 'Ireland sober is Ireland free'[88] and called for an alliance between the forces of labour and the forces of temperance. He explained how Irish workers, deprived of the opportunities for educational and social advancement available to their counterparts on the continent, had to be especially vigilant in avoiding the vice of intemperance lest it 'blunt the natural sharpness of intellect, and sap the spirit of independence'.

Whatever the statistics might say, there was ample anecdotal evidence in the year's criminal cases to link drunkenness with serious offences. A single edition of *The Weekly Freeman* carried accounts of two alcohol-related murders. John McCabe was charged with killing his 13 year-old son, Joseph, with a blow to the head from a poker. During a drunken row with his wife because she had let the fire go out and had not cooked his supper, McCabe put a poker through their front window where, pathetically, young Joseph had been weeping against the window pane and was struck by accident. McCabe was described by the police as a hard drinker. His wife 'worked in gentlemen's houses, was sober . . . and did her best to keep up a respectable home'. Despite McCabe's unreliability, the judge hesitated to impose the maximum sentence because of the hardship it would entail for his family to be deprived of its breadwinner.[89] In Bushmills, Co. Antrim, Bridget McGovern was killed by William Woods, who had earlier served a ten-year sentence for murdering another woman in Co. Derry. The two were living in the same house and were drunk on the night of the crime. The woman's body was found almost naked the following morning on a bed in the kitchen by her son who told the coroner that his mother had consumed 'a naggin and a half-pint of whiskey' the previous evening.[90]

Though much less common than before, it was still possible in 1900 to end up in prison on account of political activities. At the time, Ireland was still subject to coercion legislation. What nationalists termed the 'Whiteboy Act' was used to prosecute a United Irish League member, James Vallely, who had written to three local graziers demanding they relinquish lands held by them.[91] In July the proprietors of *The* *Kilkenny People* were arraigned for publishing a report of a League meeting in Mullinahone which had called for a boycott of the Barton brothers of Ballylin. This prosecution failed as juries were reluctant to convict under such circumstances. Later in the year, four members of Westmeath County Council were brought to Court by the Local Government Board for using Council funds to fly a green flag over a Council building in Mullingar. The Board had sought to surcharge Council members for the costs involved, but four Councillors refused to pay. They insisted on the Council's right to display symbols reflecting the sentiments of those who had elected them. In the nationalist press, the flag was seen as important:

> in keeping alive the national sentiment which, while it persists, will always operate to prevent our people from being drawn into that morass of materialism wherein most of the civilised nations of today are wallowing.[92]

3. Political Theatre in an Election Year

The leader of the United Irish League, William O'Brien, had a cow which made news in 1900. When O'Brien refused to pay an extra police tax levied in Mayo to cover the cost of additional policing the authorities said was necessitated by the threat from the League, his cow was impounded. After an effort had been made to free it from the pound, the animal was eventually sold off at an unruly auction at which League supporters gathered to disrupt the sale. The cow was purchased by James Moran, who defied the jeering crowd, clearly relishing the idea of standing up to the League's supporters and discomfiting its charismatic leader.[93] The fate of

O'Brien's cow somehow typified the theatricality of Irish politics in 1900. Much of this political theatre was supplied by the United Irish League and William O'Brien was one of the year's most prominent personalities. Founded in 1898, the League came into its own at the turn of the century, holding meetings all over the country, often in studied defiance of bans imposed by Dublin Castle. It was claimed that it had 'taken a deep hold on the people'.[94] League meetings generated considerable enthusiasm and attracted sizeable attendances. Government disapproval only served to strengthen the organisation's popular appeal. Police shorthand writers attended most League rallies checking for inflammatory statements that might sustain prosecutions.

League members delighted in playing cat-and-mouse with the police whenever meetings were banned. There were many ways in which such bans could be scorned and plenty of scope for elaborate shows of defiance. When a meeting planned for Rooskey in Co. Roscommon in January was proscribed, the local M.P. addressed a rally from the back of his moving carriage. To the amusement of the attendance, a policeman who tried to restrain him was told that there was no meeting taking place. 'We're only having a chat man. Sit down and have a smoke.'[95] The meeting continued as the carriage moved down the road accompanied by a growing throng of onlookers. Nationalists relished the spectacle of a day 'full of escapade and adventure in which the police played the undignified role of butts to the people'.[96]

A large force of police was drafted in to enforce a ban placed on a rally in Sligo called to protest at the exclusion of Catholics from a jury in a case against two nationalists. The League cunningly circumvented the ban by secretly agreeing to convene at the very early hour of 5.30 a.m. when the police were nowhere to be found. O'Brien entertained his supporters by wishing the local police inspector 'a long continuance of his deep slumbers' as he and 'his 400 chickens were caught napping'.[97] Further meetings were held in other parts of Co. Sligo throughout the day in a studied defiance of the police ban – 'another abject failure of the Castle, another splendid triumph of the League' as one commentator put it.[98] A proscribed meeting in Newmarket, Co. Cork, was again held surreptitiously at an early hour when the Dublin Castle proclamation was duly burned in the presence of a powerless police contingent who had arrived on the scene too late to prevent the crowd from massing.[99] The excitement generated by the League persisted throughout the year and a rally in Wicklow in November culminated in a police baton charge on the assembled crowd.

League activities reached a crescendo in the lead up to the National Convention which was summoned in June to set a seal of popular approval on the reunited parliamentary party and to designate the League as the party's sole support organisation. Branches were founded all over the country so that they could appoint delegates to the Convention which was attended by parliamentarians, clergy and representatives of the Corporations, Urban District Councils, Rural District Councils, Town Boards and Boards of Guardians. O'Brien's supporters succeeded, much to the disapproval of Redmond and a majority of the parliamentary party, in excluding Tim Healy's People's Rights Association from the Convention. When it took place, the Convention was described as 'representative, unanimous and enthusiastic'.[100] Redmond, who gave the League full credit for inspiring Party unity, described the Convention as the most representative gathering of Irishmen since the eighteenth century when Grattan's Parliament closed its doors.

After a decade of division, the Irish Party was reunited in 1900. For parliamentary nationalism, this was a year of raised hopes coupled with persistent personality clashes. Fed by a decade of disunity, political rivalries ran deep and the language of politics was blunt and uncompromising. Politics generated considerable passion and possessed an impressive capacity to mobilise the public in ways that now seem surprising. Visits by leading political figures commonly attracted substantial crowds. Redmond's first public appearance in Ireland since becoming leader of the Irish Party, almost three months after his appointment, sparked great enthusiasm in his Waterford constituency. 'Old feuds gave place to more patriotic rivalry and the only conflict discernible was to do the most to make the meeting a success.'[101] Special trains were laid on for the occasion and nationalists from Munster and South Leinster turned out in considerable numbers accompanied by an assortment of brass bands, celebratory banners and triumphal arches. It was as if nationalist Ireland found in the reunification of the Irish Party a cause warranting the kind of enthusiasm unionists reserved for greeting their royal guest.

Before and after the healing of the party split, relations within the ranks of Irish parliamentarians were honeycombed with suspicion and recrimination. Factionalism was so deeply rooted that, at the start of 1900, nationalist Ireland had four highly partisan daily newspapers representing rival viewpoints. *The Freeman's Journal* was the traditional voice of parliamentary

nationalism and gave its support to the majority, anti-Parnellite grouping. *The Irish Daily Independent* maintained a pro-Parnellite posture and championed the interests of John Redmond. *The Daily Nation* and *The Irish People* were controlled by interests allied respectively to Tim Healy and William O'Brien.

The reunification of the Irish Party was warmly hailed. 'The pulse of Ireland will beat faster' enthused one nationalist newspaper.[102] The choice of Redmond as leader was hailed as 'the death-blow of faction',[103] but it was nothing of the sort. The divisions that had ravaged the parliamentarians for almost a decade had not gone away and it was essential to avoid debate on contentious policy issues with their propensity to reopen old sores and sow renewed divisions. Though united again in name, the parliamentarians were far from united in spirit. Deep personal animosities quickly resurfaced and Tim Healy sought to obstruct the merger between the Party and the United Irish League. Healy accused O'Brien of using the League to dominate the Irish Party and tried to use his supporters amongst the clergy to cut across the National Convention. Popular enthusiasm for an end to political infighting, however, ensured that Healy's efforts came to nought.

Throughout 1900, Healy and O'Brien were at each other's throats, their often outrageous rivalry casting doubts on the sincerity of party unity. As the United Irish League spread to urban areas, Healy's resentment of O'Brien grew and the rancour between the two men deepened. Redmond sought to play the peacemaker but, as Healy grew more strident, Redmond sided increasingly with O'Brien and chided Healy for attacking the June Convention as 'a machined assembly, carrying out the dictates of a little clique of men'.[104] Keen to scotch the notion that the League was a one-man show, Redmond insisted that 'the League is no man's League but Ireland's'.[105] Such was the depth of Healy's disaffection that, ignoring the new logic of party unity, he fielded his own candidates against official Irish Party candidates in fourteen constituencies. The notorious rivalry between O'Brien and Healy lit up the election campaign of 1900. In September, O'Brien turned up in Healy's Louth constituency to campaign against him. The ensuing three-hour showdown was described as 'one of the most exciting election meetings ever held in Ireland in recent years'. Speaking from the same election platform, each man tried to shout the other down. 'Heavily-built men tried to pull Healy off of the platform', but he could not be budged. Stones were thrown, one of which hit O'Brien.[106] Healy held his seat in a tight contest, but most of his supporters, including William Martin Murphy,[107] Labour leader, Jim Larkin's nemesis during the 1913 Lock-out, were defeated, leaving Healy a relatively isolated figure in parliament. O'Brien quickly moved against Healy, whose continued membership of the Party he described as being 'like the presence of a poisoned bullet in the body of a man'. Despite opposition from Redmond and Harrington, in December 1900 O'Brien secured Healy's expulsion.[108] While Healy survived until 1918 as an independent nationalist M.P., and was later to become Governor-General of the Irish Free State, the 1900 election saw the end of him as a distinctive force in Irish political life.

The Healy factor was not the only fault line within the Party. There were also differences between Dillon and O'Brien. Dillon was a committed parliamentarian, convinced of the need for parliamentarians to retain full control of the political movement. For his part, O'Brien favoured a vigorous people's movement which would exercise influence over the parliamentarians and conduct extra-parliamentary agitations.

Turn-of-the-century elections were very different affairs from their modern equivalents. They were quite capable of generating intense local excitement. Arthur Griffith's paper, *The United Irishman*, was the catalyst for an early electoral challenge to the might of the reunited Irish Party when Michael Davitt's resignation from Parliament in October 1899 led to a by-election in his South Mayo constituency. Advanced nationalists saw an opportunity to elect Major John MacBride, thereby boldly underlining Irish support for the Boers and Ireland's undying disaffection from Britain. MacBride had been wounded fighting on the Boer side at Ladysmith and would inevitably have been an abstentionist M.P. The parliamentarians had no desire to criticise MacBride, but as one Irish Party M.P. put it, 'the men who came from Dublin were going to run a man who was doing good work where he is and were going to put him where he could do no good'.[109] With some support from Tim Healy, MacBride's supporters campaigned against an imprisoned member of the United Irish League, John O'Donnell. MacBride's candidacy, and the fact that this was inspired from outside Mayo, generated significant local resistance. His supporters had difficulty in holding public meetings unmolested by opponents. MacBride's most prominent backer, James Daly, Mayor of Limerick, had stones thrown at him by a crowd of United Irish League supporters in Ballinrobe.[110] On polling day, there were a handful of incidents, but, in inclement weather, less than

40% of the electorate turned out to vote. United Irish League members skilfully mobilised their supporters marching them from rural areas to polling centres. The result, a crushing 2,401 votes to 427 victory for O'Donnell, underlined the primacy of local political elites and testified to the continuing strength of parliamentary nationalism and, by contrast, the very limited appeal at the ballot box of more abrasive brands of politics.

While it has been argued that the South Mayo poll was a missed opportunity for the various strands of nationalism to coalesce under one flag in support of MacBride, it is hardly credible that the parliamentary party establishment would have been willing, so soon after its reunification under Redmond, to cede a Westminister seat to a radical figure like MacBride, however popular his exploits in South Africa may have been. The South Mayo by-election was the first test of the electoral credibility of the United Irish League, an opportunity to confirm its popular appeal that it could scarcely have been expected to pass up. The decision to stand MacBride was seen by parliamentarians as a slight on their patriotism, one they were determined to resist.

1900 was the year of the 'Khaki' election when the Conservative Government took the opportunity furnished by the Boer War to capitalise on the discomfiture of the Liberals and seek a fresh electoral mandate. Polling was spread over 14 days. The ballots in Belfast North, Tyrone South, North Louth, Cork City and Limerick took place on 4 October while the final contest was set for East Wicklow two weeks later. By the time the first Irish ballots took place, many of the English results were already known and the comfortable victory of the Conservative Government had been confirmed.

In all, 69 Irish seats were uncontested in 1900. Candidates were entitled to be, and sometimes were, elected to serve for two constituencies. Tim Healy's defeated opponent in Louth, Haviland Burke, was elected unopposed in Tullamore. The vote in South County Dublin, where Horace Plunkett was up against a nationalist and a dissident unionist, generated considerable public interest[111] and the election count attracted such attention that 'a number of ladies sought admission ... but the Sub-Sheriff, of course, politely declined to make the concession'.[112]

Electorates were small by twentieth-century standards. One Irish constituency, Galway, had a mere 2,209 electors, while even the largest, Cork City, which returned two M.P.s, had no more than 13,152 voters. As a by-product of the paucity of nationalist-unionist contests, turnout was generally low. There were only ten such contests in 1900, fewer than the number of seats that were fought out between nationalists. Parnell's brother, John, lost out on a seat when, fully expecting to be the sole candidate, he turned up for the nomination without the required election fee. A surprise challenger materialised at the last moment carrying the necessary fee and was elected unopposed. This was a curious way to bring the curtain down on the political glories of the age of Parnell!

41

CHAPTER 3

A Very Different Ireland:
How People Lived at
the Turn of the Century

The land decaying, the people dying or expatriating themselves, privation and hunger their constant companions, famine an ever-present spectre – this is civilization within a day's journey of the world's greatest capital.

An American visitor's view of economic conditions in the west of Ireland in 1902.[1]

As compared with other divisions of Britain, Ireland has a run-down, out-at-the-heels look that is depressing. Both the country districts and the towns show marked signs of dilapidation, decay and thriftlessness. There are broken walls and litter in the neighbourhood of all the villages and cities, and the land commonly has the appearance of being tilled neither energetically nor carefully.

Reflections of a visiting travel writer in 1901.[2]

The west of Ireland is depressing, but it is very beautiful … Oppressed you must be, even if you are an artist, by its bleakness and its dreariness, its lonely lakes reflecting a dull grey sky, its desolate bog-lands, its solitary chapels, its wretched cabins perched on hillsides that are very wildernesses of rocks.

Impressions of Connemara at the turn of the century.[3]

Turning the clock back one hundred years brings us into contact with a land so very different from today's Ireland. Late nineteenth-century Ireland was a country of tiny farmsteads and nasty urban tenements. It was an era when some Irish people still lived in mud cabins, and when it was not that unusual for farm animals to live under the same roof as their owners. Partial failure of the potato crop, which happened a number of times during the 1890s, was still capable of generating what late Victorian administrators coyly called 'distress', its real name being hunger. This was a time before the introduction of old-age pensions and social welfare arrangements when the workhouse, however harsh its conditions might be, was often the only place of refuge for the aged, the infirm and the indigent. Although the notion of State support for the aged was already being discussed at the turn of the century, even a politician as independent-minded as the Liberal Unionist M.P., T.W. Russell, believed a universal scheme of old age pensions to be well beyond the bounds of practicality.[4]

Around 1900, almost one in every four children born in Dublin died before their first birthday. Astonishingly, in Belfast during one four-week period there were as many deaths of children under one year old as there were of adults over 60 years of age.[5] 80% of all those who died had not yet reached the age of 60. At a time when medicine was much less advanced than it is today, one-third of all deaths resulted from chest infections. Although average life expectancy for Irish people had climbed significantly from its pre-Famine level of under 40 years, in 1900 a normal lifespan was still some 20 years shorter than it is today.[6] While, on average, people may have lived for little more than 50 years,

Ireland's population at the turn of the century contained as many as 497 centenarians. One of these, who was said to be at least 120 years of age, claimed, when questioned by a census taker, to be able to remember the French fleet sailing off the west coast of Ireland in 1798![7]

In 1900, Ireland was still marooned in an economic trough. Scarred by decades of emigration and deprivation, as well as by political and agrarian turmoil, the country was affected by a deep social and economic malaise. 'Ireland is sick almost to death'[8] remarked one observer early in the new century. It was 'a chronic eyesore in Europe'[9] according to another source, while a third noted its reputation for 'hopeless misery and incurable poverty'.[10] This was certainly not a happy picture of a land embarking upon a twentieth-century journey that would yield political independence and, latterly, significant material prosperity.

There was, however, a brighter side, with some signs of potential for revival and renewal in the new century. Contemporary police reports, with their keen eye on economic conditions as potential breeding grounds for political troubles, highlight the country's prosperity. Harvests were good, employment plentiful and wages high. A real effort was being made to grapple with the land problem that had vexed the country for decades and was, at the turn of the century, still its most contentious, potentially explosive, issue. Land hunger fed the activities of the country's principal mass movement, the United Irish League. A new Department of Agriculture and Technical Instruction had just been established in 1899 with a wide-ranging mandate to improve the country's economic well-being. The co-operative movement, founded by Horace Plunkett in 1894, was making inroads in

MICHAEL'S LANE, DUBLIN. W.L.

Tenements in Michael's Lane, Dublin. Turn-of-the-century Dublin was notorious for its overcrowded and unsanitary tenements, which bred infectious disease.

45

rural Ireland. The Congested Districts Board, established in 1891 as part of the Conservative Government's bid to draw the teeth of discontent by redressing the grievances fuelling Irish nationalism, was attempting to tackle the manifestations of chronic underdevelopment that blighted the most severely-deprived parts of the west of Ireland. The Board, with its brief to improve agriculture and encourage the setting up of industries in the country's poorer regions, acquired and distributed land to help increase the economic viability of smallholders and had sought, with some success, to develop a fishing industry along the western seaboard.[11] Yet, for all of this modernising effort, evidence of the country's economic condition remained, for the most part, depressingly negative.

1. Demographic decay

Just as had been the case ever since the Great Famine, the main symptom of the country's frailty was a demographic one. More than 50 years after the Famine, Ireland's population was still in decline. The 1901 Census, which affords a fascinating insight into Irish society as it was a century ago, put the country's total population at 4,456,546. This represented a staggering, devastating drop of over three and a half million people in just 60 years. It is true that the rate of population decline had slowed in the 1890s, but there were still a quarter of a million fewer people living on the island in 1901 than there had been just a decade earlier.[12] It was no wonder that so many people despaired about the country's future prospects.

It was not merely a case of a dwindling population. As a result of decades of emigration, marriage and birth rates were abnormally low. A turn-of-the-century Irishman over 20 years of age was more likely to be a bachelor than a husband, while almost two-thirds of all Irish women of child-bearing age were unmarried. As one early twentieth-century observer put it:

> Ireland is largely a country of late marriages and of few marriages. Emigration has drained the country to an unnatural degree of the young men and women of marrying age, and those who remain are . . . frequently unable to marry until the exuberance of life has gone out of them.[13]

In 1901, some two-thirds of the population was unmarried and the percentage of men and women in this situation was considerably higher in Ireland than in England and Wales.[14] Celibacy rates had risen steadily in the half-century after the Famine.[15] Even among Irishmen well beyond the first flush of youth, bachelorhood was a common condition. At the turn of the century, a quarter of all men aged between 45 and 55 were still unmarried. One can scarcely comprehend the frustrations this situation must have engendered among those for whom bachelorhood and spinsterhood was a matter of social and economic necessity rather than of personal choice. On account of the country's low marriage rate, late nineteenth-century Irish birth rates were depressed by European standards. Only France had a lower rate. The result of these demographic abnormalities was that the number of young people left in the country was declining in an alarming fashion.

Population decline was not uniform. Connacht's population had been slashed by almost 800,000 since 1841 while the counties of Cavan and Monaghan had lost some 13% of their people in the decade since 1891. There were even

Fish curing at Port Magee, Co. Kerry. The Congested Districts Board encouraged the development of a fishing industry in the west of Ireland.

Gweedore, Co. Donegal. Living conditions were very harsh in the Congested Districts along the western seaboard. Although housing conditions were being gradually improved, some families still lived in rudimentary mud cabins.

increases in some urban areas. Antrim, Down and Dublin were registering notable population gains. Belfast had made spectacular strides in the latter part of the nineteenth century on the back of its industrial success. With a population of almost 350,000, a leap of 27% in ten years, by the turn of the century it had dramatically outstripped Dublin as the country's largest city. Belfast people were proud of the city's achievements in establishing itself, from very modest beginnings, as Ireland's premier industrial and commercial centre.

Dublin's population was artificially low because the adjoining townships of Rathmines, Rathgar and Pembroke insisted, in defiance of geography, on retaining their separate status. Their prosperous inhabitants, who were happy to make a living in Dublin, preferred not to burden themselves with the upkeep of the city's poor. The dispute surrounding the Dublin Corporation Bill in 1900 was something of a microcosm of wider political differences. The Bill sought to extend the area of Dublin city, thereby relieving chronic congestion and providing additional financial resources for the city's maintenance and improvement, but the townships, with their large unionist populations, did not want to be absorbed by the nationalist-controlled Dublin Corporation, and fiercely resisted this move. Successful lobbying by the townships secured changes to the legislation defining the city's boundaries as it went through parliament, although they were required to combine with Dublin Corporation in providing an improved water supply and sewerage system in the interests of higher public health standards.[16]

2. The emigrant tide

During that final decade of the century, over 430,000 Irish people took the emigrant ship. In 1899 alone, as many as 32,241 people left the country, and it appeared that the emigration might even be on a rising curve again.[17] In the early months of 1900, emigration figures were boosted by the flight of young men who feared they might be conscripted for service in the Boer War. Although 25 million Europeans emigrated between 1870 and 1900, Ireland's emigration rate remained higher than anywhere else in Europe. Ireland was a demographic oddity at a time when the continent's population, substantial emigration notwithstanding, was climbing at an impressive rate due to advances in medicine and sanitation.[18] For instance, on the back of a combination of territorial expansion and natural increase, the Russian Empire's population rose by 70% between 1890 and 1911 whereas Ireland, in the same period, suffered a population drop of 5%. Europe as a whole witnessed its population rise from 293 million to 490 million between 1870 and 1914.

Those who emigrated were mainly young people in the prime of their lives. On one Cunard Line voyage, 170 out of the 195 steerage passengers bound for New York from Queenstown were young men aged between 17 and 26.[19] The bulk of female emigrants were equally young and unmarried.[20] The departure of so many young people inevitably made its mark on the society they left behind. Emigration-hit villages were left with predominantly aged populations and a conspicuous shortage of young, economically-active people. This had a negative impact on the lifestyle of rural Ireland which, in turn, encouraged further waves of emigration. In its first edition, *The Leader* complained of 'the dullness of country life' which it held partly responsible for stripping the land of so many of its people.[21] The schoolgoing population was dwindling, schools were being closed and labour shortages were pushing up wages in a stagnant economy. Schools inspectors observed that, in some areas, school attendance was being affected by farmers keeping their children at home to help out with farm work because emigration had drained the pool of agricultural labourers.

Most turn-of-the-century emigrants chose Britain or America as their destination. Thirty emigrants crossed the Atlantic to the United States for every one that chose to go to Australia. The US Census of 1900 counted 1.6 million Irish-born people who made up almost one-for-tieth of America's growing population. Behind such statistics lay a multitude of individual stories. Personal advertisements placed in a turn-of-the-century newspaper provide a melancholy insight into the human impact of decades of Irish emigration. *The Weekly Freeman* carried a 'Lost Friends' column through which readers could attempt to trace missing relatives. As the paper circulated amongst Irish communities abroad, its columns held out the hope that emigrants, who had left many years before and lost touch with their families in Ireland, might at last be contacted again. Many advertisers appear to have been ageing parents anxious for news of their emigrant offspring:

> Meany John and James; Left Toonagh, Quin, Co. Clare about twenty years ago for Adelaide, Australia . . . Sought by their father.
>
> Hayes Charles; Left Ballynew, Castlebar in 1880; last heard of 15 years ago, he was then in Chicago. . . Sought for by his mother.

Sometimes too, those who had left, or their children, were keen to trace their families who had stayed behind:

> Sullivan, Mr Florence, formerly of the Coastguard Service in Cork; last heard of in 1875, he was then residing in Ardgroom, Co. Cork; sought by his granddaughter, Mrs William F. Sheehy.[22]

The Weekly Freeman claimed to have made 75 discoveries during 1899, but, as this represents only a tiny percentage of those who were being sought, the vast bulk of searches must have ended in disappointment in an age when rudimentary communications often muddied the emigrant's trail and, in many cases, gradually eroded contact with home. A visitor to Ireland in 1900 reported meeting an old woman in Killarney who had a daughter in America and a son in Australia, neither of whom she had heard from for a long time and presumed they were dead.[23]

Emigration remained an attractive option for those eager to better themselves. In 1900, the shipping company, the White Star Line, later synonymous with the *Titanic*, whose entire fleet of passenger vessels had been built in Belfast, was advertising fares to Australia ranging in price from £14 to £21. Free farms were on offer in Manitoba, Canada. The emigrant trail was not always a rosy one, however. People who left Ireland were mindful of those at home who might be tempted to follow in their wake. An Irish gardener wrote home from Australia to warn of the dire circumstances into which many a workman had fallen there. Even the hardworking emigrant had:

> nothing to expect from his unthankful calling but a life of misery and hardship, with the Poorhouse in the end, as it is only while he is young and strong he can stand these hardships.

The writer was appalled at the number of suicides by desperate working men who 'prefer death to lying out at night and starving'. This was such a regular occurrence that, in Melbourne, men were specially appointed to drag bodies out of the Yarra River.[24]

In 1900, emigration remained a source of considerable anxiety. Turn-of-the-century commentators were acutely conscious of the problems posed by the country's plummeting population. The leading Irish Party M.P., John Dillon, sketched the problem in vivid terms:

> No war, no massacre, and no pestilence has ever inflicted so great a loss on the manhood of the country as the people of Ireland has lost within the last twenty years.[25]

The infant trades union movement was bothered by the scourge of emigration. At its 1900 congress, one speaker maintained that departures had risen to 2,800 in the previous week. By mid-September, the numbers emigrating were in excess of the figure for the corresponding period in 1899.[26] Trade Unionists looked to the recently-established Department of Agriculture and Technical Instruction to help provide employment that might stem the tide of emigration.[27]

Many Irish people who, nominally, remained at home actually spent long spells working outside of Ireland. Seasonal migration was an outstanding feature of Irish life at the turn of the century, especially in the poorer districts of the west of Ireland. In some parts of Donegal during the 1890s more than half of the population migrated each year to Scotland in search of seasonal work.[28] Cross-channel steamers were crowded in May of each year with labourers from the west of Ireland going in search of a livelihood for the summer months. They earned between 15 and 20 shillings a week and returned in September with £10 to £15 in their pockets, with which to maintain their families throughout the Irish winter until the annual cycle of migration could resume.[29]

3. Living conditions

The impact of decades of emigration was evident from the 72,582 houses registered as uninhabited in the 1901 Census. The Agricultural Labourers Act of 1883 had brought about a marked improvement in the rural housing stock. By the end of the century, 16,000 new cottages had been built on half-acre gardens. The number of the most rudimentary mud cabins had dropped from almost 500,000 in 1841 to just over 20,000 in 1891, although much of this improvement was down to the abandonment of such dwellings as a result of emigration.[30] While it was argued that there had been 'a general improvement in the classes of dwelling throughout the country',[31] living conditions were far from easy for much of the population.

Just how radically the standard of living has improved since 1900 can be gauged from contemporary accounts of Irish life around the turn of the century. Coming mainly from foreign visitors, these make depressingly dismal reading. The consistently negative impression Irish living conditions left on visitors is striking. One visitor writing about Ireland in 1901 gives a vivid description of his initial impressions of the country's poverty:

> Then there were the women with shawls drawn over their heads, and the numerous beggars and the barefoot newsboys selling green-tinted papers, and there was the

51

omnipresent donkey-cart and, scarcely less conspicuous, that other distinctively Irish vehicle, the jaunting-car with the seats hung above the wheels ... Some of the natives were no better than walking scarecrows, so dilapidated was their attire ...[32]

One might well assume the above passage to be a depiction of a deprived part of Connaught, but in fact it describes the relatively prosperous city of Cork. Other accounts confirm this dire impression of contemporary living conditions. What comes across from contemporary sources is a consistent picture of rural Ireland, characterised by extreme deprivation, seasonal migration and mass emigration. Even allowing for the foreign visitors' propensity to take special note of evidence that confirmed their expectations, this is a stark picture of the country's economic weakness at the end of a period normally viewed as one of comparative economic advancement for a dwindling population.

An American journalist, Hugh Sutherland, observed that:

> nowhere, save in a few restricted manufacturing districts, is there a condition worthy to be called prosperity ... Agriculture is the employment of eight-tenths of the population and agriculture spells destitution ... In a word, the Irish in Ireland are kept alive by the Irish who have been driven to other lands.[33]

The poverty of the west of Ireland made a particularly strong impression. In Galway, Sutherland described a typically poor family for whom 'coarse meal and potatoes form the staple diet' while in Mayo almost half of the adult male agricultural population was said to be dependent for economic survival on income earned as migrant workers in England and Scotland.[34] In Roscommon, he contrasted the sparsely-populated grasslands with the less-productive areas where the bulk of the people were concentrated:

> And here where everything conspired to cheat husbandry and make life hard, I found the people. Their cabins were on every side where the stones were sown thick in the soil ... The houses were pitifully mean, the tilled patches pitifully small. The poverty was glaring.[35]

Another traveller, Kate Douglas Wiggin, made similar observations about the west of Ireland:

> The waste of all God's gifts; the incredible poverty; the miserable huts, often without window or chimney, the sad-eyed women, sometimes nothing but skins, bones and grief ... the stony bits of earth which peasants cling to with such passion, while good grasslands lie unused, yet seem forever out of reach, – all this makes one dream and wonder, and speculate, and hope against hope that the worst is over and a better day dawning.[36]

The universal impression was one of economic backwardness:

> From the time you enter Ireland until you leave it, the towns, the farms, the inns, the shops, the cabins, all have the label of poverty. The contents of the shops proclaim it; the clothes of the people proclaim it; the poor tools with which the agriculturist and every class of labourer work, all proclaim it.[37]

A visiting angler was equally struck by the squalor he witnessed near Limerick:

> Nothing more squalid than the cabins which flank this thoroughfare could be found in Ireland. Wretched hovels with heaps of manure and slush at their doors, ducks, goats and pigs grubbing in search of offal, liquid manure running across the paths into the road, mud-begrimed, half-naked children, women in rags and tatters – these are the sights which greet us as we approach the city of the broken treaty.[38]

This visitor decried Limerick's 'abject poverty' with 'pools of slush, filth and garbage that would put to blush the dirtiest Asiatic slum'.[39]

Writing a number of years later, the French writer, Louis Paul-Dubois, was appalled by what he saw as 'a general depopulation combined here and there with sporadic overpopulation'.[40] In the Union of Westport, he found that a mere 15,000 acres (less than 10% of the land area) were being utilised for cultivation by 5,488 families.[41] He describes a typical village in the congested districts:

> A new-looking church, a school with its black sign-board, 'National School', are the only two buildings that seem able to stand erect among some fifty houses or hovels. The latter are all built on one pattern: namely a rectangle of low whitewashed walls whose surface is streaked with mildew . . . Before the low door lies the inevitable pool of liquid manure, a permanent breeding ground for infection. Within the cottage it is almost too dark to see anything, in spite of the turf fire. On one side is a recess which is used as a bedroom; on the other, shut off by a railing-work of planks, a cow chewing the cud or a black pig grunting. There are better cabins than this in Ireland, but there are also worse.[42]

People lived in extremely cramped conditions. In Achill, a family of six occupied a one-roomed house measuring twelve feet by six, for which they paid a rent of £2 a year, which included use of three acres of land. One rung up the housing ladder was the typical third-class cottage, with a kitchen/living-room measuring twelve feet by thirteen, two bedrooms and a loft. Cycling around the west of Ireland as an organiser of co-operative banks, the poet George Russell (AE), found himself depressed by the condition of Irish villages, which retained 'their primitive characteristics of untidiness and dirt'. He wondered how a people with such a rich folk tradition could put up with such squalor and advocated keeping farm animals away from the house and the removal of the cesspools and manure mounds that posed a health hazard to humans and animals alike.[43] In the opinion of Robert Lynd, who had a positive appreciation of rural Ireland and praised the standards of cleanliness maintained even by those in straitened circumstances, the Irish country town was 'one of the most deserted and indolent looking places in the world'.[44]

A Galway schools inspector reported that a very large proportion of the children he saw were poorly fed:

> It is painful to see little groups of barefooted boys and girls, miserably clad, trying to make their way on a winter's morning to the neighbouring school.[45]

Many school buildings were unsuited to the purposes for which they were being employed. 'Cabins of the rudest type' were still in use as national schools and lack of cleanliness and sanitation were recognised as problems by the authorities.[46] School buildings were often miserably cold in winter and special legislation had to be passed in the early years of the century to rectify this problem. Adverse weather, as well as outbreaks of disease, often kept pupils away from schools.

The turn of the century was an important time for Irish education. There were almost 800,000 pupils enrolled in primary schools, but average daily attendance stood at only 64% of this figure, despite the operation of the Compulsory Attendance Act of 1892. Relatively few of the country's 8,000 primary schools had a mixed staff of Catholics and Protestants, although over a third of pupils were enrolled in schools where there were Catholics and Protestants in attendance. In the primary sector, a revised syllabus was introduced at the turn of the century, with a greater accent on manual and practical instruction. The traditional system of paying teachers on the basis of results was abandoned in 1900 in favour of salary increments awarded for efficient teaching as assessed by inspectors and in accordance with a grading system related, among other things, to the average attendance at the school.[47] Music and drill were introduced to the curriculum, the latter proving especially popular with teachers and pupils alike. The vast majority of Irish children completed their education in National School and, in 1900, only 5,611 boys and 1,997 girls sat for the intermediate level examinations.[48]

The particular problems that existed along the western seaboard were well recognised by those with responsibility for governing Ireland. The Poor Law Reform Commission, which took evidence around the country between 1903 and 1905, observed that destitution had decreased considerably since the enactment of the Irish Poor Law in 1838. However, the report made no bones about the very low standard of living endured by a large proportion of the population in the early years of the twentieth century.[49] George Wyndham visited North Connaught shortly after his appointment as Chief Secretary in November 1900 and returned with stark impressions of west of Ireland poverty. Writing to his Irish-born mother, he confessed that:

> No one knows in England what 'Hell or Connaught' means ... I wish you and Pamela could have seen Srah, a heap of hovels huddled on to one soppy knoll above the bog level – in effect a simple piggery. One house had a family of five in one room 11 feet by 7 feet. In the other room a family of seven.[50]

The Congested Districts Board, which had responsibility for one-third of the island, did much to highlight the plight of the poorer regions. It published accounts of the annual income and outgoings of west of Ireland families. A family in typical circumstances might have to survive on £41 a year. Income was derived mainly from the sale of livestock, knitting and sewing and 'children's earnings as servants'.[51] Earnings were spent primarily on foodstuffs, with flour, tea and Indian meal as the most expensive items in the family's annual budget. At a minimum of 1 shilling per pound, tea was an expensive staple.[52] The only discernible luxury was tobacco which, on average, consumed 7% of annual household income. Families in 'the poorest possible circumstances', those without earnings from migrant labour, survived on as paltry a sum as £8 a year derived from casual labour and the herding of cattle. Meal and groceries accounted for their principal outlays.[53] Even in the better off areas covered by the Board:

> the standard of living was low, the diet being altogether vegetable, with the exception of salt fish or bacon at times, which was used more as a relish than as an article of food. The house, furniture and bedding were too often unhealthy, mean and comfortless, and the clothing frequently ragged and scanty.[54]

By this time, the rural Irish had given up their traditional dress, opting instead for second-hand English garments sold by itinerant dealers at fairs and markets.

A Royal Commission reporting in 1900 readily acknowledged the scale of the problem, of which the Board, with its strictly limited financial resources, could only scratch the surface:

> There are two classes in the congested districts mainly, namely the poor and the destitute. There are some shopkeepers and officials ... but their numbers are very small and there are hardly any resident gentry ... Nearly all the inhabitants are on one dead level of poverty.[55]

Until 1899, the Board had only been able to buy 25,000 acres of land to improve the lot of congested areas. At the turn of the century, in response to the activities of the United Irish League, the Board stepped up its efforts and acquired a 90,000 acre estate in Co. Mayo. These lands belonging to Viscount Dillon had 4,200 tenants, more than half of whom paid rents of less than £4 a year for land of poor quality. Many of the estate's tenants were totally dependent for survival on money earned as migrant workers. Such was the condition of the area that five-sixths of the tenants kept their cattle under the same roof as their families.[56]

While noting the squalor and deprivation of peasant life, turn-of-the-century commentators were apt to see its positive side and to believe that the search for economic development was not everything. It was not uncommon for observers to have great admiration for the forbearance shown by people in rural areas in eking out an existence on a mere pittance, living 'happy, healthy and contented lives among beautiful spaces of sea, sky and mountain' and to wonder if they would really be better off 'if they lived as men live in Sheffield or the slums of Lambeth, with £2 a week and two meat meals a day?'[57]

Stephen Gwynn looked to the cultural revival then under way to transform Ireland into a land not rich but at least no longer a by-word for misery and unthrift,[58] a view shared by Robert Lynd, who argued that only a strong nationality, buoyed by the Gaelic spirit, could lift rural Ireland out of its economic stupor.[59]

4. Urban decay

The conditions prevailing in urban Ireland were frequently deplorable. Dublin had declined dramatically from the heights of its Georgian affluence to a point where, by the end of the nineteenth century, it had gained a reputation for squalor and was infamous as the unhealthiest city in Britain or Ireland.[60] As a late nineteenth-century visitor, the poet laureate Alfred Austin, put it, 'the most indulgent imagination could

Cooperage in Killarney, Co. Kerry. Coopering was one of the traditional industrial skills that has since died out. The thatched roofs on the houses illustrate another craft.

hardly cast a halo over the unloveliness of Dublin'.[61] Another writer arriving in 1900 describes an incoming boat being met by 'a crowd of ragged gossoons, most of them bare-footed, some of them stockingless'.[62]

The city's problems derived from economic stagnation, as traditional industries declined and were not replaced by newer sources of employment, rather than from the dramatic population expansion that caused difficulties for many British cities at the time. At the turn of the century, a quarter of all Dublin families were classified as unskilled working class among whom unemployment and under-employment were rife.[63] Wealthier people had progressively fled the city in favour of the more salubrious suburbs, the houses they vacated being sub-divided into poorly-maintained tenements to accommodate the swelling ranks of the poor. Overcrowded and unregulated lodging houses catered for those who could not even afford the five-shilling rent for a tenement.[64] Newspapers advertised comfortable lodgings for respectable men from three shillings a week.[65]

The harshness of tenement life in Dublin attracted much criticism:

> The manner in which the poor are housed in Dublin is a positive danger and a disgrace to the city, and it's high time for steps to be taken to instigate a new order of things and provide the working classes with wholesome and comfortable houses.[66]

A pamphlet written in 1900 claimed that Dublin had 'some of the most wretched slums to be found anywhere' and described Harold's Cross Road as 'fringed with rows of hovels as unsightly as they are from a sanitary point of view dangerous'.[67]

Labourers generally earned between 15 and 20 shillings a week while some of the poorest families eked out an existence on an income of 10 shillings. A handbill produced by the tiny Irish Socialist Republican Party, no doubt underlining the negative for purposes of political point-scoring, portrayed 'streets thronged by starving crowds' of the unemployed and claimed that 78% of Dublin's wage earners received less than £1 a week while the middle classes had 'pawned their souls for the prostitute glories of commercialism'.[68] When he was called up to fight in the Boer War, Seán O'Casey's brother, Tom, had been earning 12 shillings a week as a temporary postman.[69]

For those with money problems, survival necessitated frequent visits to the pawnbroker where, at times, modest items of clothing were pawned to provide a family with food until the next pay day. At the turn of the century, 2.8 million pawn tickets were issued annually in Dublin alone.[70] Pawnbrokers charged five pence per pound for each month a loan was outstanding. For the more genteel in need of cash, there was 'a First Class Pawn Office' dealing in diamonds and other valuable property.[71]

The middle classes could, and did, live well. Dublin hotels advertised five-course table d'hôte meals for two shillings while a pot of tea with cream and scones cost five pence. A gallon of whiskey retailed for between 16 and 20 shillings. Single hotel rooms were available at three shillings a night 'including attendance', and with no extra charge for fires. Gentlemen's tweed suits sold for 21 shillings and it cost the surprisingly large sum of four shillings and sixpence to have them dry cleaned and pressed within three days.[72] In Joyce's story, *The Boarding House,* Mrs Mooney's clientèle of tourists, music-hall artistes and clerks from city offices paid 15 shillings a week for board and lodgings.[73] Job advertisements offered young men employment in the grocery trade at £30 per annum. The starting salary for male teachers was £58 per annum; their female colleagues were paid £10 less. The going rate for a trained nurse to run the hospital in the Fermoy Union Workhouse was £52 per annum plus first-class rations and accommodation.[74] As always there were also those with exceptional earning potential. At the turn of the century, the future unionist leader, Edward Carson, then a leading barrister, was said to have been earning something in the region of £20,000 a year.[75]

Jobs in the Royal Irish Constabulary were prized for their permanence, the social respectability that came with them and the entitlement to a pension after 25 years of service. Yet ordinary constables and their families lived lives that were far from comfortable. Giving evidence to a 1901 inquiry, a Sergeant Joseph Boyle of Naas, who had spent 20 years in the force, said he earned a net monthly income of less than £7 to support his wife and seven children. They paid £1.11s in rent and had a daily food bill of four shillings and two pence. Fuel, light and soap cost a further sixpence a day. The family could scarcely make ends meet. A four-pound loaf cost them five pence and a pound of beefsteak eight pence. Policemen faced a struggle to maintain a lifestyle in keeping with their social standing.

For the poor, daily life was unremittingly harsh. Throughout the country, 78,000 households were crowded into one-roomed accommodation while a quarter of a million other households had the benefit of just two rooms. Physical congestion was considerably greater in Dublin than in comparable British cities. Dublin crammed an average of 64 people into each acre of ground as against 20 to the acre in Bradford and Leicester.[76] At the turn of the century, only 40% of Dublin families occupied a house of their own.[77] Over a third of Dublin families, 21,000 in all, occupied a single room, a proportion that was appreciably higher than in comparable British cities.[78] There were still over 19,000 Dublin families living in fourth-class accommodation, which was defined as a house with between one and four windows occupied by two or three families, or a larger building housing four or more families.

During the 1890s, Seán O'Casey's family squeezed into two bug-infested rooms in a cottage at Dublin's North Wall. The cottage's remaining two rooms housed a couple with eight 'half-fed' children whose clothes were full of 'shreds and patches'.[79] Overcrowded tenement accommodation brought dangers other than disease. Mary Walsh, who made a living as a rag picker, died in a fire in the tenement room where she lived. The fire was caused when, reputedly very drunk, she dropped a lighted candle into the heap of rags which blanketed her room to such an extent that they initially obstructed the fire brigade's access to the blaze.[80]

Belfast made a quite different impression:

> with its industrial clamour, its new red brick that screams at you, and its electric trams that fly faster than the trams anywhere else, represents … the rush of the nineteenth century into Ireland. It is the nineteenth century in youth, however, not in decadence. Belfast has made itself too hastily … as yet an industrial camp and not a city … It will be pulled down one of these days, and

built afresh by people who love it too well to leave it like a jumble of jerry-building in a field … Belfast has grown up like a child whose parents died in its infancy, and the jerry-builders and the catchword orators have taken merciless advantage of it.[81]

In terms of its housing conditions, Belfast was appreciably better off than Dublin. Less than 700 Belfast families were obliged to make do with a single room. Factory conditions were more of a problem in Belfast, reflecting the city's industrial strengths. However, despite the city's economic success, all was by no means well on the housing front. A report compiled in 1901 noted that 52,000 Belfast dwellings had water closets while 28,000 had to make do with the unsatisfactory, older-style privies or ash pits which were already recognised as highly unsatisfactory in public health terms.[82]

Despite its notorious poverty and deprivation, turn-of-the-century Dublin had its admirers. A correspondent for the *Methodist Times* praised the city's tramway system, deeming its services to be 50 years ahead of London and unrivalled in any British city. Trams had been introduced in 1872 and the first electric tram appeared on the Ballsbridge to Kingstown route in December 1895.[83] Electric trams quickly replaced the horse-drawn and steam-driven versions and, by 1901, the city's network had been fully electrified.[84] The Dublin United Tramways Company operated its own electricity generating facilities, even offering to provide electricity to the Corporation for street lighting.[85] *Ulysses* depicts a hoarse tramway timekeeper setting trams off on their way from Nelson's Pillar to Dublin's suburbs and to Kingstown.[86] Each route's trams carried symbols identifying their

destination for those unable to read. On the whole, the country's public transport system was quite advanced with 3,174 miles of railway track including light railways constructed in the 1890s and serving hitherto isolated parts of the island. The business community complained about the quality of service provided by the various railway companies and about the high cost of getting produce out of Ireland. There were even calls from Liberal Unionist M.P,. T.W. Russell, for the railways to be nationalised.[87] Dublin also won plaudits for its network of 'commodious, cheap and clean temperance restaurants' operated by the Dublin Bread Company.[88] Travelling down Sackville Street, on the way to Paddy Dignam's funeral, Leopold Bloom and his companions pass a Temperance Hotel.

5. *Industry and agriculture*

With the notable exception of the counties of Antrim and Down, Ireland's economy was an overwhelmingly agricultural one as the new century opened. High hopes were invested in the capacity of the new Department of Agriculture and Technical Instruction to improve the country's economic fortunes. A General Council of Agriculture was established, bringing together representatives of the country's local authorities in a unique national body. This involved putting part of the responsibility for economic development into local hands. Nationalists recognised the Council as 'the first public assembly established in Ireland for over a hundred years, endowed with executive powers . . . mainly composed of men in whom the people have confidence'.[89] The Catholic Bishops urged the new Department to concentrate on nurturing the agricultural sector as opposed to the championing of industry which was looked

*New Tipperary Butter Market. New Tipper-
ary was founded by William O'Brien in 1890
as part of his war against landlordism in Ireland. At the turn of the century, O'Brien's
United Irish League was at the height of its
influence and contributed to the reuniting of
the Irish Parliamentary Party following the
Parnellite split.*

Carpet weaving factory in Killybegs, Co. Donegal. This factory was founded with support from the Congested Districts Board and drew on the traditional craft skills of the local women.

upon with less favour.[90] Taking no chances, the hierarchy ensured that it was well represented on the Department's various committees.

A handbook produced for the Irish Pavilion at the Glasgow Exhibition of 1901 confirms the impression of a predominantly pre-industrial society. The exhibitors were mainly from the handcrafts sector and there were very few Irish stands that could be described as industrial. In 1902, the Department organised a similar exhibition in Cork, an event remembered in the last verse of that well-known Cork song, *The Bould Thady Quill*. The Irish Industries Association sought to stimulate production of Irish crafts and arranged regular exhibitions of Irish goods in London and other British cities. Its strategy was to involve local gentry in promoting cottage industries, such as lace making and basket weaving amongst the peasantry. The Association's exhibitions of Irish crafts attracted London's high society. One stall was organised by the Guild of Impoverished Irish Gentlewomen. The Prince and Princess of Wales attended the Association's grand sale on St Patrick's Day 1900 and were presented with shamrock which was worn as a mark of royalty's new found fondness for gallant Ireland.[91]

Belfast's achievements were as extraordinary as they were exceptional. At the turn of the century, its shipbuilding industry was a world leader at a time when the global demand for merchant shipping was expanding rapidly. The world's merchant fleet almost doubled in size in the two decades of international economic expansion prior to the Great War.[92] In 1900, Belfast shipyards manufactured six vessels of more than 11,000 tonnes. The total tonnage of shipping produced there climbed from 45,000 tonnes in 1899 to 120,000 in 1900.[93] In April 1901, the

Harland and Woolf shipyard launched the *Celtic*, a vessel of more than 20,000 tonnes and 700 feet in length.[94]

Belfast's success does not take away from the general picture of Ireland's industrial weakness. It was readily acknowledged that, outside the large cities 'there are few towns in Ireland where any such industries exist' to warrant technical training.[95] The new Department saw the country as 'industrially depleted', suffering from a continuing 'economic drain'.[96] As a remedy, it sought to encourage self-reliance and emphasised the value of education and technical training. It acknowledged that the unusual industrial backwardness of Irish towns might require Government to become involved in actually promoting the establishment of industries. The Department's Vice-President, Horace Plunkett, was a keen advocate of industrial development which, alongside agricultural cooperation, he viewed as the route to national economic recovery. In a rousing speech to the General Council on Agriculture, which he regarded as effectively an Irish parliament with limited powers, Plunkett enthused about future challenges and prospects:

> Never before has the making and unmaking of our industrial fortunes been so unreservedly in our own hands . . . If we fail to rise to our new opportunities . . . whatever be the mission of the Irish people, it cannot be one of which material wellbeing is an essential part.[97]

Though still easily the country's predominant industry, Irish agriculture had undergone major change since the Great Famine. Tillage farming had declined dramatically and land was being devoted in increasing quantities to cattle raising.

*Pigs being driven through the streets of Water-
ford in 1897. The building on the right
belonged to a steamship company, although
sailing ships remained in common use.*

In 1855, 445,000 acres had been used for wheat growing but, by 1900, this area had been reduced to just 53,000 acres. At the same time, cattle numbers were rising to record levels – 4.6 million in 1900 – and livestock exports were on the increase, although these consisted mainly of store cattle being sent for fattening to England and Scotland.[98] The turn of the century was a time of comparative advancement for Irish agriculture with production rising by 20% between 1890 and 1910, a fact reflected in the growing volume of bank and post office deposits.[99]

The shift from tillage to pasture had implications for the size of farm holdings and the number of people employed in agriculture. In 1841, 45% of all Irish farms were between one and five acres in size but, by 1900, this figure had dropped to 12%. The number of holdings under one acre was actually on the increase on account of the Labourers Acts which set out to provide agricultural labourers with 'suitable dwellings and garden allotments'.[100] There had been an accompanying decline in numbers engaged in agriculture, from 1.8 million in 1841 to little over half of that number in 1891. The number of farm labourers and servants had tailed off even more dramatically from 1.2 million in 1841 to 258,000 in 1891.

6. The Land Question

The iniquities of the land system attracted most of the blame for rural Ireland's predicament. One turn-of-the-century commentator, reflecting on the plight of a deprived region, observed that:

> a half a million people are living under conditions which are a disgrace to civilization, and that the poverty and destitution – I have seen a little and am sick with it – are to-day

due wholly and solely to the iniquities of the land system.[101]

There was particular criticism of the practice of devoting ever larger tracts of productive land to the economically more lucrative business of cattle grazing, while squeezing too many poor people into less fertile lands incapable of sustaining them. Another source pictured the grazing lands as 'empty and bare' with not a person or a house to be seen on them. This contrasted with the 'waste lands' near the coast, and in the mountains and bogs:

> where you will see masses of hovels glued tightly against each other, very low and, as it were, half sunk into the ground, with thatched roofs of a rounded shape like the outline of an overturned boat . . . Some of them are mere huts built of dried mud. Even today there are still twenty thousand of these mud cabins in Ireland.[102]

Successive land-reform measures passed during the 1880s and 1890s had allowed around 35,000 tenants to acquire ownership of the lands they farmed and in 1900 over 5,600 loans to the tune of £1.6 million were made to tenant purchasers. While this went some way towards meeting tenants' demands, antipathy to the land system remained very strong amongst nationalist and unionist farmers alike. On the nationalist side, the land question spurred the activities of the United Irish League whose initial strongholds were in areas where small farmers hungry for land were pitted against graziers. The League targetted graziers and those who had moved on to lands vacated by evicted tenants. Its leader, William O'Brien, saw the League as a rallying

EVICTION SCENE. THE COUNCIL. 1763. W.L.

The scene of an eviction. Although the Land War was already over, land was still an emotive issue at the turn of the century. The Royal Irish Constabulary's standing in the community was affected by its role in enforcing evictions.

67

point for the outright abolition of landlordism. In the words of one nationalist commentator:

> in the creation of a great tenant proprietary lies the sole practical, certainly the sole adequate, solution of the Irish question.[103]

Unionist M.P., T.W. Russell, analysed the land problem in similarly blunt, uncompromising terms. The Irish people had, he said:

> been dominated by a land system that can only be described as systematized and legal robbery of the poor. The governed were, in the main, helots and slaves; the governors were, to a large extent, callous and heartless tyrants.[104]

For Russell, the settlement of the land question was the key to a peaceful future for Ireland. He felt that considerable progress had been made in satisfying legitimate nationalist demands, but that further land legislation was needed to complete the programme of reform. This would remove the sense of nationalist grievance engendered by the Act of Union and enable the Union to be seen in a more positive light. By the turn of the century, Russell, whose sentiments were often difficult to distinguish from those of nationalists and whose rhetoric was every bit as sharp, had lost patience with the landlord class who seemed to him hellbent on obstructing tenant purchase. Landlords, he warned, should not imagine that the:

> dark days of confiscation and wrongdoing had been forgotten. The system is written in the memories of the people. Its memories live in the slums of New York and amid the factories of New England . . . The wrongs endured have nerved the assassin's arm.[105]

Russell argued that the English Government, having created the land problem, ought to take responsibility for its resolution. Land should be classified according to its productivity and purchased for the equivalent of between 12 and 20 years rent, with the tenant repaying the state over a long number of years. Russell put the cost of such a move at £120 million, which he compared favourably with the £80 million spent on the Boer War. In 1900, he came to the conclusion that compulsory purchase from landlords was essential if the land question was to be resolved. This position gained wide support throughout rural Ulster, and brought virtually the whole of Ireland into line behind the demand to transfer land ownership to occupying tenants. With Ulster's conversion to compulsory purchase, landlords were fighting a losing battle. They had been on the defensive since the passage of Gladstone's Land Act in 1870 after which rents were increasingly subject to legal review. Irish landlords were not flatly opposed to the principle of their property being sold to tenants, but argued for more generous terms than those on offer. Many were appalled by the notion of compulsory sale.[106] Landlord representatives wanted recognition of the rights of tenants to be balanced by the landlord's right 'to receive such terms as would secure to us the full incomes we are entitled to from our judicial rents'.[107] Privately, however, many landlords must have seen the writing on the wall. Poet laureate Alfred Austin reported a majority of landlords he met to be in favour of compulsory sale and possessed of a burning desire to remain in Ireland and on good terms with their tenants.[108]

The plight of tenants evicted during the Land War evoked much sympathy. An Evicted Tenants Restoration Fund Committee was established, chaired by Cardinal Logue and with the poet, George Russell, as its Honorary Secretary. It sought to facilitate the return of evicted tenants to their lands, or to other equivalent holdings acquired by the Committee. The Committee secured a number of significant reinstatements of groups of tenants evicted many years before who had, in the interim, experienced severe hardships. This involved persuading sitting tenants to vacate lands in favour of their predecessors, and compensating them for doing so. In 1900, a Monaghan man, Peter McCarron, resumed possession of land from which his mother had been evicted twenty years earlier.[109] The raw emotions and resentments left over from evictions could still well up in a violent manner. Unionist M.P., William Johnston, provoked the ire of nationalist politicians when he tried to link the setting up of a United Irish League Branch in Bantry with the murder of William Bird, a local land agent.[110] Bird had been shot in the head and chest. A tenant whom he had evicted nine years earlier was arrested in connection with the murder.[111]

The Wyndham Land Act of 1903 went a considerable way towards resolving the land question. From then on, the end of landlordism was in sight. The measure was quick to make an impact. A Government report written a few years later acknowledged a significant improvement in the lot of tenant purchasers, especially in the previously worst-off localities. One interested observer remarked with astonishment that farmers no longer wanted credit. 'They pay cash. The money lender – the "Gombeen man" has disappeared.'[112]

7. Health and welfare

At the turn of the century, there was very little support available to cushion the poor. Recipients of outdoor relief, the only form of financial assistance available outside of the workhouse, were paid an average of a mere one shilling and four pence per week.[118] The country's 159 Poor Law Unions catered for 43,043 paupers while another 58,365 were dependent on outdoor relief.[119] In 1901, Dublin had over 5,000 workhouse inmates and a further 4,300 receiving outdoor relief.[120] In theory, anyone with a landholding of more than a quarter of an acre was obliged to surrender it in order to qualify for outdoor relief, although this condition was waived under the terms of 'distress acts' passed during the 1890s in response to rural deprivation in years of crop failure. Not all of the Irish poor lived in Ireland. In his Government role, Liberal Unionist M.P., T.W. Russell, piloted through parliament the Irish Poor Removal Bill to prevent English local authorities from sending back to Ireland those who, having spent the greater part of their lives working in England, could no longer maintain themselves. Under this new bill, no person could be returned to their place of origin who had lived more than five years in England.[121]

Conditions in workhouses were meant to discourage all but the totally destitute from seeking refuge there. Officials doubted the wisdom of making 'the condition of those who have to be supported by the community as agreeable as that of the struggling men and women of independent means' and were wary of what might happen 'if any general relaxation of irksome conditions were made'.[122] As a consequence:

> the style of building adopted for workhouses was of the cheapest description compatible

with durability, all mere decoration being studiously avoided.[123]

The country's workhouses catered for the aged and for mothers of illegitimate children together with their offspring, as well as for deserted children. All kinds of people were lumped in together. The sick shared crowded wards with the insane while all workhouse inmates wore institutional clothing as a perpetual reminder of their lowly condition. Dependent children were required to enter workhouses with their sick or destitute mothers.

The standards maintained in workhouses varied according to the competence and commitment of their management and staff. There were complaints of dirt, overcrowding and lack of sanitation. Nevertheless, some children grew up in workhouses and were reluctant to leave, if domestic service was their sole alternative. One group of workhouse visitors met:

a bright-eyed, nice looking girl of sixteen in the house who had been twice out to service and each time returned because she did not like service.[124]

There was frequent criticism of workhouse conditions. The 458 inmates of a Belfast workhouse were described in 1900 as living in conditions that fell below any humane standard:

The wards were little better than shelters without fireplaces or heating arrangements. The ventilation was very ineffective and no bathing facilities had been provided.[125]

Workhouses doubled as hospitals for the poor. At the turn of the century, Ireland had 34 infirmaries and 14 fever hospitals managed by the newly-constituted local authorities. These were insufficient to meet the needs of the population and, at any one time, about one-third of those in workhouses were there because of sickness rather than destitution. The old and the sick relied on the workhouse to the extent that the numbers of able-bodied inmates of workhouses often comprised just 10% of total occupancy.[126] In 1903, two-fifths of all deaths in Dublin took place in workhouses, lunatic asylums or prisons.[127] In areas where there was no voluntary hospital, workhouses and their dispensaries were often the only places where the poor could secure medical treatment. During 1899, the practice of using dispensaries to distribute charity relief was criticised on public health grounds. Dispenaries were described as:

habitually crowded with very uncleanly patients, many of them suffering from unfragrant sores and some of them from infectious or parasitic diseases.[128]

Roughly one-third of the population within Dublin's city boundaries lived in slums.[129] Wretched living conditions gave rise to inevitable health problems. Even by the standards of the time, Dublin was an unhealthy place in which to live. Twenty years earlier, Dublin's death rate had been lower than those of Liverpool, Glasgow and Manchester, but improved sanitation arrangements had allowed English cities to reverse this situation. By the 1890s, there were ten fewer Londoners in every thousand dying each year than was the case with the people of Dublin. This high mortality rate prompted one contemporary to remark that 'South Africa seems to be a safer place of

Buckingham Street Fire Station, Dubin.
Fire station staff and their families at
a party in 1901.

residence than Dublin'.[130] Though their death rates were high by contemporary English standards, Belfast and Cork were significantly healthier cities than Dublin.

1899 had been a particularly bad year on the health front, with a measles epidemic, outbreaks of enteric fever and a higher than usual incidence of diarrhoea pushing mortality rates up significantly. Dublin's death rate had climbed to 33.6 per 1,000 and there was a further rise at the beginning of 1900 when it reached a frighteningly high level, equivalent to an annual figure of 49 per 1,000 inhabitants.[131] While mortality statistics were lower in the country's other urban areas, in January 1900 rates as high as 38.3 per 1,000 were recorded. Although inflated by the impact of winter and an outbreak of influenza, the problem was severe enough to convince the Lord Lieutenant to commission a special inquiry into its causes. The Commission's report[132] exposes the hardships that were part and parcel of working class life at the turn of the century. It makes sombre reading. It points to a mean death rate throughout the 1890s of 29.5 per 1,000. One has only to compare this with a death rate for the 1990s of 8.6 per 1,000 to appreciate what a difference a hundred years has made to the health and well-being of the average Irish person. Contemporaries regarded infant death as an unavoidable fact of life. At the turn of the century, nine out of every hundred infants under five years of age died each year. There were considerable discrepancies between the classes. Children of middle class families were six times less likely to perish than the offspring of hawkers, porters and labourers.[133]

The chief causes of death were recorded as tuberculosis, diseases of the respiratory system and an assortment of fevers including typhoid fever and scarlatina. In 1898, there were 316 deaths from measles, 1,588 from whooping cough and 1,824 from diarrhoea. Smallpox, once a major killer, had, by this time, become quite rare as had typhus, but a newly-discovered disease, influenza, posed an increasing threat. Tuberculosis was still a growing health menace in Ireland whereas its incidence was already on the wane in England and Scotland where preventative measures – improved housing and sanitation and the removal of TB patients from crowded houses – were curbing the disease's spread.[134] Although the number of its victims was growing, cancer was far less prevalent than tuberculosis accounting for 2,657 fatalities compared with almost 13,000 for TB.[135]

The 1900 public inquiry attributed Dublin's health problems to:

> the unsanitary circumstances in which a considerable proportion of the population of Dublin lives. Large tenement houses, each room occupied by a separate family ... inadequate water closet accommodation in a foul state; backyards ill-paved and littered with refuse and excrement.[136]

The problem was compounded by the effects of poverty, 'inadequate and unsuitable food, and scanty clothing'. Insufficient refuse collection arrangements and the presence within the city of 56 slaughter houses and 700 dairies of varying standards added to the unhealthiness of the civic environment. Cork had similar problems with a multiplicity of slaughterhouses, 49 in all plus ten 'tripe and gut houses'.[137] The Dublin Sanitary Association, established in 1880, had campaigned throughout the following two decades to remove cows from the city and regulate slaughterhouses. The Local Government Board complained that numerous lanes and alleyways were in 'a filthy and neglected condition'.[138]

The situation was acknowledged to have improved during the preceding twenty years. Instead of discharging into the Liffey, Dublin Corporation was now sending 300 tonnes of refuse out to sea for disposal each day on a barge while public baths and wash houses had been built by the Corporation. Sean O'Casey gives a vivid account of conditions in a laneway near Dublin's Moore Street, half-filled with cattle on their way to slaughterhouses:

> There was a heavy reek in the air of filth and decaying blood scattered over the yards, and heaps of offal lay about watched by a restless herd of ragged women and youngsters taking their chance to dive in and snatch a piece of liver or green-slimed guts to carry home as a feast for the favoured.[139]

O'Casey's account of the desperation of the poor in their search for food resembles Jack London's depiction of contemporary England. London describes the environs of a hospital where:

> scraps were heaped high on a huge platter in an indescribable mess – pieces of bread, chunks of grease and fat pork . . . all the leavings from the fingers and mouths of the sick ones suffering from all manner of diseases. Into this mess the poor plunged their hands, digging, pawing, turning over, examining, rejecting and scrambling for.[140]

The health of the poor was affected by inadequate diet. A contemporary source highlighted the dietary plight of the poor who survived on bread and tea, potatoes and cabbage with occasional herring and bacon.[141] In stark contrast to late twentieth-century conditions, 100 years ago medical experts complained about the lack of fat in the diet of the poor who, for reasons of cost, used skim milk instead of the more expensive full-fat version.[142]

The recommendations of the 1900 report on public health in Dublin were decidedly modest. Tenements should have water on each floor and 'separate sanitary accommodation should be provided for at least every two families'! It argued that 'no stables should be let as dwellings without a licence having first been obtained from the Corporation,'[143] indicating that this type of accommodation was still in use at the time.

As a city, Dublin was not alone in posing a severe health risk to its citizens. Though Belfast provided a healthier environment and had a lower death rate, in 1900 it experienced a high incidence of typhoid fever which killed 39 people. Yet the local authorities there prided themselves on the city's improving health standards.[144] Limerick was struck by typhoid in 1902, an outbreak which was attributed to defects in the city's water supplies and to low standards of hygiene, with cesspools outside every house in the city's poorer quarters and most houses having no sanitation of any kind.[145] In London in early 1900, there were 50 deaths a day from influenza. Later in the year, Glasgow witnessed an outbreak of a much older scourge, bubonic plague. Local authorities in Ireland successfully took precautions to prevent the disease's introduction into Ireland, performing special health checks on vessels arriving from Scotland.

People living at the turn of the century had plenty of health worries other than the prevailing life-threatening diseases. The public was bothered by a plethora of lesser ailments and contemporary newspaper advertisements promoted a range of products promising medicinal relief. 'Dr Williams' Pink Pills for Pale People' boasted of having cured thousands of cases of anaemia, weakness, palpitations and 'all forms of female weakness'. Not content to rely on its own claims, the manufacturers reproduced detailed case studies highlighting their medicine's multi-faceted powers. 'Beecham's Pills' laid claim to a similar versatility, promising relief from nervous disorders, 'wind and pains in the stomach', 'giddiness, costiveness and scurvy' as well as 'disturbed sleep and frightful dreams' and what were delicately called 'female complaints'. 'Congreve's Elixir' pledged to tackle lung diseases while 'Burgess's Lion Ointment' offered 'a certain cure for ulcers, abscesses, tumours, polyps, piles and poisoned wounds of all kinds'. Coughs, bronchitis and asthma were dealt with by 'Powell's Balsam of Aniseed', 'Scott's Emulsion' and 'Potter's Asthma Cure'. For 'sick headache and torpid liver' readers were urged to employ 'Carter's Little Liver Pills'.[146] 'Warner's Safe Cure' was said to nip influenza in the bud while enriching the blood, toning up the liver and driving out 'accumulated poisons'.

8. A sporting nation

Organised spectator sport was still in its infancy in 1900. It certainly enjoyed nothing like the appeal it was to acquire during the twentieth century.

The sports news on New Year's Day contained much that would continue to be familiar to a twentieth-century readership. There were reports on Irish and English race meetings, on hockey, on rugby and on 'the Association Game'. The results from the English First Division involved teams who would survive and prosper in the coming century. Nottingham Forest, Liverpool, Wolverhampton Wanderers, Everton, Blackburn Rovers, Aston Villa and Manchester City were all in action over the previous weekend.

In Ireland, association football was strongest in the North where again the results in the Ulster Senior League could have been repeated for much of the following century – Celtic 3 Glentoran 2; Linfield 3 Cliftonville 1. The ten teams that competed in the Leinster Senior League included Shelbourne, which has survived the twentieth century. Clubs that would subsequently fade from the Irish football scene included regimental teams, the Rifle Brigade and the Liverpools, as well as Tritonville and the Freebooters. *The Leader* attacked the Freebooters for being made up exclusively of 'young gentlemen' educated in England.[147] Founded in 1881, the Irish Cup served as an island-wide competition for soccer clubs. It was dominated by Northern teams. The first team from outside of Ulster, aside from the regimental outfits, to make it to the cup final was Bohemians, who in 1895 had been beaten by a whopping 10 goals to 1 by Linfield, The club again contested the 1900 final when it fared considerably better, going down just 2-1 to Cliftonville.[148]

Ireland won its first rugby triple crown in 1899. In early February 1900, when England beat Ireland in an international rugby match played in London, an Irish newspaper wondered 'how many football victories would it take to counterbalance one defeat by the Boers?'[149] Such were the consolations of sporting failure! Later in the month, Ireland also lost to Scotland at rugby and, in a soccer international played on the same day, went down by two goals to nil to Wales which had not won a match since 1896. This was one of three soccer defeats during 1900. Nevertheless, the results were a considerable improvement on the previous year when Ireland had suffered two serious drubbings, 13-2 against England at Roker Park, Sunderland and 9-1 against Scotland in Glasgow.

This was a period of comparative weakness for the Gaelic Athletic Association which had still not fully recovered from the impact of the split between Parnellites and anti-Parnellites. Indeed, the 1898 All-Ireland Football Championships were only completed in 1900. In March 1900, the All-Ireland hurling final was fought out between Tubberadora of Tipperary and Three Castles of Kilkenny. In those days, prominent club teams represented their counties. The match was played at Jones' Road, at a stadium that would later become Croke Park (in 1900, Archbishop Croke, the GAA's first patron, was still a serving prelate in Cashel). Victory went to the Tipperary team by 7 goals and 13 points to 3 goals and 10 points before a crowd of just 2,500 paying spectators, with hundreds more watching the match from outside the ground. GAA attendances were on the rise in the early years of the century. In 1907, an All-Ireland final would attract 20,000 spectators and, by 1913, a crowd of 50,000 was recorded at Croke Park.[150]

The Gaelic football final was played in Tipperary in April between the Geraldines of Dublin and Erin's Hope of Dungarvan representing Waterford. In a hard-fought game played in bad weather conditions, the Dublin team won by 2 goals and 8 points to 4 points. The draw for the 1899 Championships had 16 counties competing at football and just 11 in hurling, with no representation from Connacht or Ulster in either

code. Surprisingly, at this time Gaelic games were weak in Connacht. Hurling and football were played with teams of seventeen-a-side and four goalposts instead of the two in the modern game.

Golf was introduced to Ireland in the final decades of the nineteenth century and soon took root. The Irish Golfing Union was founded in 1891. By 1897, there were over 100 golf courses in Ireland with many more in the making.[151] The sport became an obsession with the better-off segments of society and its popularity with women highlighted the extent to which middle-class women were asserting themselves. The

The All-Ireland Hurling Final played between Cork and Kilkenny at Dungarvan in 1905.

GOLFING BELLVUE DELGANY Co WICKLOW 9904 W L

*Family playing golf at Delgany, County
Wicklow. Golf acquired great popularity during the 1890s. It was a game which was popular with women as well as men.*

76

Irish Ladies' Golfing Union emerged as early as 1893. Irish women were on top of the golfing world at this time, winning the British Open Championship in 1899, 1900, 1902 and 1903.

1900 was the year of the second modern Olympic Games held in Paris to coincide with the Universal Exhibition. At a time when athletics had not yet succumbed to event specialisation, the Irish jumper, Patrick Leahy, won two medals, a silver for the high jump and a bronze for the long jump. In Lawn Tennis, 1900 saw the establishment of the Davis Cup, a competition that has gone from strength to strength during the twentieth century.

9. The cycling craze

At the turn of the century, in an age when motoring was still an exotic novelty, cycling was hugely popular. The modern bicycle, with two wheels of equal size, made its appearance only in the 1880s. The introduction of such refinements as gears, pneumatic tyres and brakes made for a more serviceable bicycle and cycling grew rapidly in popularity. By 1899, the US was producing 1 million bicycles a year.

In Ireland, two weekly magazines, *The Irish Cyclist* and *The Irish Wheelman*, were devoted to this popular pastime, and there was a healthy rivalry between them. There were cycling clubs throughout the country and bicycle racing was a popular sport. *The Irish Wheelman* successfully defended itself against an accusation of libel after it had criticised the standard of timekeeping at a Royal Irish Constabulary sports meeting in Belfast. At the time, cycling was a largely middle-class enthusiasm, for bicycles were beyond the reach of poorer people. The latest models cost between 10 and 15 guineas apiece. Their relatively high cost made bicycles a popular target for thieves. A woman in Blackrock, Co. Dublin was stopped by a youth who claimed to have spotted something amiss with

Two forms of early two-wheeled transport.

77

Cyclists at Waterville, Co. Kerry. Cycling was a hugely popular pastime at the turn of the century. It enabled tourists to reach remote parts of the country.

her bicycle and offered to fix it for her. Instead of putting things right, he rode away and neither the culprit nor the lady's bicycle were seen again!

Cycling gave large numbers of people the gift of mobility and cyclists visited beauty spots in groups at weekends and during holiday periods. It provided a significant boost for the tourist industry and encouraged improvements in the standard of hotel accommodation. Contemporaries saw cycling as a significant social phenomenon about which ambitious claims were made:

> The cycle is the connecting link between the town and the country; it is the key with which the busy toiler and the overworked city clerk lets himself into a clearer, brighter, happier atmosphere.[152]

It was an activity in which women could, and did, participate. There were debates in the journals about appropriate clothing for women cyclists. There were those who objected to the 'rational dress' favoured by progressive women with advanced views. *The Irish Wheelman* was less than impressed with 'the new woman' whose:

> methods only tend to bring the weaker sex down from that high pedestal which her actions and her conduct in the past have entitled her to.[153]

10. The coming of the automobile

The spread of private motoring has probably changed the face of twentieth-century Ireland,

78

and the lives of its people, more than any other innovation.

The private motor car made its appearance in Ireland as the old century drew to a close. The first vehicle to take to the roads of Ireland, a Serpollet steam car, was imported in 1896[154] soon after the passage of legislation raising the speed limit to 12 miles an hour. The first petrol-powered car arrived a few months later. Further imports followed and, within a few years, a small band of local enthusiasts – Sir Horace Plunkett among them – were out and about indulging their enthusiasm for this novel transport craze.

Before long, wealthy visitors like Alfred Harmondsworth, later Lord Northcliff, Irish-born founder of *The Daily Mail*, and Europe's first media mogul, were exploring the Irish countryside on four wheels, travelling over chronically bad roads that had been neglected during the railway age, and were ill-suited to the far-from-robust early automobiles. The steamers that crossed the Irish Sea were already catering for visiting motorists, charging three guineas to transport a one-tonne car from Holyhead to Dublin. Cars were 'slung' on board and accommodated on deck where they were covered with waterproofs during the voyage.[155]

In 1900, the first car rally took place in Ireland and a new magazine, *Motor News*, made its appearance catering for devotees of this radical new mode of transport. The Irish Automobile Club was founded in 1901, and the motor car

St Stephen's Green, Dublin. An early motorist takes to the empty streets of Dublin.

began its slow ascent towards the dominance it came to enjoy in the second half of the twentieth century.

Motoring was an exhilarating experience for those new to it. In one of his short stories, James Joyce captures the excitement roused by early twentieth-century motoring:

> At the crest of the hill at Inchicore sightseers had gathered in clumps to watch the cars careering homewards, and through this channel of poverty and inaction the Continent sped its wealth and industry.[156]

Wilfrid Scawen Blunt travelled to Paris in a friend's car to visit the Universal Exhibition, and was impressed by the vehicle's speed of 15 miles an hour but intimidated by its forbidding cost, £800.[157] Not everyone was impressed by the technological charms of the motor car. One source drew attention to the motor car's disadvantages:

> It smells; it is dangerous; it explodes; it is unsuited for leisurely conversation.[158]

Motoring was a vexatious subject at the turn of the century. When local communities throughout France sent messages to the French President on the occasion of the Universal Exhibition of 1900, according to a contemporary source:

> the chief bone of contention was not politics but automotor cars. The revolution brought about by this new method of locomotion had produced anarchy in the neighbourhood of all large towns and the County Councils were agitated by conflicting claims of valid and doubtful interests.[159]

Despite the mere handful of cars on Ireland's roads, there was already a motoring fatality in 1900 when an English visitor sustained head injuries as a result of her car overturning in the Clare Glens. She died in Limerick a few days later from what was termed 'concussion of the brain'.[160]

The automobile was still an exotic novelty on turn-of-the-century roads. Passenger travel was still dominated by railways, trams and the traditional jaunting car, or the outside car as it was known, on which passengers sat outside the carriage wheels. A turn-of-the-century traveller describes the pleasures of using an Irish 'outside car':

> You must not be afraid of a car if you want to enjoy it. Hold the rail if you must, at first . . . Your driver will take all the chances that a crowded thoroughfare gives him; he would scorn to leave more than an inch between your foot and a Guinness' beer dray; he will shake your flounces and furbelows in the very windows of the passing trams, but he is beloved by the gods, and nothing ever happens to him.[161]

In 1899, Henry Ford, the son of immigrants from Cork, founded the Detroit Motor Company which became a major automobile manufacturer and helped bring the family car within the financial reach of ever greater numbers of people. As another century draws to a close, Henry Ford's legacy poses its own problems as the popularity of motoring threatens to overwhelm the existing road network, and damage the environment, especially in the main urban areas.

Tourist car at Lake Hotel, Inchigeela, Co. Cork.

11. Tourists discover Ireland

At the turn of the century, the novel phenomenon of tourism was making its mark and Ireland was attracting attention from travellers. There were those who were enthusiastic about Ireland's potential as a tourism destination. In 1894, F.W. Crossley launched a new publication, *The Irish Tourist*, to promote tourism development. Crossley believed that, if Ireland's charm and beauty became better known, the country could attract 'multitudinous visitors' with the wealth this generated acting as 'a panacea for Ireland's ills'.[162]

Queen Victoria's visit to Ireland in April 1900 was seen as a boost to the tourism industry. It was hoped that English tourists would follow in the Queen's wake and that Ireland would come to rival Scotland and the Lake District as a mecca for Victorian tourists. Crossley argued for the establishment of an official Royal residence in Ireland along the lines of Balmoral in Scotland which, it was hoped, would encourage more frequent Royal visits. The Irish Tourist Development Association, which Crossley founded, campaigned to raise the standard of accommodation available in Ireland and to improve the quality of Irish roads.

The infrastructure for tourism had improved considerably in the last years of the nineteenth century. Access to and from Ireland had been upgraded with better rail and ferry services. The City of Dublin Steam Packet Company had introduced modern vessels which cut the travelling time between Dublin and London to nine hours with a sea journey of just two and three-quarter hours. The new vessels in service on the Irish Sea were seen as 'equal to any vessels engaged in like work in any country in the world'.[163] Within Ireland, the light rail network had been expanded and this had opened up the more remote parts of the country.

It was estimated that as many as 60,000 tourists visited Ireland each year at the end of the 1890s. Kate Douglas Wiggin wrote a lighthearted account – peppered with late-Victorian stereotypes of Ireland and the Irish, but not without the occasional insight – of a journey to Ireland in the company of two lady friends in 1900.[164] Her travels took her from Dublin to Cork, with a side journey which took in Waterford, Cappoquin and Youghal, then on to the Glens of Antrim, to Donegal, Connemara, finishing up in Meath where, after the desolate beauty of Connemara, she was pleased to be able to breathe in a 'sense of general comfort, good cheer and abundance'. The indifferent standard of accommodation and the poor quality of cuisine encountered, feature prominently in her description of turn-of-the-century Ireland as a tourism experience.

An early twentieth-century guidebook advised travellers to pack 'pyjama sleeping suits' to deal with the risk of damp sheets.[165] A not-particularly sympathetic visiting parson, the Rev. A.N. Cooper, poured scorn on low Irish standards of board and lodging, remarking that hotel accommodation was below the level of any other country in Europe.[166] On one occasion, he could not be accommodated because 'the long bed' already had four men in it and could take no more. The parson's walk across Ireland is a record of an unending search for a hearty meal and a decent place to sleep. A more robust and adaptable traveller, the poet laureate Alfred Austin, thought that Kilkee, though a dull place with standards below those of English resorts, was 'with its lean chickens, its imperfect soda-bread, and its lack of vegetables save the national potato, absolutely delightful'.[167]

Picnic at Clonmacnoise, Co. Offaly.

Holidaymakers at Tramore, Co. Waterford.

Souvenir sellers at the Giants' Causeway, Co. Antrim.

Ladies' Bathing Place, Portrush, Co. Antrim.

Visitors were often frustrated by the lack of adequate signposting and the vagueness displayed by locals as to the distances between places on a traveller's itinerary. These difficulties were compounded by the existence of Ireland's own unit of distance, the Irish mile which was equal to a mile and a quarter in English miles.

Not everyone approved of the new tourist movement. D.P. Moran's magazine, *The Leader*, was less than impressed at the prospect of deepening Ireland's connections with England through an influx of English tourists which could only advance the rampant anglicisation against which Moran campigned. Even supporters of tourism acknowledged a downside to the phenomenon. *The Irish Tourist* complained of visitors to the Glen of the Downs leaving bottles, papers and damaged trees behind them.[168]

12. Prosperity and deprivation

Visitors to Ireland at the turn of the century were shocked by what they saw. This was because they came at a time when Western Europe and the United States were wallowing in a strong sense of economic achievement which engendered great optimism about the future. By contrast, the Ireland they arrived in had hardly been touched by the wonders of this *belle époque*. Close to the heartlands of industrial Britain, the west of Ireland seemed like, and was, a world apart. The harsh conditions of Britain's industrial regions would have struck

contemporaries as part of the Darwinian struggle that sustained the economic achievements of the era. By contrast, Ireland seemed pitifully excluded from the economic currents that were, albeit at considerable social cost, delivering elsewhere what was, by nineteenth-century standards, a hugely impressive growth in prosperity.

Turn-of-the-century Ireland was a strange mixture of extreme deprivation and a growing expectation of a better future ahead. Wealth was increasing in places, but it had not spread. Rural and urban poverty remained all too apparent, the only promise of betterment for many people being to follow the emigrant trail. Economic circumstances were improving and living conditions were on the up for many Irish people, but there was no sign of the economic miracles that were transforming the fortunes of the industrialised world and, as it turned out, providing the major powers with the military muscle that was to be unleashed so disastrously not so long after on the battlefields of the Great War. While turn-of-the-century Ireland was on the verge of coming to terms with the most irksome economic problem of the nineteenth century, the land question, other European economies were moving on with their industrial development. Most of Ireland was left behind, a place apart from the European mainstream, an economic position it would continue to occupy for much of the century that lay ahead.

CHAPTER 4

Nationalist Ireland
at the Turn of the Century

Here at home, Ireland is sulking and discontented.
Irish Weekly Independent, 20 January 1900.

May not a Home Rule Ireland turn out to be a finally conquered Ireland, a willing west British adjunct of an Empire of crimes and blood and lies, of brutal and godless civilisation.
Michael Davitt in 1900.[1]

Grattan is dead and O'Connell is dead and Parnell is dead, but Emmet and Davis, Mitchell and the Fenian men are living in the twentieth century.
Arthur Griffith in 1900.[2]

Dublin is known for its Georgian architecture which reflects the golden age of the Protestant ascendancy in the eighteenth century when sufficient wealth and social confidence was available to produce the city's most memorable buildings. If Ireland's most impressive buildings are of eighteenth-century inspiration, the country's modern political ferment is, as this book attempts to show, of turn-of-the-century design. Right in the midst of the splendour of Georgian Dublin there is an area whose monuments recall that era when the political ideas that would form a central part of Ireland's twentieth-century experience were being forged in the minds of men and women who witnessed the birth of the twentieth century.

Today, St Stephen's Green is an elegant, well-maintained park, surrounded by Georgian houses. A walk through its environs calls to mind the complexities of Irish politics one hundred years ago. The Green's monuments celebrate the different political traditions that were in competition in Ireland the last time a century came to an end. Unionist Ireland is represented by a statue of the park's founder, Lord Ardilaun, who, in 1877, as Sir Arthur Guinness, sponsored the area's development as a public amenity.[3] By the turn of the century, Ardilaun, a noted philanthropist and social reformer,[4] had emerged as a staunch exponent of conservative unionism in Ireland. He had recently acquired ownership of *The Dublin Daily Express* which, under his direction, articulated a conservative unionist perspective. Ardilaun, however, was no one-dimensional conservative unionist; he was one of the initial sponsors of Yeats' Irish Literary Theatre when it was established in 1899 and also provided financial backing for the annual festival of Irish music, the Feis Ceoil.

Within the park, monuments to Constance Markievicz and the Fenian leader, Jeremiah O'Donovan Rossa, represent nationalist Ireland's revolutionary tradition as does the statue of Theobald Wolfe Tone, which advanced nationalists were planning to erect at the turn of the century to mark the centenary of the 1798 rebellion, although the monument was not completed until much more recent times. Thomas Kettle, who was killed in the Great War, is also featured, as an early twentieth-century figure from the world of parliamentary nationalism, by far the most prominent political tradition at the turn of the century. Memorials to James Joyce and W.B. Yeats recall the achievements of a literary revival that was approaching its zenith as the curtain came down on the nineteenth century. Facing Grafton Street, the imposing monumental arch at the entrance to St Stephen's Green evokes memories of the Boer War and of the competing emotions thrown up by a conflict in which many thousands of Irishmen fought in the British Army while masses of their countrymen applauded Boer victories and yearned for Britain's humiliation in South Africa. No doubt, few of the thousands who now daily pass under the arch realise that it commemorates Irish soldiers from the Royal Dublin Fusiliers, who died or were wounded while serving the British cause in South Africa in 1899 and 1900. Dublin's Boer War contribution to the Imperial Yeomanry has its more modest monument in the grounds of St Anne's Street Church.

1. Nationalist Ireland

Turn-of-the-century Ireland is often portrayed as a country in a political trough between two contrasting peaks of political turmoil. At one edge of the turn-of-the-century vista stands that summit of parliamentary nationalism represented by Parnell's leadership of the Irish party which, in the late 1880s, came close to delivering the elusive prize of Home Rule. At the opposite end of the quarter of a century before the First World War lies that other Himalayan cluster of revolution, independence and civil war which constitutes the commanding historical phenomenon of Ireland's twentieth century. Between these twin peaks lies a period of apparent tranquillity when cultural pursuits are often perceived to have monopolised patriotic attention. This book presents a picture of the turn of the century as both as the high water mark of Victorian Ireland and a time when those who would eventually sunder Ireland's British connection started to make their presence felt. Ironically, this resurgence of Irish nationalism was primed by the impact of that most Imperial of conflicts, the Boer War. This period was characterised by what I describe as a spirit of revival that was behind much of that was happening in Ireland at the time, including the much-praised achievements of the literary renaissance.

Those who lived through the period appreciated that fresh currents were astir:

> Already in 1900 the waters of Irish nationalism were beginning to rise. Two years before, Ireland had celebrated the centenary of the rebellion of 1798, an event which revived the romantic and revolutionary memories of the people. The outbreak of the Boer War ... (was) the occasion for a further recrudescence of anti-British feeling.[5]

W.B. Yeats saw great scope for the country's political transformation in the new century. In 1900, he was propagating the view that:

> we must be prepared to turn from a purely political nationalism with the land question as its lever, to a partly intellectual and historical nationalism ... with the language question as its lever.[6]

Amongst advanced nationalists, there were high hopes for the new century:

> Before the banshee croons for the century into which she (i.e. Ireland) has entered, she knows she must lie dead or reign again the finest Queen in Europe. And reign she shall.[7]

It was a period rich in innovation and political drama which saw the birth of a more restless nationalism that would not be satisfied with the prize then sought by mainstream politicians, the restoration of those legislative prerogatives expatriated by the Act of Union of 1800.

The turn of the century was a busy time for three kinds of Irish political activists – parliamentarians, protestors and patriots. While the parliamentarians were on the verge of ending the long and bitter split in the Irish Party, more vigorous brands of political activity were also making their presence felt. In an Ireland being governed with greater care than ever before by British politicians and administrators, ironically protest was becoming increasingly prominent, inspired both by agrarian as well as political grievances. In 1900, the Boer War, and a rare royal visit, opened up fresh avenues for the expression of nationalist dissension. The politics of this period repays careful examination as part of an exploration of the riddle of modern Ireland and of its tributary puzzles of nationalism and unionism.

The new century opened at what turned out to be around the mid-point of an eleven-year period of Conservative rule in Britain which did not end until 1906. This lengthy eclipse of the Liberal Party had significant implications for Ireland. Even if Parnell's Party had not suffered a catastrophic split in 1891, the combination of Conservative government in London, and the blocking power of the House of Lords, would have obstructed progress on Home Rule. Furthermore, the Liberal Party, though still formally attached to the policy of Home Rule for Ireland, had, for understandable reasons connected with the divisiveness of the issue, become decidedly lukewarm about its active pursuit. Contemporary Liberal commentators made it clear that there was no stomach for putting Home Rule back to the top of the British political agenda. Even assuming a return to power for the Liberals, there was no certainty that they could make any worthwhile measure of Home Rule happen.

Difficulties impeding Home Rule notwithstanding, nationalist Ireland was on the move again at the turn of the century. Nationalists had a new mass movement, the United Irish League; Ireland was in the throes of a cultural renaissance and producing a new literature with a strong accent on nationality; language activists were busy turning the revival of Irish into a political crusade; and opposition to the Boer War provided a rallying cause capable of galvanising

Boys' Brigade setting off from Waterford City to attend a 1798 Centenary Commemoration in New Ross.

radical nationalists and enabling them to garner public sympathy. On top of this, the Irish Party was on the verge of coming together again, thus promising a more incisive Irish presence at Westminster. In 1900, this combination of forces produced a degree of political excitement not experienced for almost a decade.

The years around 1900 have been viewed as a time of high hopes that were to vanish over the next decade or so, giving way around 1912 to a spell of conflict that divided Ireland. As one source puts it, in the years after 1900 Ireland moved 'from a phase of fusion and co-operation, when everything seemed possible, to a phase dominated by "the battle of two civilisations", when the fissures in Irish society reappeared, deeper and more unbridgeable than ever'.[8] 'The battle of two civilisations'[9] might be said to have already been under way in 1900 as the Gaelic ideal and a separatist philosophy took root among nationalists at a time when imperial enthusiasm abounded throughout Britain and in unionist Ireland. No doubt, the potential existed for the moderate strains of nationalism and unionism to come to terms with each other. Turn-of-the-century nationalism had a unique quality about it, an exuberance and inclusiveness that did not survive the impact of the revolutionary decades that followed. There was, in the years around 1900, very real potential for constructing a more expansive definition of nationality that, had it triumphed, might well have altered the course of Ireland's twentieth century.

The most potent political sentiment at the turn of the century was the emergence of a new brand of patriotism, fuelled by cultural factors. Interest in Ireland's national identity, notably its language and literature, was flowering. The new notions of nationality being hatched as the twentieth century appeared on the horizon did not mean that parliamentary politics had gone to sleep: far from it. Instead, the newer, culturally-based movements expanded the political spectrum and effectively changed the question that any Irish political settlement would have to answer.

2. Parliamentary Nationalism

Ireland's Westminster parliamentarians still occupied centre stage at the turn of the century. Parliamentary nationalism was a strange creature, at once bellicose and conservative. A contemporary summarised its split personality at this time:

> The parliamentary party had then, as always, two policies; one adapted to the House of Commons consisting of a tame and ineffective, and strictly correct, parliamentary campaign, the other extending to the advocacy of extreme measures, and destined to placate the forward men in Ireland and the United States.[10]

Members of the Irish Party fitted comfortably into the social milieu of the Imperial Parliament. One-time Party leader, Justin McCarthy, wrote a conventional history of Britain without a trace of Irish political bias.[11]

Irish parliamentarians had given ample ammunition to those wanting to charge them with pusillanimity. By dividing so deeply and decisively into Parnellite and anti-Parnellite factions, the parliamentarians compounded the difficulties posed by unfavourable political circumstances in Britain. They split over their conflicting responses to the revelation of Parnell's extra-marital relationship with Mrs O'Shea. Their divisions deepened after Parnell's death in

1891, persisting for the remainder of the decade with very negative consequences for political life in Ireland. It was not even a simple split, but a multiple clash of personalities – John Dillon, Tim Healy, John Redmond and William O'Brien – each of whom had ambitions to fill the departed leader's shoes at the helm of constitutional nationalism.[12] Joyce dramatised the political bitterness of the Parnellite split in the well-known Christmas dinner episode in *A Portrait of the Artist as a Young Man.* Set some years later, after O'Brien had left the Irish Party to found the All-for-Ireland League, Frank O'Connor's story, *The Cornet Player Who Betrayed Ireland,* gives an acute insight into how passionate and pervasive were these personality-centred political rivalries. O'Connor's tale centres on the agonies of conscience confronted by a keen cornet player who wanted to play in the best band in Ireland which, unfortunately, was sponsored by an opposing political faction.[13]

The son of a Young Ireland leader, John Dillon[14] was perhaps the leading Irish parliamentarian of the 1890s. His aim was to recreate the disciplined parliamentary party of the Parnell era under new leadership. Chronic divisions within the anti-Parnellite majority prevented the emergence of Parnellism without Parnell. Tim Healy was the principal thorn in Dillon's side. Quixotic and possessed of a very sharp tongue, Healy drew his strength from the constituencies, where he enjoyed strong support amongst the Catholic clergy. He firmly opposed the notion of a highly centralised party that had been a hallmark of the Parnell period. After Parnell's death, John Redmond assumed leadership of those parliamentarians who remained loyal to their deceased chief and who, despite their limited representation in Parliament, enjoyed the support of about one-third of the Irish electorate.[15] It was an irony that Redmond, a man of conservative instincts who envisaged a Home Rule Ireland as a willing partner in the development of the British Empire,[16] should have found himself at the helm of the more radical Parnellite strand of Home Rule nationalism, incorporating, as it did, an element of anti-clericalism. Redmond insisted that Home Rule was not a demand for separation but:

> for a Federal Union, one of the essential constituents of which was the preservation of the unity and integrity of the Empire.[17]

During the 1890s, Redmond was willing to co-operate with unionists at Westminster with a view to advancing the cause of reform and helping break down the walls of suspicion that made unionists oppose Home Rule so resolutely. William O'Brien was the final member of this quartet of Parnell's lieutenants who dominated the politics of the 1890s. O'Brien, for whom agrarian issues had primacy, drifted out of politics in 1895, but was back in business again three years later as founder of the United Irish League. For O'Brien, the key to political success was a well-honed mass movement capable of putting the people's weight behind the parliamentary leadership. In the absence of such a movement, the parliamentary movement risked being overshadowed by more adamant political forces.[18]

All attempts at reuniting the Party during the 1890s had run aground on the rocks of personality politics.[19] These efforts intensified towards the end of the decade with the new political opportunities provided by the Local Government Act of 1898 which established a network of elected local bodies, borough councils, urban district

Pilgrims at Lough Derg,
Co. Donegal, 1903.

councils and county councils, a structure of local administration that still survives. The new bodies replaced the existing Grand Jury system dominated by landlord interests. The 1898 Act was epoch-making in another, quite different, sense. It gave the vote to women for the first time and a handful of women made a breakthrough by getting themselves elected to district councils.[20]

In the first elections held under the new system in March 1899, nationalists took 774 seats and unionists only 265.[21] This resulted in nationalist political domination at local level everywhere except in Ulster. It gave a whole new group of politicians practical experience of government. Nationalists now had a fresh arena within which to wage their battle against the old order, whose prerogatives they challenged at every opportunity. There were regular disputes about the flying of nationalist flags over public buildings. In Sligo, when the High Sheriff banned the green flag, the County Council declined to supply coal to heat the Courthouse in winter.[22] Nationalist domination of local government gave unionists what they saw as an alarming foretaste of things to come, as they perceived their interests being overridden by a conservative government anxious to placate the majority nationalist community.

It was not until 1900 that the Home Rule movement began its comeback with the ending of the split in the Irish party. The immediate stimulus for the reunification of the Irish Party came from two sources: the march of events in South Africa and the emergence of a new national movement, the United Irish League which, indeed, for a time, threatened to usurp the position of the parliamentarians at the helm of the national struggle. Although the Irish Party was reunited in January 1900, it took much longer for

the divisions of a decade to heal completely and for parliamentary nationalism to redeem its lost influence. As it turned out, parliamentary nationalism would never quite regain the paramount position it enjoyed at the height of Parnell's power when his leadership, and the results it promised, were compelling enough to unite the disparate strands of the nationalist tradition.

3. The Boer War

The Boer War made a dramatic impression in Ireland when it broke out in October 1899. As R.F. Foster puts it, the War in South Africa 'focused much moderate Irish opinion into an anti-imperial mode, and provided a mobilising "cause" against the Government which helped radicalise Irish politics.'[23] Even before the outbreak of war, pro-Boer feeling was much in evidence in Ireland. A contemporary police report summarised the situation thus:

> The disaffected classes in Ireland have seized the occasion to accentuate and make public by all means in their power, their undying animosity to British interests and their determination to assist, by voice and pen, any enemy of England which may cause her trouble.[24]

The Boer War was a curious affair, a quintessentially imperial conflict that also prefigured elements of twentieth-century warfare.

Some of the war's British personalities would go on to become twentieth-century icons. There was the Kerry-born Kitchener, a leading British General in South Africa who would later become synonymous with the First World War when his finger-pointing, moustached image adorned 'Your Country Needs You' recruiting posters. Almost a century after the Boer War, his association with Kerry, where his father had been an unpopular land agent, was still capable of generating controversy there.[25] Winston Churchill, the cigar-smoking Second World War Prime Minister, spent the Boer War reporting from South Africa for a British newspaper. The war also attracted the poet laureate of imperialism, Rudyard Kipling, as well as Sherlock Holmes' creator, Arthur Conan Doyle, who published his own account of the conflict.[26] The man who went on to become Mahatma Gandhi, when he moved to India to lead the independence movement there, spent the Boer War as a stretcher bearer on the British side. A notable opponent of the war was the Welsh radical, David Lloyd George, who matured into a powerful force in British politics and, as Prime Minister, presided over the negotiations in 1921 that created the Irish Free State.

In Irish terms, future republican leaders, Arthur Griffith and James Connolly, cut their political teeth opposing the Boer War, but there were others who took a different stance. Erskine Childers, later the most adamant of Irish republicans who was executed by the first independent Irish Government, left his post as clerk of the House of Commons in London to serve in the Imperial Yeomanry in South Africa, a force that was the brainchild of the future Irish Chief Secretary, George Wyndham. Roger Casement, executed in 1916 for attempting to import German arms for use in the Easter Rising, spent much of the war as a British Consular official in Southern Africa and disliked the Boers for their treatment of the native African population.[27]

Guinness brewery proprietor, Lord Iveagh, paid for a hospital ship to look after war casualties.[28] The future Premier of Northern Ireland, James Craig, served as a Captain in the British Army in South Africa. The writer, George Bernard Shaw, was asked by the Fabian Society to probe the moral and political dilemma thrown up by the war and to come up with a distinctive Fabian position on the conflict. On account of the war fever that swept Britain at the time, opinion was divided even among the radical Fabians who might have been expected to express outright opposition to an imperial conflict. Never one to shirk an intellectual challenge, Shaw produced a pamphlet on *Fabianism and the Empire,* in which he put forward an ingenious argument justifying a position of neutrality on the part of the Fabians. He concluded that:

> the moral position of the Boers and the British is precisely identical in every respect . . . Two dogs are fighting over a bone thrown before them by Mrs Nature, an old established butcher with a branch establishment in South Africa. The Socialist has only to consider which dog to back; that is which dog will do the most for Socialism if it wins.[29]

Amongst turn-of-the-century Irish nationalists, there was almost universal admiration for the independent-minded Afrikaners and a corresponding antagonism towards imperial Britain. It was realised that the conflict, whose chief architect was British Colonial Secretary, Joseph Chamberlain, blamed by many in Ireland for derailing the first Home Rule Bill in 1886, had placed Britain in a troublesome situation. The British were fighting a war against a determined and resourceful enemy far from home and in the face of hostility from the other European

97

powers. When Boer leader, President Kruger, fled to Europe he was fêted enthusiastically in France and granted a private audience with the Queen of the Netherlands. The predicament created by Britain's isolation was keenly appreciated. In the opinion of one authoritative English publication, the crisis was on a par with the Napoleonic Wars one hundred years before:

> Europe, from Calais to Constantinople, was not less hostile to England in 1900 than in 1801 . . . although none of its nations was actually in arms against her.[30]

The same source confessed that the war had confronted Britain with:

> difficulties for which our forces were unprepared and which our rulers had never foreseen. The light-heartedness with which we entered upon the struggle for supremacy in South Africa had been sadly clouded.[31]

Was it any wonder that so many Irish nationalists scented an opportunity for political gain on the back of Britain's beleaguered position? John Dillon told the House of Commons that by beating down the Boers Britain was:

> creating for yourselves, as a result of this war, far away in the southern seas, 7,000 miles away from your shores, another Ireland which will be infinitely more difficult to hold down than the Ireland which is so close.[32]

There were few Irish nationalists who would fail to warm to the spectacle of a people struggling against the odds to assert their independence and,

in the process, challenging the might of the British Empire. Speaking in the House of Commons, Tim Healy said it was natural that Irishmen should see in the Transvaal 'the figure and form of Irish nationality' and gloated that 'the defeat of the Home Rule Bill was revenged at Spion Kop', the scene of a notable British setback.[33]

Advanced nationalists saw in the war the ugly face of British imperialism. Arthur Griffith, Maud Gonne and James Connolly were all active in the Transvaal Committee, set up to rally support for the Boer cause. They organised a public demonstration against Joseph Chamberlain when he came to Dublin in December 1899 to receive an honorary degree from Trinity College. In her memoirs, Maud Gonne recalls the excitement of addressing the banned meeting from the back of a horse-drawn carriage driven by James Connolly and how, as they passed the gates of Dublin Castle, guarded by just two sentries, Connolly asked if they should seize the Castle.[34] As it turned out, 16 years were pass to before Connolly would help capture a Dublin public building. Joyce's Leopold Bloom recalled the scene when police charged the crowds:

> That horse policemen the day Joe Chamberlain was given his degree in Trinity he got a run for his money. My word he did! His horse's hoofs clattering after us down Abbey Street. Luck I had the presence of mind to dive into Manning's or I was souped. He did come a wallop, by George. Must have cracked his head on the cobblestones.

Bloom was less than impressed by the demonstrators and spotted the ambiguities associated with Irish reactions to British wars:

Maud Gonne. In 1900 Maud Gonne was involved in the Transvaal Committee, which campaigned against recruitment for the Boer War.

-Up the Boers!

-Three cheers for De Wet.

-We'll hang Joe Chamberlain from a sour-
apple tree.

> Silly billies. Mob of young cubs yelling their
> guts out . . . Few years' time half of them
> magistrates and civil servants. War comes on:
> into the army helterskelter: same fellows
> used to whether on the scaffold high.[35]

Joyce was not the only Irish writer to concern himself with the Boer War. Oliver St John Gogarty, then a young poet and medical student, created a stir when a Dublin magazine published a nondescript poem of his extolling the war deeds of 'The Gallant Irish Yeoman'. There was great demand for the magazine when word got around that the first word of each line of the poem spelled out an unflattering phrase, 'The whores will be busy'.[36]

The outbreak of war highlighted the strongly anti-imperialist views that existed among nationalists. As one source put it:

> We have a horror of the creed of the Impe-
> rialist. We recognise that it is immoral, and
> that it is the cause of untold human misery,
> and of incalculable expense to the Imperial-
> ising countries.[37]

Michael Davitt was a pivotal late nineteenth-century figure who combined many facets of the nationalist tradition through his involvement successively in the physical force movement, in agrarianism and in parliamentary politics as a Westminster MP. Davitt bitterly criticised what was going on in South Africa as:

a war for the meanest and most mercenary aims that ever prompted conquest or aggression, and it will remain in history as the greatest crime of the nineteenth century.[38]

So strong was Davitt's abhorrence of the war that he resigned his seat at Westminster and travelled to South Africa to witness the conflict at first hand. His sympathetic reports from the Boer Republics were regularly featured in the pages of the main nationalist paper, *The Freeman's Journal*. The 'magnificent struggle' of the Boers was seen as an example to Ireland. As he put it when writing to W.B. Yeats, 'we are 25,000,000 of Celts in the world population! The Boers are 150,000!!'[39] Whatever the Boers could achieve, surely Ireland could match or exceed. His massive tome on the war, *The Boer Fight for Freedom*, concludes with a searing indictment of England's role in the world:

> England, by her money markets and press
> and commerce; by her howling hypocrisy in
> pulpit and Parliament; has successfully mam-
> monized the world. By her rationalistic mis-
> sionaries, her newspapers, and the influence
> of her wealth, she has morally debased
> Christianity . . .

He lashed out at the world's other powers for being passive spectators of 'the most dishonourable and unchristian war which has ever disgraced a civilized age'.[40]

News from the Transvaal brought crowds onto the streets of Dublin[41] and, throughout the country, nationalist-dominated local authorities passed resolutions expressing admiration for the 'plucky Boers' and hoping that the British side would succumb to humiliating defeat.[42] Resolutions at

GAA Conventions[43] expressed support for the Boers. At a United Irish League rally in Cahir in July 1900, the 'deep-throated chorus of applause that greeted any reference to the gallant Boers' was a feature of the gathering.[44] Dublin Castle nervously eyed the remarkable spread of pro-Boer sentiment and the attempts of secret societies to capitalise on the situation by recruiting new members. At the start of the war, the RIC's Inspector General, Andrew Reed, was taken aback by what he saw as the intensity of 'seditious and treasonable spirit towards England'.[45] It appeared to the police that the *frisson* caused by the outbreak of war had counteracted the conciliatory impact of the local government reform of 1898.

Seán O'Casey recalls his youthful ambivalence about the war when his brother, Tom, was called up by the Dublin Fusiliers and sent to South Africa. O'Casey, who had a Protestant upbringing, depicts the war's impact on the home front:

> Ireland had become a place of stormy argument, with Dublin as its centre. Every man, woman and child fought battles hour by hour, either for the British or the Boers. Transvaal flags were in everyone's house, in everyone's window or in everyone's hand. At times spontaneous processions formed in the streets, marched through the city booing every redcoat that passed, and often coming into collision with the irritated police. All fancy-goods shops and newsagents were filled with Boer symbols; streams of ribbons flashing the colours of England's enemies flowed through every street and sparkled in every second window . . . a story went everywhere that De Wet

was really Parnell come to life again, and up in arms against the English.[46]

There were some nationalists who had qualms about supporting the Boers in their war against many thousands of Irish-born British soldiers, but these were very much a minority. D.P. Moran saw the danger of the Boer War distracting attention from the pursuit of Ireland's priority objectives. For Moran, it was Ireland and all things Irish that had first call on the energies of nationalists. The United Irish League's newspaper took a similar line:

> any Irishman ought to be ashamed of prating enthusiasm for the Boers of the Transvaal until he has first acquitted his conscience by doing his own share . . . for the country that has first claim on his energies and his blood.[47]

Mayor Strange of Waterford, a Redmond supporter, was another nationalist who stood against the pro-Boer tide, refusing to attend any public function that might entail an expression of support for the Boer cause.[48] The writer, T.W. Rolleston, a Home Rule supporter, decried nationalist support for the Boers on the grounds that Ireland had:

> a place and power at the centre of the Empire which puts Home Rule, financial reform or anything else we like within our grasp as soon as we make up our minds to a steady self-consistent effort on constitutional lines.

Rolleston argued cogently that a Home Rule Ireland would play a central part in the management of the Empire and considered that the nationalist movement had lost its way by wandering down an anti-imperial *cul-de-sac*. Nationalists should take 'active possession of a heritage which at present we are madly throwing away'.[49] Stephen Gwynn was another who was ready to combine a passion for Home Rule with a certain fondness for imperialism. Although proud to call himself a nationalist, he stressed that there was nothing irreconcilable about his nationalism. If Ireland had the same status as Canada, he would be as avid an imperialist as anyone else. He argued that 'when Ireland has the same reasons (i.e., as Canada) for being imperialist, patriotism in Ireland will take on the same aspect'.[50] One effect of the Boer War was a definite dimming of the Empire-orientated tradition in parliamentary nationalism and the corresponding reinforcement of a national sentiment strongly antipathetic to Englishness and its imperial expression.

The outbreak of the Boer War impacted heavily on the fortunes of the Irish Party. At the start of January 1900, the Parnellite faction resolved to press for a restoration of Party unity. It was realised that, for the first time since the end of the Napoleonic Wars, Britain was faced with a serious threat to its Empire. Redmond, writing to the Committee charged with trying to reunite the Party, expressed an awareness of the 'extraordinary change of circumstances' brought about by the outbreak of war and felt this strengthened the case for nationalist unity.[51] There was a feeling that 'Ireland's opportunity has at length arrived',[52] a clear expression of the adage that England's difficulty could become Ireland's opportunity. One of the first acts of the reunited Irish Party was to authorise John Redmond to move an amendment to the annual Queen's Speech, asserting that the Boer War was unnecessary and unjust and should be brought to a close by a recognition of the independence of the Transvaal and the Orange Free State.[53] It has been suggested that opposition to the Boer War was vital in cementing a highly fractious Irish Party in the tentative early stages of its evolution after the healing of the Parnellite split when divisions might otherwise easily have resurfaced.[54]

In 1900, Irish M.P.s at Westminster were very much in the minority in opposing a war which aroused patriotic passions in Britain that were too powerful for mainstream British liberalism to resist. Irish hostility to the war made its mark on British opinion. Lord Salisbury, addressing a meeting of the Primrose League in London, saw the war as a lesson in the dire consequences that could stem from permitting a disloyal government in Ireland to accumulate arms under the umbrella of a Home Rule administration.[55] The Primrose League which, in 1900, had around 1,500,000 mainly middle-class members throughout Britain devoted to the constitution and the Empire, voiced what was probably the dominant 'spirit of the age' in Britain at the turn of the century. Nationalist Ireland's animosity stood in stark contrast to the support for Britain's war effort that came from the self-governing British colonies, Australia, Canada and New Zealand, although an acute observer might have drawn an important lesson from the granting of political autonomy to them and their impressive loyalty to Britain in her hour of military need.

As many as 30,000 Irish soldiers served with the British Army in South Africa and there were some 3,000 Irish casualties in the war.[56] John Redmond was conscious of the bravery shown by Irish troops in South Africa even while their homeland was being denied self-government.[57] Many of the key military figures of the war, Roberts, Kitchener and Generals White, French,

Knox and Kelly-Kenny had Irish connections. For St Patrick's Day 1900, *The Belfast Newsletter* carried a drawing of a shamrock containing images of the leading Irish officers serving in South Africa. Irish newspapers paid particular attention to a despatch from Lord Roberts to the effect that the 13th Battalion of the Imperial Yeomanry, one of the many Irish contingents in South Africa, had been forced to surrender by a superior Boer force.[58] The members of the Imperial Yeomanry were middle-class volunteers who had to bear all the costs associated with assignment in South Africa, including the supply and transport of their horses, up to the formidable sum of £170. A member of the British cabinet, the Duke of Norfolk, resigned his position to go on active service while a war loan attracted 39,000 investors who subscribed ten times the amount of the loan.

Nationalist considerations notwithstanding, there were inevitably many whose reaction to the conflict was conditioned by their connections with the British military. As one contributor to the radical paper, *The United Irishman,* revealed:

> In the very neighbourhood in which I reside poor men and women are to be found to whom it would be dangerous to say a word derogatory of England's invincibility. They have relatives among the Fusiliers etc. who are at present fighting in South Africa, and they are proud of the fact.[59]

The presence of Irish troops in the British Army in South Africa did not stop *The United Irishman* from maintaining a passionate interest in the fortunes of the pro-Boer Irish Transvaal Brigade and a deep hostility to British actions in South Africa. The Transvaal Brigade consisted mainly of Irish people already living in South Africa, together with a collection of Irish-Americans and Irish-Australians. Very few of its members came directly from Ireland specifically to serve the Boer cause and the brigade's numbers probably never exceeded 300.

The conflict in South Africa, in which Irish people fought on both sides, was a uniquely divisive issue in Ireland. For Unionist Ireland, the Boers, religious affinities notwithstanding, were an enemy who threatened the stability of the Empire to which unionists gave ardent allegiance. Irish unionists professed themselves baffled by the attitude of their nationalist compatriots, shouting themselves hoarse in 'incoherent resolutions cheering on the enemy'. As one source put it, despite the spate of concessions delivered by constructive unionism:

> the moment we get to grips with our enemy, they are apparently longing to be at our throats.[60]

Ulster Unionism's parliamentary leader, Colonel Saunderson, was a particularly keen supporter of the war and an outspoken critic of the pro-Boer proclivities of nationalist M.P.s. Unionist-dominated Councils in the north of Ireland passed strong, anti-Boer resolutions.[61] Trinity College students publicly rejoiced at news of British triumphs in South Africa and this led to occasional raucous altercations in the streets around Trinity's unionist bastion. Branches of the Orange Order signalled their support for the British war effort. Among unionists, there was inevitable pride in the exploits of Irish officers such as General Sir George White, a Ballymena man, who successfully commanded the beleaguered British garrison at Ladysmith until it was relieved by a force spearheaded by the Dublin Fusiliers.[62] A combined force of Irish soldiers – Inniskillings, Dublin Fusiliers and Connaught Rangers – suffered total losses of 400 men in the fighting around Ladysmith. Queen Victoria sent a telegram to their commanding officer praising the 'splendid fighting qualities' of her brave Irish soldiers.[63]

In Ulster, the Boer War proved particularly divisive. British defeats prompted celebratory bonfires to be lit on the Catholic Falls Road.[64] Rumours of the relief of Ladysmith in late February brought throngs of loyalists onto the streets in the centre of Belfast in celebration and rowdy elements smashed windows in Catholic buildings.[65] Stones were thrown from nationalist districts and the police had to intervene to keep the rival factions apart. In May 1900, word of the lifting of the siege of Mafeking, which aroused unprecedented popular enthusiasm throughout Britain, sparked off further attacks on Catholic buildings in Belfast.

Those who joined the Army were not necessarily ardent admirers of Queen and Empire. Cardinal Logue wrote to the newspapers in February 1900 about the case of a man named Duffy who, with four months left to serve in the militia reserve, had been summoned to Monaghan and feared he might be despatched to South Africa despite the fact that he had never volunteered for overseas service.[66] When the Kerry militia left Tralee in May on their way to South Africa many did so reluctantly while 'cheering loudly for the Boers' and singing *The Fenians of Cahirciveen*. Some displayed Boer emblems while others disappeared into the crowd of 3,000 which had turned up to see them off and never left at all.[67] When the Clare Militia departed for South Africa, John McInerney, a nationalist politician from Limerick,

was arrested for being drunk and disorderly, while shouting 'three cheers for Kruger' at the departing soldiers.[68] When the 125 members of the 'hunting contingent' of the Irish Imperial Yeomanry left the North Wall for Holyhead in March, they were seen off by an enthusiastic band of loyalists who later clashed with nationalists as they made their way back to Trinity College waving Union Jacks and singing *God Save the Queen*.[69] A Galway soldier, Martin Dunne, wrote home a graphic description of the realities of war during an attack on Boer positions near Ladysmith. The final line of his letter underlines the ambivalence experienced by Irishmen soldiering under the British flag:

> It was an awful sight to see us walking over our dead and wounded comrades, but still we could not help them not knowing the moment we would be shot ourselves . . . we went in the rale ould Irish style and the Boers who pluckily stuck to their position had to suffer with cold steel . . . the Boers are great men and when we go home if we come through it all right I will tell you all about it. I wish this will arrive safe and find you in the best of health and spirits, and that old Ireland will yet be free.[70]

Already disliked for political reasons, the Boer War's unpopularity deepened further with the announcement of taxation increases to offset spiralling war costs. Excessive taxation was one of the grievances perennially levelled by Irish nationalists against the government in London. A Commission of Inquiry in 1896 had appeared to bear out the charge that the Irish public was making too great a contribution to the Imperial coffers. This had briefly united nationalists and unionists in a common demand for a fairer taxation regime.

To pay for the Boer War, income tax was increased to one shilling in the pound (i.e., 5%) while beer, spirits and tobacco were subjected to increased levies. The total additional burden on the Irish taxpayer was estimated at £1 million. There were complaints that wine, the preference of better-off people, had not been hit. While these impositions may have pleased the growing temperance lobby, they were deeply unwelcome to the representatives of the licensed trade who pressed Irish parliamentarians to ensure that the increases would not continue to be levied after the war's end. They blamed the decline of the distilling industry on repeated rises in taxation. It was pointed out that the number of distilleries in Ireland had dropped from over 90 in 1835 to just 29 at the turn of the century. By the middle of 1900, the total cost of the war was being put at £100 million and Irish nationalists could be heard to complain that 'British jingoes, drunk with slaughter, still applaud the most shameful, and the most costly war in the annals of England'.[71] The war did, however, bring some economic benefits. Irish horses were in great demand with 'all the good, bad and indifferent beasts of the island' being snapped up at horse fairs around the country.[72]

4. The United Irish League

The United Irish League was founded by William O'Brien in Westport in January 1898. Its original purpose was to mark the centenary of the Rising of 1798, but it soon took on a more ambitious character. O'Brien saw popular confidence in the effectiveness of parliamentary agitation being shaken by the continuing divisions within the Irish Party and conceived the League as a tonic to restore the flagging fortunes of parliamentary nationalism.[73] With its policy of opposing land grabbers and seeking the return of land from graziers to tillage farmers, the League had great appeal amongst small farmers in the west of Ireland. As it became intertwined with the revival of the Irish Party, the League quickly spread to most parts of the country. By 1900, it was estimated to have had up to 80,000 members[74] and published its own national newspaper, *The Irish People*.

By profession a journalist, and for years a close ally of Parnell's who had broken with him very reluctantly, O'Brien was determined to engineer a coming together of the warring parliamentary factions.[75] From the League's inception, he was at pains to involve Parnellites in his new organisation. When it was launched in 1899, *The Irish People* looked towards a movement:

> wide enough to give free play to every school of honest nationalist conviction from the believer in a Gladstonian Parliament to the believer in an Irish Republic.[76]

The League orchestrated a resumption of agrarian agitation and, for a time, seemed poised to shift the focal point of nationalist Ireland away from Westminster and towards direct, if largely peaceful, action on the ground in rural Ireland. Although the League was eventually subsumed by the Irish Parliamentary Party, and O'Brien transformed himself into a resolute advocate of conciliation and nationalist moderation, in its early days the organisation encompassed more radical elements. Members of the revolutionary Irish Republican Brotherhood were associated with the League and elements drawn from local secret societies were available to enforce its authority against targeted graziers and 'land grabbers'.[77] The administration in Dublin worried about the influence of secret societies within the League, especially in its early stages when many Catholic priests appeared to be standing aloof, thus making it easier for revolutionary elements to exert an influence. The authorities watched anxiously for signs of a possible full-scale resumption of the Land War, but this never came. In some places, advanced nationalists looked askance at the League as yet another brand of feeble parliamentarianism and there were incidents of League meetings being disrupted by more radical elements.

In 1900, the League was a remarkable political phenomenon, and one that was quintessentially Irish. It was much more of a national movement than a conventional political party. It was the latest in a line of mass movements dedicated to mobilising popular opinion and mounting a challenge to the established order. As it had to accommodate a broad spectrum of interests within its ranks, the organisation's strength lay in its 'broad brush' nationalism. The League was strong on organisation and was effective in mobilising its membership, giving nationalists a vehicle through which to express themselves politically. In twentieth-century Ireland, political success has belonged to those Parties (Sinn Féin between 1917 and 1922 and latterly Fianna Fáil) who applied the 'national movement' formula epitomised by the United Irish League. The League can be viewed as the last successful attempt to combine parliamentary nationalism with a brand of mass agitation. The combination of parliamentary and extra-parliamentary activity had been a feature of the political careers of Daniel O'Connell in the 1820s, 1830s and 1840s and of Parnell in the

1880s. A later movement like the Irish Volunteers was not, to quite the same extent, an integral part of the parliamentary nationalist family.

In political terms, 1900 was William O'Brien's year. His new movement had become a major political force and was widely credited with creating the conditions for reuniting the Irish Party. While the League's activities attracted copious attention from Dublin Castle's Crime Branch, it managed to remain on the right side of the law and retained its essentially peaceful and constitutional character. In January 1900, O'Brien boasted that, although the League had been two years 'in active vigorous existence', there had not been 'a single agrarian murder in the whole province of Connaught'.[78] As with previous agrarian-based Irish mass movements, the League made its mark by threatening and ostracising perceived wrongdoers, even if it was not possible to replicate completely the passions of the Land League era in the more prosperous circumstances prevailing at the turn of the century. The fear of retribution from the League dissuaded many people from renting farms from which previous tenants had been evicted and, in September 1899, there were 2,500 such properties which remained unlet. Some tenants were even prevailed upon to surrender tenancies they had acquired following evictions. Maud Gonne was present for one such public surrender by a man named Hughes in September 1899.[79] Nonetheless, confidential police reports throughout 1899 and 1900 testify to the essentially peaceful condition of the country notwithstanding the impressive spread of the United Irish League and the anti-English feeling generated by the Boer War.[80]

The League afforded the parliamentarians vital grassroots support, credibility and legitimacy. Its policy platform demanded full national self-government, educational equality for Catholics through the establishment of a University which they could in conscience attend, and preservation of the Gaelic language. The League's agrarian origins were reflected in its insistence on the abolition of landlordism, provision of cottages and allotments for agricultural labourers and reform of the ground rent system. Support for the promotion of Irish-made products foreshadowed later trends in nationalist thinking.[81] While the League was eventually subordinated to parliamentary ends, throughout 1900 the pages of the main nationalist newspapers testify to the enormous popular enthusiasm this new organisation inspired throughout the country. O'Brien returned to Parliament at the October General Election and, though never entirely comfortable as a parliamentarian, for a time he became one of the most influential figures in the restored party.

Nationalist Ireland had changed during the years when the parliamentarians were absorbed by their internal divisions. The reunited party represented the public face of Irish nationalism, but beneath the parliamentary surface of political life new national passions were helping to fashion the intellectual climate within which the parliamentarians operated. While these new trends posed no serious threat, as yet, to the ascendancy of the parliamentary party, already in 1900 the seeds of its eventual disintegration were being sown. Perhaps the most powerful manifestation of the changed climate was the campaign for the revival of the Irish language.

5. *The Gaelic League*

The bid to revive the Irish language was in full cry at the turn of the century, with Douglas Hyde and the Gaelic League as its prime movers. The League was a remarkable phenomenon which gripped middle-class Ireland in the early years of the twentieth century. The patriotic urge embodied by the League was underpinned by a new pride in Ireland, in its language, its culture and its potential in the new century. Earlier Irish movements had been political, revolutionary, religious or agrarian in focus. This was none of these. A predominantly urban movement spawned by intellectuals rather than political activists, the League's long-term political impact was to be quite profound. Founded in 1893 and centred mainly in Dublin and the bigger provincial towns, the League's popularity burgeoned between 1898 and 1901.[82] The number of League branches rose from 43 in 1897 to 600, with a total membership of 50,000, in 1904.[83] It succeeded in encouraging large numbers to attend Irish language classes including in London where 2,000 Irish exiles were taking its classes. In 1900, the League's journal, *An Claidheamh Solais,* was arguing the case for the revival of the language and contributing to the stream of Irish-Ireland ideas that flowed so strongly at the turn of the century.

In his 1899 book, *A Literary History of Ireland,* Hyde reflected on the condition of the Irish language at the turn of the century. At the time of the 1891 census, over three-quarters of a million Irish people were bilingual while some 66,000 could speak Irish only. For Hyde, the blame for the precipitate decline of Irish lay firmly with the educational system and especially with the Board of National Education which, motivated by 'a false sense of Imperialism' and drawing its members from those who were ignorant of the Irish language and literature, had pursued the aim of 'utterly exterminating' the language.[84] This complete exclusion from the education system of the

Irish language and Irish history had been disastrous in pedagogical terms. As a result:

> bright-eyed, intelligent children . . . with all the traditional traits of a people cultured for fifteen hundred years . . . come out at the end with their natural vivacity gone, their intelligence almost completely sapped, their splendid command of their native language lost for ever, and a vocabulary of five or six hundred English words, badly pronounced and barbarously employed, substituted for it . . . the unique stock-in-trade of an Irish speaker's mind, is gone for ever and replaced by nothing.[85]

Hyde wanted Irish speakers to be taught through Irish at school and then to acquire the English language through this medium.

The status of the Irish language in the education system was becoming a battlegound for nationalists. When, in 1900, new regulations were issued by the Commissioners of National Education, these were praised for abolishing the discredited system of paying teachers by results, but there was much criticism from the Gaelic League of the lack of provision for Irish language teaching. The new regulations' sole acknowledgement of the language was an acceptance – one bound profoundly to enrage language enthusiasts – that Irish should, where practicable, be used with Irish-speaking pupils as 'an aid to the elucidation and acquisition of English'.[86] The League organised a protest meeting addressed by the novelist George Moore to demand bi-lingual education in Irish speaking areas and to insist that Irish become a subject in all higher primary school classes unless there were objections from parents.[87] In the view of

the Gaelic League, new arrangements for intermediate education, also promulgated in 1900, actually weakened the standing of Irish within the post-primary sector. Hyde had become embroiled in lively exchanges with Trinity academics led by the Greek scholar, John Pentland Mahaffy, on the status of Irish within the education system. Mahaffy and Trinity's Professor of Languages, Robert Atkinson, maintained that almost all writing in Irish was either religious, indecent or obscene. Hyde, however, canvassed the views of leading British and continental scholars who vouched for the linguistic pedigree and educational value of Irish. Nationalists, for whom Trinity was 'the canker of the higher education system', cheered Hyde for taking on his *alma mater* and scorned Mahaffy and his colleagues as 'the blinking torch of jaundiced ignorance'.[88] As a result of the League's campaigns, the numbers studying Irish in secondary schools more than trebled between 1899 and 1902.[89]

Francis A. Fahy, the well-known composer of the earlier, less well-known version of the song, *Galway Bay*, produced a Gaelic League 'Cathecism' outlining the League's philosophy and motivations. According to Fahy, the League's chief aim was to halt the steady anglicisation of Ireland as native traditions in language, culture, literature, music and sport were being abandoned in favour of those imported from England. This trend was seen as injurious from 'moral, religious, national and industrial standpoints'. As President of the League's London branch, Fahy had very strong views on the menace of anglicisation and the importance of the language movement. He saw the spectre of English influence everywhere, not just in the decline of Irish, but also in the popularity of English Christian names, the impact of popular

English literature and 'the inanities of the English concert hall and the vulgarities and veiled indecencies of the London music hall'. Even the polka, the waltz and the barn dance were viewed as insidious, as they threatened to replace 'the immemorial dances – the graceful reel, jig, planxty and country dance'. The Cathecism went on to point out that:

> The majority of our 'respectable' people are slavish imitators of English fashions and manners; the majority of our upper classes are distinguishable in no respect from Englishmen, and are without any knowledge or regard for Irish history or literature; the rank and file of our English-speaking people lose more and more of their distinctive attributes as an Irish race.[90]

The League, it was argued, had 'awakened the national conscience to a sense of shame for past delinquencies', 'widened and intensified the popular idea of Nationality' and was involved in 'building up an Irish Ireland, self-contained, self-centred and self-reliant'.[91] Elsewhere, Fahy argued for the importance of the language revival to the national movement. It was the language that would act as the most powerful bulwark of nationality:

> Hatred born of unredressed wrongs alone, must vanish with their amelioration, and nationality, built upon it alone will, when the props are taken away, come down with a crash.[92]

The League intended 'to build up again the nation on the basis of the ancient tongue of the Gael'.[93]

While the Gaelic League, led by Hyde and an outstanding young Irish historian, Eoin MacNeill,[94] was demonstrably non-sectarian and non-party political, its advocacy of the Irish language as a badge of nationality had undeniable political resonance. As Hyde argued in August 1899, by anglicising themselves Irish people had:

> thrown away . . . the best claim which we have upon the world's recognition of us as a separate nationality.[95]

Hyde was by no means alone as a Protestant Irish language enthusiast. James Standish O'Grady, described by Lady Gregory as 'a fenian unionist' and whose work had done so much to stimulate late nineteenth-century interest in the heroic glories of ancient Ireland, decided to carry an Irish language column in his *All Ireland Review* when it was launched in 1900.[96]

At the turn of the century the Gaelic League functioned as an outstanding propagandist for a new definition of nationality sustained by factors other than the sense of economic and political grievance that had been the mainstay of nineteenth-century Irish nationalism. While the demands of parliamentary nationalism could perhaps have been accommodated within existing constitutional arrangements, Gaelic League nationality was a headier cocktail, founded on an intrinsic Irishness manifested primarily through the Irish language. As one contemporary Gaelic Leaguer put it, the Irish language was 'the one invincible barrier against national disintegration' and 'the surest and most powerful bond of a distinctive nationality'. D.P. Moran was unequivocal about the League's mission.

Whatever their politics, whatever their motives, the work of the League is to make the population of Ireland Irish.[97]

The activities of the Gaelic League were putting the Irish language firmly on the map of public debate. Horace Plunkett, while devoting himself wholeheartedly to the business of Ireland's economic renewal, appreciated the Gaelic League's positive impact and its contribution to wider national advancement. Though not himself a language revivalist, Plunkett valued the League's contribution to the general revival of Ireland's fortunes:

A passionate conviction is taking root that if Irish traditions, literature, language and art are allowed to disappear, it will mean the disappearance of the race; and that the education of the country must be nationalised if our social, intellectual, or even our economic position is to be permanently improved.[98]

While Irish parliamentarians had not hitherto evinced a great deal of interest in the Irish language, by 1900 they were starting to embrace some of the rhetoric of the language revivalists. In May, the struggle of the Gaelic League was being described in mainstream nationalist circles as:

a struggle against degeneracy and corruption, a struggle carried on by all small nations that are threatened with extinction by powerful ones.[99]

In July 1900, the Irish Party engineered a parliamentary debate on the Irish language at Westminster. John Redmond maintained that there were 70,000 children attending National Schools who had Irish as their first language. There was growing pressure from the managers of schools in Irish-speaking areas for greater recognition for Irish within the educational system. The attitude of the Chief Secretary, Gerald Balfour, was unyielding. According to Balfour, only 38,000 people were recorded in the 1891 Census as having Irish as their sole language while the number who were down as being bilingual had dropped by some 240,000 in 10 years. There was, he argued, no national demand for the revival of Irish and, he added, 'any such movement would be a retrograde movement'.[100]

The League's importance as an incubator of separatism is underlined by the fact that its executive, meeting in July, was chaired by the future leader of the 1916 Rising, Patrick Pearse, who, though still only 20 years old, was already in his second year as a member of the League's executive and was secretary of its Publications Committee.[101] The meeting considered 120 resolutions urging Irish M.P.s to resist changes to educational rules that did not make proper provision for Irish teaching in national schools. The relative modesty of its ambitions is illustrated by the passing of a motion calling on the Irish Party to secure provisions in the Intermediate Education Bill for Irish 'to rank equal to Greek for marking purposes'.[102] Pearse was also present when a delegation from the League made a presentation to a meeting of Dublin Corporation in April 1900.

The battle lines were drawn on the language issue. Modern Ireland was seen by Gaelic Leaguers as drifting rudderless, its prized national habits vanishing and being supplanted by values derived from the 'penny dreadful', the 'shilling shocker' and the 'low music hall ditty' imported

School boys at Derrycreagh, Co. Cork. The National School system was heavily criticised by Nationalists for its neglect of Irish subjects but it did help to dramatically improve literacy rates in the latter part of the nineteenth century.

from London which outraged decency and common sense.[103] Gaelic-based nationality was posited as an effective bulwark against what Yeats later called 'the filthy modern tide'. Yeats himself had a similar perspective on the value of the Irish language. The Catholic priesthood were, he felt, coming to understand that the language was:

> the only bulwark against the growing atheism of England, just as we men of letters have come to understand that it is the only barrier against the growing vulgarity of England.[104]

The utilitarian arguments favouring the English language, implicitly accepted by mainstream nationalism and by the Catholic church throughout the nineteenth century, were now being faced by a potent set of counter-arguments attuned to the spirit of the late nineteenth century. In the Gaelic League scheme of things, the revival of Irish, highly ambitious though it might be, was both achievable and essential if Ireland was to preserve its identity and resist the encroachment of modern vulgarity and all that went with it. The stakes were high. The legacy of turn-of-the-century nationalism, in which the Gaelic League's influence was pivotal, was to highlight Ireland's uniqueness and the distinctiveness of its twentieth-century destiny. Combined with the harder-edged remnants of the Fenian tradition, this romantic image of Ireland would go on to stoke the fires of revolution under the Irish shadow of the twentieth-century's first cataclysm, the Great War.

6. The Leader *and the idea of an Irish Ireland*

There was another significant turn-of-the-century development when, in September 1900,

D.P. Moran's crusading magazine, *The Leader*, made its debut. David Patrick Moran, still just 30 years old, had returned to Ireland in 1898, having worked as a journalist in London where he had become a member of the Gaelic League. Back in Ireland, he contributed a series of articles on the philosophy of Irish Ireland to the *New Ireland Review* edited by the Dublin Jesuit, Fr Thomas Finlay.[105] The emergence of *The Leader* gave Moran free rein to promote his strongly-held views on the need to create an Irish Ireland.

A relentless critic of anglicisation in all of its manifestations, Moran waged a dogged battle against everything in Irish life he considered bogus or insincere. Possessed of a harsh and biting journalistic talent, he was dismissive of the reunited parliamentarians; he opposed the ideals of the literary revival, nicknaming George Russell (AE) 'the hairy fairy';[106] and disliked the extremist strand in nationalism. The first edition of *The Leader* spelled out what he stood for:

> a self-governing land, living, moving and having its being in its own language, self-reliant, intellectually as well as politically independent . . . developing its own manners and customs, creating its own literature out of its own distinctive consciousness, working to their fullest capacity the natural resources of the country, inventing, criticising, attempting and doing.[107]

Expressed in these terms, his Irish-Ireland creed had much to recommend it and, at this time, Moran could be considered a contributor to the literary revival, with whose ideals, however, he quickly parted company. In his columns, Moran railed against gutter literature and castigated what he called 'the English mind in Ireland'. The Irish education system, he believed, was killing the country's nationality. He wanted to secure the revival of the Irish language and 'everything else Irish that it is possible to revive'.[108] The note struck by Moran resembled that of Douglas Hyde when he called for an end to 'the Englishing of Ireland', except that Moran expressed himself in far more polemical terms.[109]

Notwithstanding the impressive practical streak in his nationalism, with its emphasis on economic and industrial development, Moran's impact was undoubtedly a divisive one. Whether he was reflecting a rising climate of opinion within nationalist Ireland, or leading the way himself, his definition of an Irish Ireland was undeniably exclusive and tendentious. A belligerent exchange he had with George Russell (AE) in 1904 typifies his uncompromising outlook. Russell took exception to the bellicose tone of Moran's writings which he saw as symptomatic of a negative trend in Irish public life. In AE's eclectic view of the world, the life of a country ought to be 'in its heretics, its doubters of all accepted faiths and formulas' whereas in Ireland 'everything is howled down except facile orthodoxy'. He felt that 'if the nationality of the Irish mind can only be preserved by unargumentative abuse of the other side, the sooner it is let perish the better'.[110] Moran would have none of this. His was a stinging, mocking riposte, delivered in a menacing tone. The literary revivalists were a coterie. With their 'amateur paganism, Celtic note drivel', they had been left out in the cold by Irish Ireland:

> they are not of the mere Irish; they cannot and will not think, but they gabble 'thought' like ducks gabble 'quack quack'.[111]

Moran was prone to dismiss Irish Protestants as bigots and sourfaces, and was proud of his bellicose style:

> Well we have cried bigot and will continue to cry it; we are spoiling for an argument.[112]

With its militantly Gaelic and Catholic character, Moran's image of Irish Ireland was to become arguably the dominant ideology of the new Ireland during the first half of the twentieth century. It rejected any notion of a composite national identity that might have been more appropriate to a society as deeply divided by history, traditions and religion as Ireland was when it entered the new century.

7. Catholic Ireland at the turn of the century

In the eyes of the Catholic Church, 1900 was the century's last year and, to mark the occasion, Pope Leo XIII, who was approaching his 90th birthday and was in his twenty-second year as Pontiff, declared a Holy Year. This was launched with 'a striking exhibition of the fervour and devotion'[113] on the part of Irish Catholics. The nationalist press saw the Holy Year as an opportunity for the Irish people to demonstrate afresh the strength and depth of their Catholic faith. To mark the occasion, around 500 Irish pilgrims travelled to Rome in October. The pilgrims began their journey with early morning mass at 6 am and were seen off from Westland Row railway station by a large crowd, with the band of the Rathmines Boys' Brigade carrying the papal flag and playing Irish airs. At Kingstown, there were shouts of 'God Save Ireland' as the pilgrims boarded the Holyhead ferry, the Connaught, where they recited the *Ave Maria* on the vessel's deck. The pilgrims spent the night in London before travelling on to Brussels and across the continent by rail to Rome.[114]

In contrast with its fortunes in other parts of Europe, where the Church was in retreat under a tide of urbanisation and an increasingly secular popular culture, Catholicism was burgeoning in turn-of-the-century Ireland and could afford to view the onset of the new century with some confidence. The 1890s had been a period of active church building as relative prosperity generated the required resources. 1895 had marked the centenary of the establishment of Maynooth College, the Church's first great breakthrough after the tribulations of the eighteenth-century's anti-Catholic 'penal laws'. The intervening hundred years had been one of steady advancement for the Catholic Church and, by the turn of the century, it was in a very strong position.

An editorial in *The Irish Catholic* in January 1900 voiced satisfaction with the gains registered by the Church during the nineteenth century. Bit by bit, civil and religious liberties had been won back and a rosy future beckoned. This held out the prospect for Ireland of the 'full concession of her national claims and her consequent admission to a rightful share in the councils of the Empire'.[115] Buoyed by the apparent eclipse of revolutionary nationalism, and of Parnellism, turn-of-the-century Irish Catholicism was more or less fully in tune with the mainstream nationalist tradition. While there had been initial doubts about the United Irish League, by 1900 the Bishops were expressing 'fullest sympathy and support' on condition that its campaigns were 'conducted on just and orderly and constitutional lines'. In a 1900 pastoral letter, the Bishops recognised that Ireland had passed through a political agitation which 'was little less than a revolution'. While acknowledging that some

evils had been done, they were 'for the most part superficial and transient, and left hardly a trace upon the national character'.[116]

While the traditional episcopal Lenten Pastorals saw the outbreak of the Boer War as having tempered 'the spiritual consolations which the opening of a new century brings',[117] the hierarchy expressed satisfaction with the Church's lot. Education was seen as a considerable plus point. At primary and secondary levels, the battle for denominational education had been won. Primary education was, after its controversial beginnings, now 'as denominational almost as we could desire', while the Intermediate Education Act of 1878 was admired by church leaders for 'its frank recognition of the denominational principle'. Only in the absence of a University acceptable to Catholics was there still ground to be made up. The University question had been a source of public controversy in Ireland throughout the nineteenth century, with the Catholic Church fiercely criticising the 'godless' Queen's Colleges and insisting that State funding be made available for Catholics to study in a Catholic atmosphere.[118] By 1900, British political opinion was warming to the idea which enjoyed the backing of, among others, the Deputy Prime Minister, Arthur Balfour. The Catholic Bishops called for the issue to be 'made a test question in every Catholic constituency' which should elect men capable of advancing 'this most important and sacred cause'.[119]

Impressive advances notwithstanding, the church was not without its worries as the new century arrived. Chief among these was 'the steady vulgarisation and anglicisation, not only of Irish political but also of Irish social life'.[120] Of particular concern were the:

pernicious consequences which result from the reception into Catholic houses of the filthy and immoral literature which is poured forth in ever increasing quantities from the printing presses of England.[121]

The Bishops were also appalled by low standards in the theatre where some plays were regarded as 'unfit for persons of either sex to witness'.[122] The threat to faith and morals posed by indecent literature would continue to send ripples of alarm for much of the twentieth century. In 1900, parish priests were exhorted 'by combined and persistent action' to put an end to this unholy trade'.[123]

The Church's response to this threat was to encourage the propagation of a literature that would be 'at the same time healthy and interesting'.[124] The Catholic Truth Society was founded in 1899 to counter the threat posed by the 'cheap and dangerous reading which was coming in increasing quantities from England' which 'made no troublesome demands on the intellect, but appealed to the interests of a lower order which were unfortunately more easily aroused'.[125] The Society's first Secretary was an up-and-coming young cleric, Dr Daniel Mannix, who went on to become a long-serving Archbishop of Melbourne. Throughout his life, Mannix maintained a fervent interest in the affairs of Ireland, and used his position in Australia to support the nationalist cause.

In the same year as the Catholic Truth Society was founded, a New Ross-born priest, Rev. James Cullen, set up the Pioneer Total Abstinence Association with a mission to fend off the social evil of intemperance, which was blamed on the profusion of public houses. Gambling, indulgence in the stock market and 'the desecration of Sunday by horse racing' were also a cause for concern.

The establishment at the turn of the century of two new organisations was symptomatic of the determination of churchmen not to let the ascendancy of the faith slip in the face of twentieth-century challenges. The Catholic Primate, Cardinal Logue, epitomised the confidence of the turn-of-the-century Church and was not slow in proclaiming what he saw as the Church's prerogatives. In his view, there was:

> the strictest union between the cause of faith and the cause of fatherland.

Attempts to break the faith-fatherland axis would not work as there could not be:

> a complete separation between the spiritual work of the clergy and the secular work of the laity.[126]

This attitude would find many echoes in the pronouncements of twentieth-century clergymen.

During 1900, the Irish Catholic Bishops convened the second Maynooth synod whose audit of turn-of-the-century Catholicism produced a highly positive balance sheet. The generation since the first synod in 1875 had seen the 'onward march of Catholicity'.[127] The Synod's conclusions acknowledged that Ireland was in a spiritually impressive condition, but expressed anxiety that the Irish people might not always be as faithful as they had been in the past. They pointed out that the persecutions of Irish history had 'acted as a shield against the attacks of unbelief which . . . were making such havoc throughout Europe'.[128] The Bishops feared that the intense preoccupation with the:

purely human questions that are now at issue, with the spread of education, the diffusion of literature, the unrestrained circulation of every current, however bad or irreligious, of modern thought, the mind of our people may lose the fine edge of its faith and it may enter on to the path that had led other nations to their spiritual ruin.[129]

The turn-of-the-century Irish Catholic Church was an organisation in triumph, possessed of a devoutly loyal flock, yet intensely watchful of threats to faith and morals. It was deeply suspicious of the irreligious leanings of the world outside of Ireland. The Church's turn-of-the-century attitudes, with its aversion to English influences, combined with those of Irish Ireland and of the Gaelic League to shape Ireland's intellectual climate along insular lines for much of the twentieth century.

8. Advanced Nationalism

The year 1900 saw the emergence of another political force destined much later, and in a guise not intended by its founder, to play a major part in the outflanking of parliamentary nationalism. Arthur Griffith helped found an organisation called Cumann na nGaedhael (The Society of the Irish), an umbrella group bringing into a loose federation the network of cultural and political clubs that had mushroomed during the 1890s. This body was relaunched in 1905 as Sinn Féin, but its original name was to resurface as the Irish Free State's first governing party in 1922.

Born in Dublin in 1871, Griffith was active in the network of literary and cultural clubs that emerged in Dublin in the 1890s, especially the Celtic Literary Society founded in 1893 by his friend, William Rooney.[130] In 1896, Griffith emigrated to South Africa only to return two years later to found his own weekly newspaper, *The United Irishman*, which became a vehicle for his ideas of national self-reliance and Gaelic revival. Griffith's paper attracted an impressive range of contributors, including W.B. Yeats and the novelist, George Moore. Griffith's nationalism, though undeniably of an advanced, separatist brand, was highly eclectic. While Moran was critical of much of the legacy of nationalism, Griffith took a more benign view. He prized the achievements of Grattan's Parliament (1782-1800), of the United Irishmen of 1798, of the Young Irelanders, of the Fenians, and even of the Hungarians for their success in extracting a dual monarchy from a reluctant Habsburg Empire. His pragmatic streak, with its emphasis on industrial development, echoed the attitudes of D.P. Moran, as did his staunchly Catholic outlook which would later bring him into conflict with W.B. Yeats when Griffith denounced Synge's *Playboy of the Western World*. At the turn of the century, Griffith took an anti-clerical line and promised Yeats support against Catholic critics of his play, *The Countess Cathleen*.

Cumann na nGaedhael capitalised on the revivalist spirit that existed at the turn of the century and sought to direct these energies into a political channel. It stood for 'the rooting of the whole Irish people in Ireland, the weakening of every force and influence that tends to drive them into exile or make them unworthy of their fathers while they remain at home'.[131] The organisation was committed to total de-anglicisation and the attainment of a sovereign, independent Ireland. It attracted a range of advanced nationalists, the old Fenian, John O'Leary who became its President, Maud

Gonne, who combined with Griffith in drawing up its original programme, and her future husband, Major John MacBride, who was appointed Vice-President.[132] W.B. Yeats suggested the holding of bi-annual festivals to be called Bealtine and Samhain.[133] A police report on its first committee meeting derided its committee members as 'two habitual drunkards, two "corporation scavengers", two schoolboys and a cardriver'.[134] Leaving aside the inevitable prejudices of the police source, it is clear that the power of such organisations lies not in their membership, but in the quality and influence of their ideas.

As part of her ongoing onslaught on British interests in Ireland, Maud Gonne set up Inghinidhe na hÉireann (Daughters of Erin), to work for 'the re-establishment of complete independence' for Ireland. Reflecting the mood of the period, Inghinidhe na hÉireann concentrated on cultural activities, including the provision of classes for children in the Irish language, history, music and dancing. It aimed to counter what it saw as low English literature and committed itself to combatting English influence in every way possible including discouraging army enlistment.[135] As Maud Gonne was becoming President of Inghinidhe na hÉireann, newspaper reports announced the marriage of Constance Gore-Booth to the Polish nobleman and musician, Count Markievicz. The new Countess was said to be on her way to Paris where, as an up-and-coming artist, she had established a studio. She would later outstrip even Maud Gonne in her nationalist fervour and would become the first ever woman Minister in an Irish Government, a distinction she was to hold for 60 years.

Other new organisations with political potential were emerging. The nascent Irish Labour movement had registered a measure of success in local elections in 1899, and, through James Connolly's recently-established Irish Socialist Republican Party, was represented at the 1900 Paris Congress of the Socialist International.[136] Dublin Castle kept a careful watch on the development of the new labour movement. The Ancient Order of Hibernians, a successor to the tradition of Ribbonism, was gaining adherents amongst nationalists in the North. These developments were making political life in nationalist Ireland much more diffuse than it had been during Parnell's ascendancy when the very real prospect of the attainment of Home Rule had served to impose discipline and to direct all political energies into a single parliamentary channel.

One older organisation – the Irish Republican Brotherhood – still survived, albeit well in the background. Its membership was estimated to have been around 8,000 in 1900, a considerable tally for a secret, and illegal, organisation of this nature, especially as this figure did not include its membership in the Dublin area.[137] Police reports reveal that the organisation was well and truly infiltrated by informers who provided details of who attended meetings and what was discussed. Dublin Castle believed that there were at least 12,000 members of Secret Societies available to support a physical force policy if the opportunity arose.[138] In 1900, an attempt was made to secure for the Fenian, Thomas Clarke, a position as an inspector in Dublin Corporation, but Clarke failed to get elected and left the country again only to return in 1907 to help put in place the organisation that eventually inspired the Easter Rising of 1916.

The Irish Republican Brotherhood had strong links with the Gaelic Athletic Association, whose fortunes were, however, still at a fairly low ebb because of the disruption caused by the Parnell split in which the GAA, to its cost in terms of clerical and public support, had pursued a consistently pro-Parnell line. The GAA's 1900 Annual Congress was probably the least well attended in the Association's history with just 30 delegates present, representing a mere 8 counties.[139] While the GAA's comeback began at the turn of the century, it was only in the last years of the century's first decade that the Association's fortunes underwent a genuine revival with an influx of Gaelic League members.

The welter of activity in nationalist circles was not hugely significant in 1900 in terms of political power and influence. It did, however, highlight the diversity that had entered into the nationalist tradition. There was a clear distinction between the parliamentarians and those of a more advanced nationalist outlook who viewed the Boer War not just as a joyful embarrassment for Britain, but also as a real example to Ireland, even if, as yet, no one seriously believed in the feasibility of a direct Boer-style military challenge to Britain.

9. Irish women press for political rights

Suffragism, with its quest to get the vote for women, came into its own in the early years of the twentieth century. In Ireland, it was essentially a branch of the movement that existed in Britain.

In the 1890s, women seeking political rights were inspired by the dramatic advances being made in the antipodes where New Zealand women secured the vote in 1893. This was followed by similar developments in Australia and in some parts of the United States. According to one turn-of-the-century Irish source, women

had 'by their moral and refining influence . . . largely contributed to the purification of the political atmosphere'.[140]

Although women were not allowed entry into Trinity College, by 1900 some 20 women had managed to be appointed as local authority inspectors responsible for sanitation and school attendance. Irish women recorded some limited political advances in the closing years of the nineteenth century. From 1896, women were entitled to serve on the Board of Guardians of the country's 159 Poor Law Unions which supervised the running of workhouses. Within a few years, there were around 100 women guardians. Women were viewed as having a contribution to make to the running of workhouses on account of their expertise, for example, with regard to the care of children who made up a not insignificant proportion of the workhouse population and whose moral welfare in those unhealthy confines greatly bothered philanthropists.

The Local Government Act of 1898 represented a landmark for women's political rights in Ireland. For the first time, qualified women were given the right to vote in local elections and to stand as candidates for urban and rural district councils. It was estimated that around 100,000 women became entitled to vote.[141] The first local elections under the new rules were held in 1899 and brought political success to a significant number of women. 85 women candidates were elected as Poor Law guardians, 31 as rural district councillors and four as urban district councillors.[142] Women were still barred from serving on borough councils such as Dublin Corporation and, of course, the parliamentary franchise was still some way off.

Turn-of-the-century suffragists were a far cry from their radical successors. In Ireland, it was a relatively tame upper middle-class movement, predominantly unionist in political outlook, with a modest level of ambition. Divisions between nationalists and unionists complicated the pursuit of suffragist goals although a women's franchise bill did pass its first stage in the House of Commons in 1897, but failed to become law. In Parliament, the measure had prominent Irish supporters from both national-ist and unionist traditions, an eclectic mix – Davitt, John Parnell, Carson, Lecky and T.W. Russell. The Ulster Unionist MP, Johnston of Ballykillbeg, was the Irish movement's staunchest supporter at Westminster. In Britain, senior Conservative figures such as the Prime Minister Lord Salisbury and Arthur Balfour backed moves to give votes to women.

The new century seemed to Irish suffragists to hold promise of further progress for women, although expectations were hardly revolutionary. As one Irishwoman put it, with considerable modesty of ambition:

> we can entertain no doubt that, long before the year 2000 has dawned, upon our succes-sors every artificial barrier restricting the free political action of our country women will have been removed.[143]

Even staunch supporters of the suffragist cause could be unintentionally condescending. Thomas Haslam was married to one of Ireland's most prominent suffragists, who had been a founder member of the Dublin Women's Suf-frage Association in 1876, and was one of 25 Irish people who signed John Stuart Mill's peti-tion in 1869 which first urged that women be enfranchised. Offering a masculine view of the issues involved, he opined that:

> there is not a lady in this room who, in my judgment, is not morally entitled to every right and political privilege which I, as a *man*, am *naturally* entitled to.[144]

This passage exposes views that were a far cry from the principles of sexual equality that came to the fore during the latter part of the twentieth century. The first European country to grant women the vote was Finland in 1906. Irish-women made the breakthrough in 1918. By then, women in Ireland had become prominent in another area of political life courtesy of the revolutionary upheavals of the period.

10. Political Ireland in 1900

In 1900, despite the not inconsiderable blandish-ments of constructive unionism, a raw sense of political and historical grievance racked nation-alist Ireland. Notwithstanding the very real trans-fer of political authority implied by the Local Government Act of 1898, the demand for at least some measure of national self-government remained undimmed. The emergence in 1900 of the new Australian Commonwealth was noted in Ireland where it was contrasted with the very dif-ferent treatment of Irish political demands. The implications of the Boer War were also keenly felt. For the first time in almost a century, Britain was vulnerable and needed Irish soldiers to mas-ter the Boer Republics. Suddenly, after almost a decade of disarray, the Irish parliamentarians at Westminster saw a new opportunity to assert themselves. The reunification of the parliamen-tary party injected renewed life into the demand for Home Rule, even if, by the end of the year, the re-election of the Salisbury Government deflated expectations and marooned the Home Rule movement for a further crucial decade.

Even if the turn of the century could not match the headline-grabbing events inspired by the tumult of Parnell's last years, nor of the revolutionary decade between 1912 and 1922, an examination of the year 1900 exposes all too clearly the perennial instability at the heart of Irish politics in the late nineteenth and early twentieth centuries. While there was insufficient raw material to fuel a violent political upheaval, there was also little sign of contentment anywhere on the political landscape. In 1900 the land question continued to breed dissatisfaction. The reforms of the 1890s had tinkered with this problem, but there were enough jagged ends to spur the development of the United Irish League and turn it into a potent movement capable of mobilising large numbers of Irishmen to challenge the established agrarian and political order.

The demand for a state-funded Catholic University, strongly resisted by Protestant interests, highlighted the rise of a more assertive and self-confident brand of Catholicism spurred on by a resurgent Church. This dispute was a continuation of a controversy stretching back to the establishment of the Queen's Colleges and beyond. In 1899 Arthur Balfour had made a move to grant Irish Catholics a university of their own, but this idea floundered in a flurry of angry opposition in Britain to the State endowment of an institution that would operate along essentially confessional lines.[145] The absence of a Catholic University cut across the interests of an increasingly prosperous and self-confident Catholic middle class and their demand to have their grievance redressed symbolised their burgeoning challenge to a fearful and defensive unionist establishment.

The activities of the Gaelic League had turned the nineteenth-century decline of the Irish language into a serious charge against British rule in Ireland. The language issue generated enormous passion and enthusiasm, albeit on the part of a comparatively small number of activists who, however, proved themselves more than capable of making their mark. The Irish language was the most powerful symbol of Ireland's cultural distinctiveness. The implications of its decline, and the demand for its revival, inspired a new breed of nationalist dissension.

The visit of Queen Victoria, at the end of her long reign, brought to mind the profound sense of historical grievance that would ultimately ensure that nationalist Ireland would not be satisfied with the kind of political compromise that might have been capable of commending itself to early twentieth-century Irish unionists. A passage from a nationalist newspaper, written during the Queen's visit, pulls together the litany of grievances that delineated Irish nationalism at the turn of the century:

> With national self-government denied; with the Catholic religious orders still proscribed; with the right to carry arms denied to every Irishman; with a perpetual Coercion Act for Ireland only on the statute book; with Irish Catholics treated as pariahs in the matter of higher education; with Ireland robbed of at least £4 million annually; with the memory of the last 60 years of famine, misgovernment, revolt, repression and misery; the ceremonies of today (the Queen's arrival) are a triumph over a conquered people – 'a dance in chains'.[146]

In 1900, at a time when political compromise might have been feasible, nationalist Ireland and unionist Ireland were steadily drifting ever further apart. Meanwhile, Britain was, at the height of its imperial obsession, 'imperially brain-washed'[147] and occupying a different planet entirely from an Ireland pockmarked by communal grievance and dissatisfaction. In the thick of the Boer War, imperial Britain, with its Conservative government, was in no mood to acknowledge the demands of nationalist Ireland, nor to respond to them. As Britain wallowed in the imperial idea, Ireland acquired a new and deeper sense of its own nationality that would serve to widen the gulf between Britain and Ireland and between nationalists and unionists in Ireland, until this fault line became well nigh unmanageable.

CHAPTER 5

Irish Unionism at the Centuries' Crossroads

Ireland is in a plastic state. We can mould her almost at our will provided that we go on doing something. We must give the Irish something sensible to think about and work for.

George Wyndham, Chief Secretary for Ireland.[1]

I am a landlord, a Protestant and a unionist. I hold to my class, my creed and my political faith. I believe that Unionism must justify itself in its results or wither under a policy of mere negation.

Reform-minded unionist, the Earl of Dunraven.[2]

But during the welter of contention which prevailed after the fall of Parnell, there grew up in Ireland a wholly new spirit, born of the bitter lesson which was at last being learned. The Irish still clung undaunted to their political ideal, but its pursuit to the exclusion of all other national aims had received a wholesome check.

Horace Plunkett.[3]

During more recent years, notwithstanding great measures designed for the good of Ireland, no body of opponents has been converted into supporters, the defences of unionism in Ireland have been seriously impaired, and a sense of injustice, whether well or ill founded, is almost universal among those who ought to be, and who desire to be, the cordial friends of an Irish administration.

A conservative unionist perspective on turn-of-the-century politics.[4]

In 1887, when Victoria Park on Killiney Hill was acquired by the Queen's Jubilee Memorials Association to mark the fiftieth year of the reign, the unionist community's political ascendancy was already being seriously challenged. In the year before the jubilee, Britain's Prime Minister, William Ewart Gladstone, had introduced the first Home Rule Bill designed to confer a measure of self-government on Ireland. From that date stems so much of the modern history of Ireland – the struggle for and against Home Rule, the gaelicisation and radicalisation of Irish politics in the wake of the prolonged delay in advancing nationalist aspirations by parliamentary means and, of course, the Ulster question.

Because Irish independence has been a political reality for most of the twentieth century, it is easy to overlook the fact that, when the century dawned, Ireland was still a province of Victorian Britain. It was a country where those who wanted to preserve the Union with Britain retained a decisive grip on the levers of power. While Irish unionists did not see their fortunes as entirely positive, by most standards they were in a comfortable position in 1900. Though very much a numerical minority, economically they were easily the dominant grouping. People of unionist outlook still owned most of the land of Ireland. Moreover, in the north-eastern counties of Antrim and Down where, alone in Ireland, industrialisation, and the prosperity associated with it, had taken root, unionists were in a clear majority.

In constitutional terms, their position also seemed secure and there was no certainty that Ireland's political status would ever be radically changed. Mainstream nationalism was seeking what amounted to regional autonomy for Ireland within the Imperial British State. Britain's governing majority was adamantly opposed to Home Rule, while their Liberal opponents, who formally favoured it, had been divided and vanquished. As a serious political issue within the British system, Home Rule was no longer on the agenda. At the beginning of 1900, the political party that championed the cause of Home Rule was, nine years after the death of Charles Stewart Parnell, still divided, its effectiveness severely blunted. There could be no guarantee that the dispirited elements of the once-powerful Irish Party would ever be in a position to prosecute the claim to a separate Parliament in Dublin. Even as advanced a nationalist as Arthur Griffith was, in the early years of the twentieth century, satisfied to aspire to an Austro-Hungarian style dual monarchy.

In the late Victorian and Edwardian period Britain's political establishment, supported by sections of Irish unionism, made its most ambitious effort to pacify Ireland and might very well have accomplished this task. Its inability to do so, the product of failing political nerve on the part of a waning administration, is part of the story of turn-of-the-century Ireland. The Government's strategy of weaning Ireland away from Home Rule by supplying a diet of reform was the central reason why many Irish unionists felt a real sense of disgruntlement as the new century dawned.

1. British Ireland

In 1900, 100 years after the Act of Union put an end to the centuries-old separate Irish Parliament and established a Union between Great Britain and Ireland, the politics of the two islands were deeply intertwined. The ruling class (for such a thing did exist in 1900) on both islands formed a single entity. Ireland was honeycombed with landed aristocracy. The Irish peerage was extensive. There were two Dukes (Abercorn and Leinster), ten Marquesses (Clanricarde, Conyngham, Donegall, Downshire, Ely, Headfort, Londonderry, Ormonde, Sligo, and Waterford), and 61 Earls in addition to a host of holders of lesser titles.[5] Twenty-five Irish peers sat in the British House of Lords. The class to which the Irish aristocracy belonged was at the height of its self-confidence following decades of unrivalled Imperial expansion. Coinciding as it did with the outbreak of the Boer War, this period can be seen both as something of a zenith of British imperialism and also, considering the difficulty encountered in subduing the Boers, the beginning of Britain's protracted retreat from the responsibilities of Empire.

There was an end-of-an-era atmosphere at the very top where the long reign of Queen Victoria was drawing to a close. After 63 years on the throne, the Queen would only just see out the year before dying in January 1901. The Marquis of Salisbury, the last member of the House of Lords to become Prime Minister, was approaching the end of his very successful political career (he had been Foreign Secretary under Disraeli and continued to occupy this post for most of his own three terms as Prime Minister) during which he had been perhaps the chief architect of the Conservative Party's opposition to Home Rule for Ireland.[6] Salisbury presided over what has been termed 'the last government in the Western world to possess all the attributes of aristocracy'.[7] It was also a Government with an unassailable position in Parliament, for the Conservatives had won a resounding General Election victory in 1895. To put it into a late twentieth-century context, Salisbury's parliamentary majority of 152 seats was similar in scale to what the British Labour Government enjoyed after its landslide victory in the 1997 General Election.

Salisbury's deputy, Arthur Balfour, who was also his nephew, would succeed him in 1902. Balfour had served as Chief Secretary for Ireland from 1887 to 1891.[8] Balfour's predecessor in his Irish post, Sir Michael Hicks-Beach, was, in 1900, Chancellor of the Exchequer in the Salisbury Government. The Ministry of War slot in the Cabinet, a position of great importance in Imperial Britain, was occupied by an Irish peer, Lord Lansdowne who, later in the year, succeeded Salisbury as Foreign Secretary.[9] These high-level connections with Ireland serve to underline the contemporary importance within the British system of the top Irish political post, and the salience of Irish affairs in late Victorian Britain.

In the late nineteenth century, the Irish question had impacted heavily on the party political divide in Britain. Under Gladstone's leadership, the Liberal Party had embraced Home Rule for Ireland only to fail to get it past the House of Lords after the measure had finally been approved by the House of Commons in 1893. Earlier, in 1886, Gladstone's Liberals had seen their parliamentary majority crumble when the vote on the first Home Rule Bill resulted in almost one-third of the Liberal Party's MPs opposing the measure and abandoning their traditional Party home. Some years later the dissidents went on to form a coalition government with their erstwhile conservative opponents.[10] While the Liberals returned to power between 1892 and 1895, they did not manage to recover their former strength.

The Liberal Party schism conditioned British politics for a generation as conflicting attitudes to Home Rule became one of the distinguishing traits of the two main Parties and paved the way for two decades of Conservative ascendancy. While they continued to adhere to Gladstone's Irish legacy after his retirement from politics in 1895, for practical and electoral reasons the issue of Home Rule did not come to a head again until 1910 when a Liberal Government came to power relying for its parliamentary majority on Irish nationalist support.[11] At the turn of the century, opposition in Britain to Home Rule was often tied up with Imperial considerations. Those like Joseph Chamberlain, Colonial Secretary in 1900, who had broken with the Liberal Party, did so mainly because they viewed 'the fight for the Union' as 'only a chapter in the greater fight for the Empire'.[12]

Despite being part of the United Kingdom politically, Ireland was a place apart. It had a separate administration with the Lord Lieutenant at the top of the pyramid of power. At the turn of the century, this office was occupied by the Earl of Cadogan who, when in Dublin, resided at the Vice-Regal Lodge at the Phoenix Park. It was there that the 80 year-old Queen stayed during her visit to Ireland, the house having been modified to meet her needs. During his spells in residence at the Phoenix Park, the Lord Lieutenant was the focal point of the city's social life. A contemporary account captures something of the opulence of Vice-Regal entertainments at Dublin Castle:

> It was a brilliant scene when the assembled guests awaited their host and hostess, the shaded lights bringing out the satins and velvets, pearls and diamonds, uniforms, orders and medals. Suddenly the hum of voices ceased as one of the aides-de-camp who preceded the Vice-Regal party announced 'their Excellencies' . . . we passed through the beautifully decorated rooms to St Patrick's Hall in a nicely graded procession, magnificence at head, humility at the tail.[13]

Aside from his ceremonial role as the Queen's representative, the Lord Lieutenant had extensive statutory powers and the authority to make a wide range of Irish appointments.[14] Cadogan was not held in the highest regard within the Irish administration. As one insider put it:

> He puzzled me immensely. The most childishly simple and elementary things it was almost impossible to get him to understand but his brain had curious patches of brilliancy, and complicated, difficult matters . . . he would take in at once.[15]

A member of the House of Lords, Cadogan, unlike many of his predecessors, also had a seat in the British Cabinet, a fact which naturally enhanced his political influence. While Cadogan favoured recourse to coercion when faced with the challenge from the United Irish League, he was, nonetheless, considered to have 'shown a degree of sympathy with popular aspirations' not usual among former occupants of his post. Throughout 1900, Cadogan fretted about evidence of sedition appearing in police intelligence reports which his Chief Secretary took in his stride, declining to exaggerate the threat posed by the United Irish League and the secret societies who were bent on exploiting pro-Boer and anti-English sentiment. Cadogan's reputation for relative impartiality was enhanced by his appointment as his private secretary of Lord Plunkett, son of the former Church of Ireland

Archbishop of Dublin, who, in nationalist eyes, was 'not one of those Irish Unionists who are always unionist and never Irish'.[16]

The Chief Secretary's Office was the hub of British rule in Ireland and, accordingly, relations between Chief Secretary and Lord Lieutenant were frequently strained. Much like a modern Prime Minister's Department, all aspects of the administration of the country passed through the hands of the Chief Secretary and his staff at Dublin Castle, except that there were no cabinet colleagues with whom to share the burdens of authority. The archives of the Chief Secretary's Office[17] show many trivial matters (such as requests for leave from magistrates) being referred to it for adjudication and decision. The Administration's Crime Branch had a key role in monitoring opponents of British rule in Ireland, especially those thought to have seditious intentions.

As the year 1900 opened, the Chief Secretary, Gerald Balfour, had occupied his post for five years. A brother of Arthur Balfour's, he was the one who was said to have coined the memorable phrase about 'killing Home Rule with kindness'[18] which summarised the prevailing approach to Irish affairs of the ruling Conservatives. While Balfour denied responsibility for it, nationalists were quick to trumpet the phrase as evidence of the Government's malign intent. Though aristocratic and deeply conservative in outlook, Gerald Balfour was responsible for a raft of reforming legislation during his tenure in Ireland.

The Chief Secretary for Ireland was the political head of the British administration in Dublin, a post usually of Ministerial rank within the British system. However, as Cadogan was a Cabinet member, Gerald Balfour was not. As a Member of Parliament, however, the Chief Secretary represented the Irish Administration in the House of Commons where he frequently crossed swords with Irish nationalist MPs during debates on Ireland and at question time. A comment made by Balfour in 1900 summed up the approach he took to his Irish responsibilities. He maintained that his aim was:

> to get at the very root from which home rule was supported and sustained by remedying all legitimate grievances.[19]

After the General Election of 1900, Balfour, whose reforming policies had made him the butt of Irish unionist criticism, and whose health had declined during his time in charge of Irish affairs, was replaced by his cousin, George Wyndham, who had previously served in Ireland on Arthur Balfour's staff when he was Chief Secretary. The arrival on the Irish scene of Wyndham, who was by temperament a romantic imperialist, was seen at first as a victory for Conservative unionism. Wyndham made a strong impact on turn-of-the-century Ireland. Yeats' early collaborator, Katharine Tynan, was enthralled by his personality and felt that he 'belonged to a more romantic age'.[20] A later biographer maintained that 'when George Wyndham died, romance died from English politics'.[21] When appointed to his Dublin post, he spoke to his friend, the Countess of Fingall, of his intention of pulling off a grand slam of a Land Act, a University Act and devolution.[22] Wyndham proved to be one of the most successful Irish Chief Secretaries, even if, as things worked out, he only managed to complete the first leg of his political grand slam. With the passage of the 1903 Land Act that carries his name, he went a long way towards settling the vexed question of land ownership, for so many years a potent source of political discontent in Ireland. In the opinion of the quixotic nationalist MP, Tim Healy, Wyndham's 'sympathies with Ireland were immense'. As Chief Secretary, 'his ambition', as recorded by Healy, 'was to make an international settlement between the island he administered and the island of his birth'.[23]

Appointed Chief Secretary after the General Election of October 1900, Wyndham came to Ireland somewhat reluctantly, having revelled in his wartime assignment at the War Office. It was not long before he warmed to the task of governing a land with which, as a great-grandson of the eighteenth-century United Irishman, Lord Edward Fitzgerald, he had strong ancestral ties. Wyndham was an active Chief Secretary with a mind of his own. According to one sceptical account, Wyndham was forever 'bubbling over with new and brilliant conceptions'.[24] Another observer described him as 'frank, excited, brilliant, epigrammatic, sanguine, visionary'.[25] Wyndham beheld Ireland with great romantic enthusiasm, and not a little sympathy for its people's woes. As he saw it, his new home was:

> a land of sorcery; false but so fair that the adventurer willingly dives beneath the waters . . . I swim the Celtic twilight but through the green and golden witchery comes the piercing appeal of grinding and hopeless poverty.[26]

Notwithstanding its strong natural affinity with the unionist community, and its equally strong antipathy to nationalist aspirations, the Salisbury Government had tried to steer a course between the irreconcilable demands of the two traditions.

It was supremely difficult to satisfy nationalists with anything short of Home Rule, while unionists were appalled at the spectacle of Government concessions to their ungrateful, inveterate political foes. As one conservative unionist saw the competition between unionism and nationalism:

> two ideas, essentially antagonistic, will confront each other – now as in 1886 – until one or the other has obtained the mastery.[27]

As their functions within the British political system frequently kept the Lord Lieutenant and the Chief Secretary away from Ireland, much day-to-day responsibility for Irish affairs rested with the Under Secretary, who was permanently resident in Dublin. Although this had once been a political post, by the end of the nineteenth century the Under Secretary had become the most senior British civil servant in Ireland. In 1900, the post was held by Sir David Harrel, an Irish-born former chief of the Dublin Metropolitan Police force, who was highly thought of by his superiors and whose political affiliations were well concealed. As one source put it:

> I could not work out whether Sir David Harrel was a Home Ruler or not. He did his duty as an official and never attempted to interfere in policy.[28]

Harrel's son was assistant Police commissioner during the Howth gun running in 1914 and called out the army in a vain effort to prevent the Irish Volunteers from getting their hands on the smuggled weapons. He was forced to resign on foot of the fallout from this incident.[29]

Within the Irish Administration, there were some 40 offices, boards and Departments.[30] Some survived the advent of independence in recognisable form, for instance the Land Commission, the Department of Agriculture and Technical Instruction and the Local Government Board, while others such as the Congested Districts Board and the Quit Rent Office were distinctive products of the nineteenth-century Irish administration.

One of the most prominent British institutions in Ireland was the Royal Irish Constabulary (RIC) which, combined with the Dublin Metropolitan Police, had a membership of 12,000 men, a decline of 3,000 since 1883 as a consequence of the country's relatively peaceful condition in 1900. Turn-of-the-century Irish policemen complained bitterly about their working conditions, maintaining that their earnings had fallen behind those of artisans who had benefitted from rising wage rates in the closing years of the nineteenth century. RIC men argued for being placed on a par financially with the London Metropolitan Police Force, something they claimed was justified on account of the difficulties inherent in policing a politically volatile island where policemen did not enjoy the same co-operation from the public as they did elsewhere in Britain.

A Committee of Inquiry reporting in 1901 granted some modest increases in allowances but rejected the RIC's main pay claim. The report acknowledged that RIC recruits were of an 'exceedingly good stamp' unlike their counterparts in other parts of Britain where a wider range of employment opportunities drew potential candidates away from a career in policing. The RIC remained an attractive career option for young Irishmen, not so much

for the salary, rising as it did to the not very princely sum of £70 a year for ordinary constables, but on account of the entitlement to a full pension after 25 years service. This was a considerable asset in an era before the arrival of old age pensions. Recruits, many of whom were policemen's sons and who had to be unmarried or widowed without children, often joined up at 17 years of age and, after six months training, were assigned to a Station where they became significant figures in the social hierarchy of small-town and rural Ireland. One-quarter of the force's officer class of 250 was English, while most of those born in Ireland were graduates of Trinity College, sons of landlords and army officers.[31]

An armed, paramilitary force who were present on such emotive occasions as evictions, the RIC were inevitably the butt of nationalist criticism, especially at times of heightened political excitement. Nationalist MPs were only too willing to draw attention to any police excesses or misdemeanours. The various 'coercion' laws designed to counter the threat from secret societies were deeply resented. A Sergeant Sheridan, dismissed from the force in 1901 for allegedly concocting evidence against innocent suspects for crimes committed by his own accomplices, was the subject of a sustained campaign on the part of the United Irish League.[32]

A key position in British Ireland was that of Commander-in-Chief of the British Forces, which had a total strength in 1901 of 27,000, and whose headquarters were at the Royal Hospital, Kilmainham. Since 1893, this post had been held by General Lord Frederick Roberts, the exotically-titled Earl of Kandahar and Waterford, who was born in the Indian garrison town of Cawnpore, but whose family hailed

A revivalist preacher addressing a crowd under police protection.

from Waterford.[33] A veteran of Britain's Army of India, Roberts, a man of diminutive stature, was acclaimed by Rudyard Kipling as, 'a pocket Wellington':

> Clean, simple, valiant, well-beloved,
> Flawless in faith and fame,
> Whom neither ease nor honours moved
> An hair's breadth from his aim.[34]

In January 1900, Roberts, decorated for his exploits during the Indian Mutiny and later in Afghanistan, was on his way to South Africa to command the British Forces in the Boer War.[35]

A perhaps over-confident Britain had suffered serious and surprising setbacks in the closing months of 1899. From his post in Dublin, Roberts, whose son was killed during the British defeat at Colenso, had entreated Cabinet members to give him the task of saving the day in South Africa. Roberts' character may be gauged from the stoic manner in which he faced up to the loss of his son. A telegram he and his wife sent to Queen Victoria, in response to a message of condolences from her, remarked that 'our loss is grievous, but our boy died the death he would have chosen'.[36]

With Kitchener as his deputy, Roberts, though 68 years of age, succeeded in pushing back the Boer forces and went on to capture Bloemfontein and Pretoria and to annex the Orange Free State before returning to Britain in triumph at the year's end. He was the last person to have an appointment with an ailing Queen Victoria just days before her death. It was as if she had clung on to life just long enough to encounter the hero of Britain's last imperial war. Towards the end of his long life (he died in 1914 from a bout of pneumonia contracted while vis-

iting British troops in the trenches of the First World War), Roberts lent his support to Edward Carson and his Ulster unionist followers in their resistance to Home Rule. He sympathised with those army officers involved in the Curragh Mutiny of 1914 when they made it clear that they would not impose Home Rule on Ulster.

When Roberts was sent to South Africa in 1900, he went there to take over from Sir Redvers Buller, who was being blamed in some quarters for the reverses suffered at the hands of the rampant Boer forces in the early months of the war. Buller, too, had a significant track record in Ireland, having once been Under Secretary, and also Special Commissioner in the west of Ireland during the Plan of Campaign phase of the Land War. He had been sent to the west in 1886 with a mandate to snuff out boycotting and quell agrarian unrest. Buller, who believed in combining coercion with conciliation, was remembered by one nationalist writer as someone who had come to conquer Ireland, but had himself been conquered, leaving Kerry as 'a convinced Land Leaguer'.[37]

On New Year's Day 1900, Roberts' replacement in Ireland was announced. The new Commander-in-Chief was Queen Victoria's third son, the 50 year-old, Arthur, Duke of Connaught, who had had a distinguished military career and was once mentioned as a possible Lord Lieutenant of Ireland until it was decided that, in view of the post's political sensitivity, it would not be a suitable position for a member of the British Royal Family. The Duke had pressed to be assigned to war duty in South Africa, but this had been resisted by the Government.[38]

As the year 1900 began, British Ireland was preoccupied with the progress (or lack of it) of the war in South Africa. News from Ladysmith,

Kimberly, Mafeking and the Modder River filled the headlines in *The Irish Times,* the most Empire-minded of the country's newspapers.

2. *Unionist Ireland*

Prior to the mid-1880s, supporters of the Union had normally backed the British political party of their choice. The extension of the franchise and the threat of Home Rule had encouraged unionists to organise themselves politically.[39] For the 1895 General Election, the Dublin-based Irish Unionist Alliance had campaigned actively in Britain in support of pro-unionist candidates. It was not surprising that unionists directed their campaigning efforts at the British electorate for, in Ireland, their political position was parlous. They lacked any island-wide democratic basis for their economic and political ascendancy, and this inevitably bred a sense of unease about their future in a political climate increasingly influenced by democratic principles.

Despite, or perhaps because of, the lack of any serious threat of Home Rule, at the turn of the century the unionist consensus, so effective in times of crisis, was showing signs of fraying at the edges. Irish unionists were not at all at ease with their government. The Government was torn between the need to appease the nationalist majority in Ireland and the interests of its unionist political allies. Five years after the conservatives, with strong backing from unionist Ireland, had trounced the Liberals at the polls, there was considerable disappointment among unionists at what they saw as the dubious fruits of Conservative rule. It was a source of considerable disenchantment that the Government had failed to reciprocate unionist loyalty and seemed to feel compelled to placate popular demands at the expense of its natural supporters in Ireland.

They were dismayed at the Salisbury Government's pursuit of policies that offered little comfort to those in Ireland who were pro-Union in outlook.

In the conservative unionist view, the Government had bowed to nationalist agitation and delivered a series of concessions, on land and local government, that had damaged unionist interests. One unionist pamphlet even compared their plight to the sensational case of Alfred Dreyfus, a French Jewish officer imprisoned for alleged espionage by a French legal system, responding to pressure from right-wing nationalists and royalists. Irish unionists blamed Gladstone for inventing the pusillanimous strategy of 'seeking to appease Irish rebels at the expense of Irish loyalists' which had become 'almost the settled policy of the Imperial Parliament in dealing with the Irish land question'.[40]

Unionists felt alienated by the very same government policies that had failed to impress nationalists. The Land Act of 1896 and the Local Government Act of 1898 were regarded by many as bridges too far. It seemed to them that their own government was bent on rewarding nationalist dissension and yielding to illegal agitation. Local government had fallen into the hands of disloyal nationalists who in 1900 were showing their true colours by passing resolutions supportive of the Boer cause. A Catholic University looked like it was next on the list of concessions. Could self-government be far behind?

The Government's willingness to concede land reforms to tenants dismayed Ireland's overwhelmingly unionist landlords who organised themselves within the Irish Landowners' Convention to resist further tenant-orientated legislation. Landlords, who saw their traditional position being eroded, found this new order difficult to tolerate. They tried to hit back through their position of influence within the House of Lords where they pressed for a Royal Commission to look into the losses sustained by Irish landlords. Landlords insisted that the method employed for valuing land and fixing rents judicially was unjust, weighted too much in the tenants' favour.

Speaking in the House of Lords, Lord Templetown asked if the concessions granted had satisfied tenants. No, he replied:

> they are continually looking for bigger reductions of rent. In the west of Ireland, too, another of those pestiferous organisations which aim at robbing landlords of all of their rights has arisen, and has been doing its utmost to promote agitation.[41]

In the eyes of conservatives, landlord and tenant could readily sort out their differences, but:

> Priests, on the one hand, and demagogues on the other, are everlastingly agitating them, and seeking to use them for their own ends . . . they have not the strength to resist the wiles of the cleric and the 'arts' of the patriot.[42]

Their preferred remedy was the 'firm hand' of government:

> Pass righteous laws, administer them fearlessly, and let it be clearly understood that there will be no deviation from the justice of the law for the sake of sentiment, and then the Irish people will be governed as easily as any people in the world.[43]

The problem for conservatives was that, in a changing world, this kind of solution could no longer be as rigorously applied as before. They saw their interests being sacrificed as part of a bid to 'kill home rule with kindness'. As landlords saw it, the undermining of their class would 'weaken one of the best guarantees for order and stability in Ireland'.[44] As it turned out, the resurgence of conservative unionism around 1900 was a last roll of the dice for the landlord interest in Ireland. Further land reform and a changing political environment in Britain saw to that.

Irish unionists were by no means united on their response to the land question. Predominantly unionist tenant farmers in the North, whose interests were similar to those of their nationalist counterparts throughout the island, were understandably supportive of land reform. The land question had the potential to bridge the constitutional divide and unite nationalists and northern unionists in a common quest to overhaul Ireland's controversial system of land ownership.

The recently-enacted reform of local government, followed, as it was, by the routing of unionists in local polls outside of Ulster, had delivered a hammer blow to unionist self-confidence. It had brought about a significant shift in the balance of political power in Ireland. As *The Irish Times* put it:

> throughout the entire south of Ireland, the effect of this measure has been to transfer county government from the control of unionists to the control of nationalists[45] who were, after all, the sworn enemies of the Union.

With regard to local government reform, it was not just a case of Irish unionists being at loggerheads with nationalists and British Government policy. Within Irish unionism, there were also north-south strains on this issue. Local Government reform had been welcomed by many northern unionists, who saw it as an opportunity to wrest control of local politics from conservative figures unresponsive to popular concerns. Indeed, all Ulster Unionist MPs had supported the Local Government Act when it was introduced in 1898, leaving the member for Trinity College, the historian W.E.H. Lecky, as its principal opponent. Compared with the rest of the country, where total nationalist domination was the norm, local government elections in Ulster were a much more equal struggle and the local political spoils were shared between nationalists and unionists. Political differences meant that northern local authorities were places of often heated debate by contrast with the South, which, for the most part, a broad nationalist consensus reigned. Northern preparedness to endorse changes in local government arrangements was deeply resented by southern unionists. Whereas northern unionist representatives generally reflected the interests of their electorates, mainstream southern unionism had virtually no parliamentary voice.

At the General Election of 1895, only 22 non-nationalists succeeded in being elected throughout the island.[46] Of these, just four MPs (two seats for Dublin University and one each for St Stephen's Green and South County Dublin) represented constituencies located outside of Ulster. So predictable were the results of Irish elections in most constituencies that only a handful of seats were contested between nationalists and unionists, fewer, indeed, than the number of intra-nationalist and intra-unionist contests. At the turn of the century, one of the Dublin University seats was held by the future

Ulster unionist leader, Edward Carson, who continued his political ascent in 1900 when he became Solicitor-General in Salisbury's administration.[47] Quintessentially a southern unionist, Carson had been an MP since 1892 and had served briefly as Solicitor-General of Ireland. While he had strongly opposed Gerald Balfour's 1896 land legislation as an assault on landed interests, Carson was a supporter of the idea of a separate Catholic University, one of the main demands of nationalist Ireland at the time. When Carson became Solicitor-General, his appointment, together with that of the Marquis of Londonderry as Postmaster-General, was viewed by conservative unionists as a sign of Government willingness 'even at the eleventh hour, to do something for the unionists of Ireland'.[48] However, this gesture did not succeed in stemming the annoyance with government policy felt by many unionists in the South. As one newspaper put it, 'the chiefs are lying still and contented, but the rank and file are in full revolt'.[49] Speaking on the occasion of Carson's re-nomination to Parliament, one member of the Trinity electorate, a Reverend Phineas Hunt, claimed that 'there has never been a worse government for this country'.[50] Just as Gladstone had brought down the church, the Conservative Government had done likewise to the landlords with their land bills and the Local Government Act which 'deprived the landlords and the gentry of every influence they ever had'.

At the turn of the century, Southern unionism was divided between those who endorsed the government's conciliatory overtures towards nationalism and those who favoured robust resistance to popular demands. A contemporary unionist source sketched the differences within unionism.

We have on the one hand those who feel themselves slighted and aggrieved by the policy of the Government . . . On the other hand, there are a newer and more liberal class of unionists who believe in conciliating the majority, in giving them a fair share of all benefits, making them as contented as they can be made, and the country as prosperous as possible, so removing all the real causes of the desire for Home Rule.[51]

These two strands of unionist opinion came into conflict in 1900 as Conservative unionists resolved to hit back at a Government they believed had betrayed them. Their principal target was Horace Plunkett, seen by conservatives as an arch-advocate of constructive unionism.

3. Constructive Unionism

Constructive unionism, seen as an effort to placate Catholic and nationalist sentiment in Ireland, was not exactly new. Catholic emancipation in 1829, Church of Ireland disestablishment in 1869 and Gladstone's land act of 1870 were some of the earlier manifestations of the British Government's enduring need to placate Irish nationalist opinion if the country was to be governable. In the 1890s, what came to be known as constructive unionism evolved as the Conservative Government's riposte to the Liberal Party's endorsement of Home Rule. The principal achievements of this 'constructive' policy were the setting up of the Congested Districts Board in 1891, the passage of the 1896 Land Act, the Local Government Act of 1898, and the establishment of the new Department of Agriculture and Technical Instruction. Coinciding as it did with the emergence of the new Department, and the arrival of a new and dynamic Chief Secretary, the turn of the century

may be seen as marking something of a high-point of constructive Unionism.[52]

The effort to win nationalist acceptance of the Union through conciliatory reforms was not just a British Government political strategy,[53] but also had its adherents among Irish unionists, the most accomplished of whom was Horace Plunkett. On his return from a spell in Wyoming in the late 1880s, Plunkett had set out to spread the gospel of agricultural co-operation as a remedy for Ireland's economic woes. In 1895, he brought together an all-Party Committee during the Westminster Parliamentary recess. What became known as the Recess Committee reported in 1896 and engendered a rare measure of political consensus between nationalists and unionists behind its proposal for the setting up of a Department of Agriculture and Technical Instruction. In 1896, the report of the Childers Commission revealed that Ireland had been making a contribution to the Imperial Exchequer of some £2,750,000 more than its wealth warranted. This grievance resulted in the formation of an all-Ireland committee which, for a short time, raised the possibility of a united approach by Irish politicians to issues not impinging on the constitutional question.

Horace Plunkett epitomised constructive unionism and his fortunes underlined its inherent difficulties. Plunkett analysed the Irish problem in a novel way, asking himself what was at the heart of the country's difficulties and then suggesting ways in which this could be remedied. While others might view Ireland as a constitutional problem, Plunkett saw the economic condition of Ireland as the source of the country's social and political ills. His was an economic solution to an economic problem; he wanted to foster economic advancement by engineering co-operation

between different types of Irishmen. Fundamentally, he believed that economic improvement was best achieved within the framework of the Union.[54] Plunkett insisted that traditional politics had failed Ireland to such an extent that, while Britain had forged ahead throughout the nineteenth century, Ireland had regressed economically. Nationalist politics, with its insistence on blaming the British connection for all of Ireland's ills, had dulled the Irish mind and yielded nothing but economic ruin. As Plunkett saw it, however, all was not lost. He detected a more constructive spirit on the rise, 'a new philosophy of Irish progress',[55] which carried the promise of substantial material advancement in the new century. Plunkett wanted to bring people together on the economic front where nationalists and unionists could unite in their common interest in the country's well-being. Looking at the various efforts at national revival under way as the new century arrived, he sensed that there was an essential unity among those 'striving for the upbuilding of a worthy national life in Ireland'.[56] Plunkett's assertion that 'the most important part of the work of regenerating Ireland must be done by Irishmen in Ireland'[57] was not far removed from the Irish-Ireland philosophy of D.P. Moran, even if the political conclusions they drew from these opinions differed radically.

While undeniably a unionist, Plunkett, who had been a Member of Parliament since 1892, was critical of the negative inclinations of

Coleraine, Co. Derry. 12 July Orange Parade crossing the River Bann.

conservative unionists with their relentless devotion to the *status quo*. Inevitably, his emphasis on the need for change did not endear him to everyone within the unionist community.[58] Plunkett believed that the constructive unionist policies pioneered by the Balfour brothers, had been 'the greatest ever tried in Ireland'.[59] Some unionists had been displeased by his habit of occasionally siding with nationalists at Westminster, for example by supporting an amnesty for Fenian prisoners. Moreover, he appeared to adopt an ambivalent attitude to the Boer War which was seen as a litmus test of imperial and unionist orthodoxy.

In the run-up to the election of October 1900, moves were made to unseat Plunkett as MP for South County Dublin, perhaps the sole constituency outside of Ulster with a natural unionist majority. The push against Plunkett was led by Lord Ardilaun. The young James Joyce evidently paid attention to Ardilaun and describes him in *Ulysses* as someone who had 'to change his shirt four times a day, they say. Skin breeds lice or vermin'. Joyce maintained a healthier interest in a story about Ardilaun's brother, Lord Iveagh, to whom he had earlier sold his interest in the Guinness brewery, cashing a cheque for a million pounds, an amount equal to 'fifteen millions of barrels of porter'.[60]

In his push against constructive unionism, Ardilaun had the support of Edward Dowden, a recent sparring partner of W.B. Yeats on the subject of Irish literature, about which Dowden, a distinguished Trinity don, was dismissive. Together, they orchestrated a campaign against Plunkett in Ardilaun's newspaper, *The Dublin Daily Express*. The issue for which Plunkett came under heaviest fire was his appointment of a Catholic, and former member of the

Land League, T.P. Gill (coincidentally a former editor of the *Express* before the paper was acquired by Ardilaun), as his deputy at the Department of Agriculture and Technical Instruction. This move, which Plunkett stood firm on, alienated a significant number of his unionist supporters. Aside from the displeasure directed at Plunkett himself, the conservative unionist attempt to unseat him was designed 'to show their dissatisfaction with the general policy of the Irish government'.[61]

At the October General Election, Plunkett was opposed by a more orthodox unionist, Francis Elrington Ball, and, despite Plunkett's comparative renown, a split in the unionist vote was sufficient to hand the seat to the nationalist candidate, John Joseph Mooney. Conservative unionists were willing to sacrifice a scarce southern seat in order to register their disapproval of Plunkett's, and by association, the Salisbury Government's brand of unionism. At the same election, the only other Dublin unionist MP outside of Trinity College, James Henry Campbell, who represented the Stephen's Green constituency, also lost his seat to a nationalist. Plunkett received support from many prominent Ulster Unionists, while the Duke of Abercorn, head of the Irish Landowners Convention, voiced opposition to the bid to oust him. Plunkett's electoral eclipse made a considerable impact. The historian, W.E.H. Lecky, remarked that henceforth 'Ulster unionism is the only form of Irish unionism which is likely to count as a serious political force'.[62]

Following his defeat, Plunkett was prevailed upon to stand in a by-election in Galway in 1901, where he opposed a nationalist candidate for a seat vacated by a unionist MP, Martin Henry Morris, when he became Lord Killanin.

Having run into unionist opposition in Dublin, Plunkett now had the hostile attentions of the Irish parliamentary party trained on him. Michael Davitt, who might have been expected to have some sympathy for Plunkett's efforts to improve the lot of Ireland's downtrodden peasantry, proclaimed that a vote for Plunkett was a vote for Irish landlordism 'with all its blood records in the process of the extermination of the Irish nation'.[63] In the minds of many nationalists, there was no doubt that Plunkett was 'the more dangerous enemy of the National idea' than the conservative landlord grouping who believed in 'killing Home Rule with unkindness'.[64] John Dillon denounced Plunkett as a carpetbagger[65] and he was routed at the polls by Arthur Lynch, an Australian of Irish descent.

After graduating from the University of Melbourne, Lynch had travelled to Europe, Africa and America before becoming a journalist with the newly-established *Daily Mail,* a newspaper derided by Lord Salisbury as 'a journal produced by office boys for office boys'.[66] He went on to fight on the Boer side in South Africa as a Colonel in the Second Irish Brigade.[67] When Lynch arrived in England to claim his seat, he was arrested and charged with treason. As Solicitor-General, Edward Carson was part of the prosecuting team which secured a conviction resulting in the death penalty which was commuted to life imprisonment although, in the event, Lynch only served a few months of his sentence. Ironically, by the time the First World War came around, Lynch, by then a sitting nationalist MP, was an enthusiastic advocate of Irish enlistment in the British Army.[68]

Despite his electoral reverses, the Conservative Government kept Plunkett on as head of the new Department and he continued, with some

success, to build the co-operative movement. However, when the Liberals were returned to office in 1906, Irish nationalist MPs pressed for Plunkett's removal from his Department of Agriculture post.

The Earl of Dunraven was another unionist who aspired to build a bridge of political and economic reform across the divide between nationalism and unionism. A renowned yachtsman, Dunraven made a vigorous attempt to cultivate a centre ground in Irish politics but sailed into the eye of a political storm. In 1900, as a member of the Imperial Yeomanry raised from the grouse shooters and foxhunters of Britain and Ireland, Dunraven had gone to fight in the Boer War, where he had been struck down by dysentery and returned without seeing any military action.

On return from South Africa, Dunraven resolved to devote himself to remedying Ireland's ills within a reforming unionist framework. His priorities included land reform, the establishment of a University acceptable to Catholics and:

> the obtaining for Ireland of such an extension of self-governing powers as would give Irish people full control over all purely Irish affairs.[69]

In 1902, Dunraven was behind the convening of a Land Conference which brought together landlord and tenant interests, nationalist and unionist alike, around the same negotiating table. The Conference, attended by John Redmond, William O'Brien, Tim Harrington, then Lord Mayor of Dublin, and the Liberal Unionist MP, T.W. Russell, paved the way for the 1903 Land Act which, in five years, enabled over a quarter of a million tenants to buy out their holdings. Despite the involvement in the Land Conference of three prominent nationalists, the measure was eventually repudiated by the Irish Party, and this precipitated William O'Brien's retirement from Parliament. For Dunraven, the Land Conference typified a spirit of reconciliation which, had it triumphed further, might have satisfied all of Ireland's legitimate aspirations.

Buoyed by relative success on the agrarian front, Dunraven turned his hand to the constitutional arena and, through the Irish Reform Association, whose platform was intended as 'a rallying point of moderate opinion', produced a complicated scheme of devolution for Ireland.[70] This envisaged Irish parliamentarians having a degree of control over the country's finances and other local business.[71] While Dunraven's relatively modest scheme fell well short of Home Rule, it still managed to generate a heated controversy in which the Chief Secretary, George Wyndham, became embroiled. This came about when it was revealed that his Under Secretary, Anthony Mac-Donnell, a Catholic Irishman who had formerly been a senior official in British India, had assisted Dunraven in crafting his devolution proposals. Many unionists, and not just arch-conservatives, were enraged at the idea of the Government's most senior civil servant engaged in what seemed like a conspiracy to undermine the Union. One senior unionist termed the devolution scheme 'Home Rule on the sly'.[72] Although Wyndham attempted to distance himself from the ideas developed by Dunraven and MacDonnell, the controversy dragged on through the final months of 1904 and, when it threatened to bring down Balfour's administration, Wyndham was forced to resign in March 1905. His departure, which effectively ended a political career that had seemed destined for higher office, signalled the death knell of constructive unionism. It marked the end of a ten-year period during which a Conservative Government in London had laboured hard to deliver concessions aimed at mollifying nationalist opinion.

Whereas the land question had been susceptible to reform, political change proved a far more obdurate proposition. The outcry that surrounded this so-called devolution crisis underlined the peculiar intractability of the political divisions affecting Ireland. Orthodox unionists saw proposals for devolution as another betrayal of their interests by a Government that was supposed to be on their side. The crisis left them 'animated by the same grim resolve as in 1886' when the prospect of Home Rule first surfaced to menace their interests. For nationalists, devolution did not measure up to their idea of Home Rule, and that was that as far as they were concerned. Michael Davitt described the scheme as 'a miserable makeshift', while for John Dillon it was 'an insidious attempt to sap and destroy the force and vitality of the nationalist movement'.[73]

With the collapse of his devolution initiative, Dunraven was left to rue the decline of what he saw as the 'patriotic spirit' that had manifested itself in early twentieth-century Ireland and 'enabled any Irishman, whatever his creed or class might be, to help his country'.[74] Writing against the depressingly-violent backdrop of the War of Independence, and looking back on the early years of the century, Dunraven mused about

what might have happened had advantage been taken of the good feeling between the classes in Ireland and between Great Britain and Ireland, that existed twenty years ago . . . if politicians, British and Irish, had had any vision, or even common sense, if, indeed, it had not been for almost criminal folly, all the horrors of recent times, and all the bitter legacy of hate resulting from them, would have been avoided.[75]

The experiences of Plunkett, Dunraven, and indeed Wyndham, were salutary ones. Their inability to maintain the momentum of constructive unionism underlined the difficulties inherent in constructing a viable centre ground in Irish politics. Such efforts tended to be spurned by unionists while nationalist politicians saw the entire tradition of constructive unionism as a threat to the sacred cause of Home Rule. While circumstances at the turn of the century seemed conducive to moderation and reform, in reality there were too few people willing to abandon traditional positions in order to explore alternative visions of Ireland's future.

4. Unionism in Ulster

The controversies surrounding Plunkett and Dunraven were not the only examples of conflicting trends within Irish unionism at the turn of the century. The arrival of democratic local government had exposed strains within Ulster unionism while, at the same time, highlighting the sectarian competition at the core of Ulster's politics. The controversy about local government reform drew attention to the different interests of Ulster unionists and their political allies in the rest of Ireland. There was a fundamental divide between the predominantly landlord-dominated tradition of southern unionism and the very different situation in Ulster, where unionists were in a numerical majority and unionism was a mass movement.[76] Even in Ulster, however, as one source puts it:

> despite the common bonds of Protestantism and British origin, class and political

divisions were often in danger of undermining unionist cohesion there.[77]

In Ulster, opposition to mainstream unionism came from a number of quarters. There were those who believed that reform, to the benefit of unionists as well as nationalists, could be pursued without endangering the Union. There were others who disliked the unionist leadership for seeming to be an episcopalian elite indifferent to Ulster's Presbyterian community. Protestant tenant farmers had no great love for the landowners who tended to dominate Unionism, even in Ulster. There were also radical, working class challenges to a conservative unionist political establishment.

In 1900, liberal Unionism, which combined attachment to the Union with support for reform, still had a strong foothold in Ulster. Its leading figure was the South Tyrone MP, T.W. Russell, who, for a time at the beginning of the century, threatened to fragment the unionist tradition by introducing into Ulster a more radical brand of politics, driven by socio-economic rather than constitutional considerations.[78] A staunch unionist and a strong temperance advocate, Russell was sharply critical of the historical record of British government in Ireland, although he warmly endorsed the policies sponsored by Balfour and Wyndham as Chief Secretaries, and considered that the raft of reforming legislation passed during the 1890s, 'completely justifies the existence of the Unionist Party'.[79] He predicted that, in the eyes of future historians:

> the case against England, viewed from a nineteenth-century standpoint, will be as damaging as it well can be.[80]

Royal Avenue, Belfast. By the turn of the century, Belfast had become the largest city in Ireland, outstripping Dublin on account of its status as a leading industrial centre.

142

Such views were hardly likely to endear him to conservatives, and the *Belfast Newsletter* rounded on him and called him a 'political pervert'.[81]

For Russell, constructive unionism held the key to political harmony in Ireland. He asked 'does any sane statesman imagine that the Union can be permanently maintained without the assent of the majority of the Irish people?'[82] The Local Government Act of 1898 was hailed by Russell as 'the greatest measure passed since the Act of Union'.[83] As he saw it, what was needed to complete the work of constructive unionism was a further wave of land reform, a settlement of the university question and the establishment of more equitable financial relations between Britain and Ireland.

Russell had taken a courageous stand in favour of a Catholic university, supporting proposals sponsored by Arthur Balfour to settle a controversial cause championed by nationalists and opposed by a majority of unionists. As part of the price of his nomination to contest the 1900 election, Russell was obliged to promise his constituents not to pursue the university question any further, to abstain in future parliamentary votes on the subject, and to resign from any Government that sought to accede to Catholic demands for a university of their own.[84] The notion of State-funded denominational universities was anathema to many Irish Protestants. As the *Belfast Newsletter* put it, 'we are all determined that the higher education of our country shall not be subjected to the deadening influence of the Papal hierarchy'.[85]

His dissident opinions on higher education notwithstanding, Russell's main focus was the land question. According to Russell, the key to bringing the majority around to accepting the Union was land reform. His efforts had been largely responsible for goading the Government into passing the 1896 Land Act, having directed a campaign of protest among Ulster's Protestant farmers in 1895. His scathing criticisms of the existing order might easily have come from the pen of a nationalist politician, the difference being that Russell wanted to resolve the land question as a means of preserving the Union.[86] For Russell, to buy out Irish landlords:

> is to buy out the fee simple of Irish discontent. Land-purchase is true Unionist policy. The Union is best maintained and preserved by doing away with those grievances which imperil its existence. Chief of these is the Irish Land System. And he is a true Unionist who seeks, as I do, to destroy it.[87]

In 1900, Russell predicted that if the land question remained unresolved, it would ruin the landlord class, but would, in addition, 'soon make the Ulster tenant into a rebel'.[88] In a speech delivered during the 1900 General Election campaign, Russell came out in favour of compulsory purchase, an idea that proved to be as popular among Ulster's unionist tenants as it was in the rest of the country. Russell's stance was backed with varying degrees of enthusiasm by most Ulster Unionist MPs, but was firmly rejected by Government. His public comments at this time were full of fire and foreboding. He observed that 'we are lighting a fire in Ulster today which will not easily be put out'.[89]

Russell's outspoken stance on the land question inevitably brought him into conflict with important forces within unionism. In 1900, landlord influence within the Government secured Russell's removal from the junior Ministry he had held since 1895. Russell proceeded to take his case to Ulster's rural constituencies, initiating an agitation that had some parallels with that of the United Irish League. The campaigns of the Ulster Tenants' Defence Association created conditions conducive to the passage of the Wyndham Land Act.[90] In 1907, the new Liberal Government appointed T.W. Russell to succeed Horace Plunkett at the Department of Agriculture and Technical Instruction where, with his land reform credentials, he was more acceptable to nationalists. Russell continued in this post until 1918, by which time Irish politics had been transformed beyond recognition. By then, there could be no turning the clock back to the gentler tensions and controversies of the year 1900.

At the 1900 General Election, the Irish Unionist leader, Colonel Edward Saunderson, whose outlook was the very antithesis of Russell's, was challenged for his seat by an independent unionist, James Orr. Saunderson was a dogged defender of landlord interests and a strong believer in the virtues of Empire. However, he was much criticised by Liberal Unionists for his conservative, elitist politics. An expert sailor and keen golfer, this relatively obscure parliamentarian was, curiously, on good terms with the German Emperor. In the summer of 1900, they dined and played tennis together on the occasion of a regatta in Kiel.[91] At the polls in October, his opponent took 2,468 votes to Saunderson's 3,579, which was quite a shock for the most senior Unionist figure at Westminster who had held his North Armagh seat since 1885, having been unopposed at most elections. Opposition to land reform was at the root of Saunderson's electoral difficulties. At the election of 1900, around 1,000 unionist farmers defected to the independent candidate and

Saunderson owed his survival to support amongst urban workers and rural handloom weavers in Lurgan and Portadown, where a monument to his memory stands today.[92]

Political allies of T.W. Russell went on to record by-election victories over official unionist candidates in 1902 and 1903 and in the General Election of 1906.[93] The leader of the Belfast Protestant Association, T.H. Sloan, triumphed as an Independent Unionist in South Belfast in 1902. However, a subsequent attempt to elect a Labour candidate, William Walker, with working-class Catholic support foundered on the constitutional question when opponents exploited the fact that some of his British Labour supporters, including his election agent, the future British Prime Minister, Ramsay MacDonald, were known supporters of Home Rule.[94]

5. Unionist Ireland in the Age of Revival

As was the case among Irish nationalists, something was afoot in unionist Ireland at the turn of the century which, had it taken flight, could well have altered the course of Ireland's twentieth century. With an active Chief Secretary and a hunger for land reform striking a chord with both nationalist and unionist tenant farmers, there was sufficient political imagination in existence to tackle the land question.

In the late Victorian period, Irish unionism had seemed capable of reaching out across Ireland's constitutional divide. Against a backdrop of comparative calm on the constitutional front, and with a strongly unionist government in power in London, some unionists were keen to search for common ground with nationalists. Liberal Unionism retained a foothold in Ulster. The work of Horace Plunkett found support within both political traditions. The prospect of economic betterment held out by his policies had an appeal that could transcend political differences. Working-class unionism seemed capable of asserting itself in Ulster and challenging unionism's conservative leadership.

The constructive spirit exemplified by Plunkett, Dunraven and Russell, might well have produced further gains for the largely unexplored middle ground in Irish politics. Unfortunately, unionist Ireland was facing in several different directions. There were thoses who wanted to conciliate nationalists. There were others who called for stiff resistance in defence of unionist interests. Then there was Ulster unionism, which was itself in flux at the turn of the century. Ultimately, only the Ulster version of Irish unionism counted for anything as the twentieth century wore on.

Perhaps the single most significant impact of the devolution crisis was that it roused Ulster unionism into a more watchful state. This prompted the establishment of the Ulster Unionist Council which, as the century nears its end, is still the ruling body of the Ulster Unionist Party. The Council was founded at a time when the differences between southern unionism and unionism's Ulster variant were becoming more and more apparent. The seeds of the disintegration of Irish unionism as a significant, island-wide political movement, and the consolidation of Ulster Unionism, were being sown at the turn of the century.

Disenchanted though they may have been with the Government, conservative Irish unionists had nowhere else to go with their support. Nonetheless, the existence of such sharp dissension within unionism highlights the difficulty of engineering any sort of political accommodation in such a deeply divided society. The significance of the turn-of-the-century push against constructive unionism, and its proponents in Ireland, was that it contributed to the ultimate demise of a policy that had promised so much and delivered a not inconsiderable quantity of reform. The electoral defeat of Horace Plunkett, and the removal from Ministerial office of T.W. Russell, drew attention to the conservative trend that was reasserting itself within unionist Ireland at this time. By 1905, the heyday of constructive unionist had well and truly passed. The Irish Reform Association's venture into devolution had backfired; George Wyndham had departed as Chief Secretary; and the influence wielded by Plunkett and T.W. Russell had waned.

Queen Victoria's reception in 1900 offered a keen insight into the political realities of the time. The visit inspired great unionist enthusiasm, constitutional nationalists were in two minds and there were those who availed of the visit to highlight Ireland's generally dismal record during the Queen's reign. Dublin's streets were splendidly decorated to greet the Queen. Beyond the cheers and the banners of this imperial heyday, however, lay the burgeoning reality of a new and assertive Irishness that was destined to partially sunder Ireland's British link before the new century was too much older. This, coupled with the eclipse of constructive unionism, would sweep away the promise of a vibrant middle ground briefly offered at the crossroads of the nineteenth and twentieth centuries.

A letter written by Wyndham to Dunraven at the time of William O'Brien's retirement from Parliament, following the Irish Party's decision to turn its back on the Wyndham Land Act, summarises the doomed ideals of constructive unionism:

An Ireland that has said goodbye to faction could win almost anything. We live in an age of transformation. Irish education, Irish industry, Irish nationality, her pride of place, all hang in the balance and must all be lost if she alone will not change with the changing years.[95]

As it turned out, early twentieth-century Ireland was not ripe to dispense with faction. As for change, that was on the way alright, although not in a form anticipated by constructive unionists, nor by parliamentary nationalists for that matter.

CHAPTER 6

The Dawn of Achievement for
Irish Literature

To transmute the anti-English passion into a passion of hatred against the vulgarity of a materialism whereon England founds her worst life ... has always been a dream of mine.

W.B. Yeats in 1900.[1]

No man, said Nolan, can be a lover of the true or the good unless he abhors the multitude; and the artist, though he may employ the crowd, is very careful to isolate himself.

James Joyce in 1901.[2]

For most Irish people living at the turn of the century, their reading material did not include the poems of W.B. Yeats, the novels of George Moore or the plays of George Bernard Shaw. Literacy rates rose significantly in the late Victorian period, reflecting the educational impact of the much-criticised national schools system. Census returns commonly show families where the parents and children were literate while the grandparents were unable to read or write. In 1901, however, one in every seven Irish persons over the age of five remained illiterate.[3] According to one contemporary account, popular reading matter consisted primarily of the weekly newspapers, which included supplements containing fiction geared to their readers' tastes. If books were found at all in the cottages of labourers and small farmers, these were most likely to be *The Irish Penny Readings*, the sermons of Father Burke, *The Lives of the Saints*, and A.M. Sullivan's *Story of Ireland*. Charles Lever's novels, such as *Charles O'Malley* and *Charles Burke of 'Ours'* were also popular. Many households had such songbooks as *The Harp of Tara Songbook* and *The Brian Boru Songbook*, collections of sentimental and patriotic songs. The Centenary of 1798 boosted interest in patriotic balladry and the singing of such political ballads as *The Rising of the Moon, God Save Ireland* and *The Wearing of the Green*, as well as *Moore's Melodies*, was a popular activity. Street ballads devoted to topical subjects were sold by wandering dealers for a halfpenny apiece.[4] Cheap publications from England circulated in abundance, fuelling fears that Ireland was in danger of losing its own identity. Copies of *Tit Bits, Home Chat, Pearson's Weekly, Answers* and *Woman's Life* were to be found even in the remotest parts of the country. Their circulation

had quadrupled in the space of ten years, sales of these English titles greatly outstripping those of their Irish competitors, *The Emerald, The Shamrock* and *Irish Bits*.[5]

Many contemporaries fretted about the impact on popular culture of the 'yellow press' and the ready availability of cheap, low-calibre literature. Churchmen worried about the influx of irreligious influences and, in 1899, were spurred into setting up the Catholic Truth Society which set about publishing material matching Catholic standards of literary taste. During 1900, the Society produced 59 penny pamphlets, with such diverse titles as *The Catholic Church in the Present Century, The Round Towers and Holy Wells of Ireland, Reasons for Holding the Catholic Faith*, and *How the Angel became happy and Frank Forrest's Mince Pie*. Between them, these sold 650,000 in their first year in print.

There was an intensely creative spirit in the air as Ireland prepared to enter the twentieth century. Irish literature was on the move, approaching the peak of its achievement as some of the twentieth-century's greatest writers were coming into their own. The Irish Literary Revival, which aspired to create a distinctively Irish tradition of writing in English, was already in full cry, even if its finest moments, in the later poems of W.B. Yeats, in the novels of James Joyce and in the plays of Seán O'Casey and John Millington Synge, still lay ahead. In 1900, Yeats, now 35 years of age and approaching full maturity as a writer, was busy trying to create an Irish literary theatre. Joyce, still a precocious undergraduate, was starting to make his way as a writer, hoovering up experiences of turn-of-the-century Dublin that would fire his later work. Synge had just commenced his visits to the Aran Islands where he would garner material

A young James Joyce (right) with two of his university class-mates, George Clancy and J.F. Byrne. Clancy (Davin in Joyce's A Portrait) *was Mayor of Limerick when he was killed by the Black and Tans during the War of Independence.*

for use in his great plays. Lady Augusta Gregory was discovering her vocation as a writer, while George Moore, having established a reputation for himself in London and Paris, was on the verge of returning to Dublin to commit himself to the cause of Irish literature and, curiously for someone of his literary background, to the Irish language.

Far from discarding the literary heritage of the nineteenth century, the writers of the literary revival were, for the most part, determined to resurrect the romantic tradition in literature and put it to work on Irish themes, thus creating what they saw as a new literature for a new century. What comes across most forcefully is their determination to define and express a reinvigorated national consciousness that would differentiate them from the English literary mainstream and act as an antidote to the cosmopolitan mass culture of the 1890s. There is a palpable yearning for an Irish identity capable of deflecting the unhappy realities of the modern world.

The turn of the century was a period when Irish literature and nationalism came together in an alliance that promised much. In 1900, the literary movement's principal figures, Yeats, George Russell (AE), Augusta Gregory and George Moore were, despite their backgrounds, all more or less at home within the broad nationalist tradition of the day which appeared to satisfy their artistic and personal needs. Viewed in the light of the disenchantment subsequently experienced by Yeats, AE and others with the evolution of the nationalist tradition as it acquired a sharper, more abrasive profile, the turn of the century comes across as a halcyon period for cultural nationalism, a plateau from which the highest peaks of individual creativity could be tackled.

The creative spirit of this age was a radically different one from the tortured sensibility of the twentieth century. The pages that follow trace the writer's fascination with Irish themes and look at the roots of the differences that would drive a wedge between Irish writers and mainstream nationalism as the new century unfolded. The strength of the modern Irish literary tradition will be more readily understood against this backdrop.

As this chapter argues, the ethos of the Irish literary revival was essentially a conservative, even backward-looking, one while, at the same time, the writers allied themselves with a nationalist political tradition that was moving, in a radical direction. This temporary alliance tells us something about Irish literature and Irish nationalism at this juncture. It was only when modern Irish literature dispensed with nineteenth-century romanticism, and the idealistic nationalism that went with it, to embrace the twentieth century with all its attendant frustrations and uncertainties, that the summits of creative achievement were scaled. Despite the turn-of-the-century literary enchantment with nationalism, the foundations of the subsequent falling-out between the writers and the political establishment, which culminated in the restrictive censorship introduced by the independent Irish State in the late 1920s, were already being laid. While enthusiasm for all things Irish was undoubtedly strong, differences were already emerging on the direction that Ireland, and its literature, ought to take in the new century. The Gaelic League, with its desire to revive the Irish language, was gaining in strength and prominence. *The Leader* magazine, with its commitment to an Irish-Ireland, was quick to proclaim the need for a national literary tradition that would express itself principally, or even exclusively, in the Irish language.

The intellectual atmosphere of the Ireland of 1900 was highly charged. The breadth and quality of the contemporary cultural debate was arguably more impressive than it has been at any time since. In its own terms, the country was undergoing a real renaissance in politics, in the arts and even, haltingly, in the economic sphere. As the new century loomed, it seemed as if the writers were more absorbed with public debate than with their creative writing. To explore the ideas of turn-of-the-century Irish writers is, therefore, to delve into the political arena once more for, as the new century arrived, the question of identity was becoming central to the new, still inchoate, nationalism that would fuel the subsequent revolutionary upheavals that shaped twentieth-century Ireland. In a society steadily drifting away from Britain, despite a concerted effort on the part of the London Government to improve Ireland's lot, Irish writers reflected, and helped magnify, this British-Irish drift.

1. George Moore and James Joyce: the clash between the 'national' and the 'modern'

Old and new trends in literature were in competition as Ireland's nineteenth century petered out. There are two very different Irish books that have the turn of the century as part of their subject matter. George Moore's *Hail and Farewell*[6] and James Joyce's *Stephen Hero*,[7] both effectively memoirs of turn-of-the-century Ireland, are poles apart in style and outlook.

Moore's book is the work of a nineteenth-century man of letters, essentially a Victorian view of the Irish revival. Its focus is on the author's discovery of the lure of Irish literature and nationalism. *Stephen Hero*, an early version of *A Portrait of the Artist as a Young Man*, but containing much material omitted from the final product, is a fictionalised account of Joyce's life as a turn-of-the-century student and emerging writer. While not a fully mature work, it is manifestly a twentieth-century one, foreshadowing as it does some of the literary devices employed in Joyce's later output. In their attitudes to Irishness and nationality, the two books are fundamentally at odds. Moore, with his turn-of-the-century enthusiasm for all things Irish, presents himself as a writer jaded with cosmopolitan influences and as a new champion of the national ideals of the literary revival. By contrast, Joyce's autobiographical character, Stephen Dedalus, mounts a robust challenge to nationalism and adopts a pugnaciously European pose.

Looking back on the year 1900, in *Hail and Farewell*, Moore describes how 'the Englishman that was in me . . . had been overtaken and captured by the Irishman'. The author had caught 'the disease that overtakes all Irishmen sooner or later' which he described as 'a sort of spiritual consumption'.[8] Its symptoms included abhorrence of 'shameful and vulgar' English materialism and opposition to the 'sensual cosmopolitanism' and 'heartless lust for gold' that marked the high imperial outlook that prevailed in England during the Boer War.[9] Moore felt 'he had been summoned to Ireland' as 'the Boer War had made any further stay in England impossible to me'. Moore's earlier work had borne no particularly Irish imprint, and indeed he had written disparagingly about Ireland in *Parnell and his Island* (1887). Yet in 1900, he was determined to live in Ireland, to break the 'English mould' of his mind and become a Gaelic League propagandist. He was to spend ten years in Dublin, where he wrote a collection of short stories, *The Untilled Field*, specifically for translation into Irish and a significant novel with an Irish theme, *The Lake*. Now largely neglected, this novel has its similarities with Joyce's *A Portrait of the Artist as a Young Man*. In *The Lake*, Father Oliver Gogarty denounces a young schoolteacher from the altar on account of an extra-marital pregnancy. This precipitates her flight to England where she falls in with an agnostic scholar, causing the priest severe pangs of conscience which are relieved only by means of a prolonged correspondence and his progressive infatuation with the wronged teacher. Just as Joyce attempts to fly the nets erected by religion and nationality, *The Lake* is preoccupied with Father Gogarty's tortured attempts to cast off the responsibilities of his priestly vocation and face up to the betrayal of his people's trust that his apostasy represents in a society where religion and nationality are deeply intertwined. As the priest exclaims on the eve of his eventual departure for a new life in America:

> in Ireland, the priest is a temporal as well as a spiritual need. Who else would take an interest in this forlorn Garranard and its people, the reeds and rushes of existence?[10]

Writing about Queen Victoria's 1900 visit, Moore said that 'chill politeness' was the extent of Ireland's obligation towards the ageing monarch who came as a recruiting sergeant 'with a shilling between her forefinger and thumb'. The price of Irish soldiers for the war in South Africa should, he said, be an Irish Government at College Green, site of the country's eighteenth-century parliament abolished by the Act of Union of 1800.[11] Moore,

the erstwhile cosmopolitan man of letters, cultivated a curious advocacy of an Irish language he could not speak. He saw the revival of the language as necessary 'if Ireland is to preserve her individuality among nations'.[12] London was too old and too wealthy to stimulate new creativity[13] while English, corrupted from universal use, was on the way to becoming, like Latin before it, a language 'unfit for literary usage' and 'limited to commercial letters and journalism'.[14] In her letters, Maud Gonne voiced similar sentiments about the English language. Though, by his own estimation, too old to learn Irish himself, Moore promised to ensure that his brother's children would do so! For Moore, Ireland, 'a small nation that has not yet achieved its destiny', was still in a phase of youthful national enthusiasm rich in artistic vision and intellectual awakening.[15] While Moore was espousing these anti-imperial sentiments, his brother was fighting in the British Army in the Boer War. Colonel Maurice Moore later became a member of the Senate of the Irish Free State and was present to challenge Yeats when he made his famous Senate speech opposing the prohibition of divorce – 'we against whom you have done this thing are no petty people'.[16]

George Moore's strange transformation in 1900 did not have an entirely happy outcome. He was never quite at ease in Ireland; he quarrelled with Yeats over their collaboration on the play, *Diarmuid and Grainne;* fell out with most of his literary and language revival allies; and got his revenge through caustic profiles in *Hail and Farewell*. As Joyce suggests in *Ulysses,* that unsurpassed portrait of early twentieth-century Dublin, Moore was too quixotic to be taken seriously in his chosen role in Ireland. He left in 1911 to return to England.

Joyce dismissed Moore's new-found nationalism as an impulse that 'has no kind of relation to the future of art'.[17] In *Stephen Hero*, the young aesthete, Stephen Dedalus, embraces European influences and is determined to confront the orthodoxies of nationalist Ireland. Joyce wanted to be a European writer rather than an Irish one in the manner of the literary revival. His attitude is captured by the aphorism 'Ireland – an afterthought of Europe'.[18] He had the kind of familiarity that Yeats, Moore and Lady Gregory could never have with the realities of middle-class Catholic Ireland which was becoming the mainstay of the new nationalism. For much of his book Joyce, as Dedalus, conducts a haughty dialogue with Gaelic/Catholic/Irish-Ireland and is scathing about the ideals of what he termed the 'irreconcilable party' in Ireland:

> The liberty they desired for themselves was mainly a liberty of costume and vocabulary, and Stephen could hardly understand how such a poor scarecrow of liberty could bring serious human beings to their knees in worship.[19]

The young Joyce, staking out his ground on the national question, was wary of Irish orthodoxies well before Yeats fell foul of the conservative ethos of early twentieth-century Irish nationalism. Joyce's perspective is that of a self-conscious artist who, familiar by birth and upbringing with the insides of Catholic nationalism, was determined to shine an unflinching and unflattering light on them. At the turn of the century Joyce was a lone, little-known voice of scepticism as the more established writers embraced new concepts of nationality with some relish. He was acutely conscious of all that separated him from the literary revivalists. In *A Portrait of the Artist as a Young Man* whose concluding pages, containing some of his most memorable lines, delve into turn-of-the-century debates about literature and nationalism, Joyce contrasts his own forward-looking approach with that of Yeats' character, Michael Robartes, who:

> remembers forgotten beauty and, when his arms wrap her round, he presses in his arms the loveliness which has long faded from the world. Not this. Not at all. I desire to press in my arms the loveliness which has not yet come into the world.

Joyce made a precocious début in print with a piece on 'Ibsen's New Drama' published in April 1900 in a prestigious periodical, *Fortnightly Review*, for which he earned the sum of 12 guineas.[20] While still a student, he was sufficiently self-assured to write to the aged Ibsen, proclaiming that 'I have claimed for you your rightful place in the history of drama', praising him for his 'absolute indifference to the public canons of art, friends and shibboleths', and admiring the manner in which the Norwegian dramatist walked in the light of his 'inward heroism'.[21] Joyce was of a different cast of mind from Yeats and his generation. Even as an eighteen year-old in 1900, he was militantly *avant garde* and a staunch admirer of the realist tradition in contemporary European drama. Nevertheless, in 1899 he had taken a stand against his fellow students when they objected to Yeats' *The Countess Cathleen* for what was seen as its representation of the Irish people as 'a loathsome brood of apostates'. Joyce refused to sign the letter of protest they despatched to *The Freeman's Journal*.[22]

In January 1900, Joyce delivered a resounding affirmation of his view that everyday contemporary realities were the proper material for drama:

> Even the most commonplace, the deadest among the living, may play a part in a great drama. It is a sinful foolishness to sigh back for the good old times, to feed the hunger of us with the cold stones they afford. Life we must accept as we see it before our eyes, men and women as we meet them in the real world, not as we apprehend them in the world of faery.[23]

Though he was still a student and fledgling writer, Joyce's 1900 lecture might be seen as mapping out the literary creed he would pursue with imposing results for the rest of his life. It was one in which the quasi-mystical romanticism of the literary revival would have no part. While Joyce's endorsement of literary realism foreshadowed the dominant tradition of the new century, in 1900 he was exceptional in his interest in the everyday realities of the modern world as raw material for literature, for the bulk of Irish writers still operated in a decidedly nineteenth-century aesthetic environment.

Despite his youth, Joyce was not slow to take on more celebrated figures. In an intemperate pamphlet published after his essay, *The Day of the Rabblement*, was refused publication in a college magazine, Joyce unleashed a withering attack on the literary revival's flagship, the Irish Literary Theatre. Whereas others might scold Yeats and his collaborators for not being Irish enough, in Joyce's eyes their sin was to be excessively Irish and too willing to pander to popular, 'nationalist' tastes. It was the new theatre's fondness for exclusively Irish material that provoked him to unleash an attack on the entire movement spearheaded by Yeats. In the view of the young purist, the literary revival had become 'the property of the Rabblement of the most belated race in Europe'. He failed to understand why artists would want to make terms with the Rabblement. The new theatre had been making good headway until it had 'surrendered to the popular will'. Modern artists should, he felt, look abroad for inspiration. Though Joyce admired Yeats' best work, he criticised the 'treacherous instinct of adaptability' that had led him astray. In his most disdainful voice, Joyce argued:

> if an artist courts the favour of the multitude he cannot escape the contagion of its fetishism and deliberate self-deception, and if he joins in a popular movement he does so at his own risk.[24]

This charge against Yeats of excessive populism sits strangely alongside the poet's subsequent advocacy of an elitist political creed.

2. The crossroads between literature and nationalism

The crossroads between literature and nationalism was a crowded place in turn-of-the-century-Ireland. In 1900, Lady Gregory, under Yeats' influence, was on her way to becoming an influential Irish writer. Hers was a striking example of the appeal nationality had for Irish literary figures at the time. Daughter of a Protestant landowning family and widow of a former Governor of Ceylon, in 1893 she had written a pamphlet called *Phantom's Pilgrimage: or Home Ruin*, which predicted that devastation would follow in the wake of Irish Home Rule.[25] Despite her continuing friendships within the British aristocracy, Lady

Gregory emerged in 1900 as an admirer of the Irish rebel tradition[26] when, in a magazine article, she surveyed with approval the history of the patriotic ballad and its lionisation of Irish political rebels from the United Irishmen to the Fenians. Her diaries of the time show her brimming with enthusiasm for the idealism of the national revival while being determined to stay aloof from political entanglements. She 'found every year an increased delight and happiness in Ireland'.[27]

Literature counted for quite a lot in the Ireland of a century ago. Creative writing exercised a powerful influence over the ever increasing number of people who were literate. Despite a wealth of literary activity, however, the turn of the century was not actually a time of great accomplishment for Irish writing. With the exception of a few of W.B. Yeats' lyrics, none of the Irish writing from the years between 1899 and 1901 has stood the test of time. Even in the case of Yeats, who was then on the verge of supreme literary achievement in the new century, the major compositions that occupied him during these years: a novel, *The Speckled Bird,* a dramatic poem, *The Shadowy Waters* and his collaboration with George Moore on the play, *Diarmuid and Grainne,* are not in the first rank of his work. Even if they were not producing great writing, Yeats and his associates made a significant contribution to the debate that was then under way about the country's identity, and its future in the new century. They were preoccupied with defining their ideals for Ireland and produced two collections of essays on the subject, *Literary Ideals in Ireland* (1899) and *Ideals in Ireland* (1901). Lady Gregory described the latter as an effort 'to show those who look beyond politics and horses in what direction thought is moving in Ireland'. The writers were active contributors to the various newspapers and journals concerned with cultural and political matters – *The United Irishman, The New Ireland Review, The Leader, An Claidheamh Solais,* and *The All-Ireland Review.*

James Standish O'Grady, who launched *The All-Ireland Review* in January 1900, saw it as a vehicle for 'the new forces in the new Ireland now emerging'.[28] Though unionist in politics, O'Grady castigated the Anglo-Irish aristocracy for having failed to provide leadership. The entire population, nationalist and unionist alike, had fallen under the spell of what he called 'the Great Enchantment'. For O'Grady, it was the heroes of early Irish literature, notably Cuchulainn, which his work had done so much to bring to public attention, who provided the cure for this contemporary malaise.

In 1900, the debate about Irish nationality was coming to the boil. In his contribution to *Ideals in Ireland,* D.P. Moran argued that:

> Ireland will be nothing until she is a nation . . . she will never accomplish anything worthy of herself until she falls back on her own language and tradition and, recovering there her old pride, self-respect and initiative, develops and marches forward from thence.[29]

Moran would soon turn decisively against what he saw as the mistakes of those who wrote in English rather than Irish. His insistence on the primacy of the Irish language inevitably departed from the typical Irish literary perspective that:

> if Irish writers do not deviate into an imitation of English literature, but cling close to the spirit of their native land, they do well

for their country when they use the English tongue.[30]

This gap between Irish-Ireland attitudes and the outlook of Yeats and his circle was set to widen as the new century took root and attitudes hardened on both sides. The writers of the literary revival sought a hybrid nationality capable of encompassing Gaelic and English elements. For its part, the Irish-Ireland tradition clung to the concept of Ireland as a nation with a mission to stand aloof from the modern world and in which only the Gaelic tradition had a valued place. This belief in Ireland's cherished individuality, resistant to the materialism of the wider world, was one to which the writers of the Irish literary revival strongly subscribed and indeed helped to fashion even if they demurred on Gaelicism..

It was not just the writers who seemed to have their finger on the pulse of Ireland in 1900. The poet's brother, Jack B. Yeats, was making a mark as an artistic exponent of the new found 'Irish spirit'. His 1900 exhibition, 'Sketches of Life in the West of Ireland', was described as 'a living breath of Irish life' and its creator was viewed as 'the most sympathetic interpreter of the artistic side of the Irish renaissance'.[31] There were many painters giving artistic expression to the new spirit that had entered into Irish life. This was a time of substantial achievement for Irish art. Many of the most accomplished modern Irish painters were active at the turn of the century. Nathaniel Hone was the senior figure

An early twentieth-century production of The Shadowy Waters, *which W.B. Yeats published in 1900.*

in the Irish art world. Younger artists like Roderic O'Conor, William Orpen, Walter Osborne, William Leech and Paul Henry were coming under the spell of European influences and producing works of great quality, or on the verge of doing so.

3. Popular theatre

While turn-of-the-century Ireland shines brightly with the achievements of the Irish literary renaissance, it is worth recalling that in 1900 there was, as always, another more popular side to cultural life. As the year began, the plays being performed on the Dublin stage were not the products of the literary revival, but rather a mixture of pantomime, cabaret and popular drama. Of the six main theatres whose performances were reviewed in the national press at the beginning of 1900, only the Queen's Theatre in Brunswick Street, the prime venue for what passed for 'Irish' theatre in the late nineteenth century, was featuring anything that could be classified as an Irish play. This was *The Colleen Bawn* which had been written by Dion Boucicault in 1860.[32]

Boucicault, one of the most popular English dramatists of the nineteenth century, represented an earlier, and now decidedly outdated, tradition of Irish drama which Yeats' new theatrical movement set out to supplant. Despite the 'stage Irish' character of his plays (and Boucicault had been a prolific dramatist with some 140 works to his credit), tailored as they were to the tastes of mid-Victorian audiences in Britain and their preconceived notions of Irishness, the mainstream nationalist press enthused about the 1900 production of *The Colleen Bawn*, with its sentimental Irish theme. One of its actors, Tyrone Power, came in for special praise for his performance as Myles na Gopaleen.[33] Power, whose grandfather had been a renowned Irish actor, was soon to move to Broadway where he became what, in the idiom of the period, was termed 'a matinée idol' and would later star in early silent films. Even the reviewer in the advanced nationalist paper, *The United Irishman,* confessed to a fondness for Boucicault's Irish plays, *The Shaughran* and *Arrah-na-Pogue* as well as *The Colleen Bawn*.[34]

Tyrone Power was not the only leading actor to grace the Dublin stage in 1900. Later the same year, the leading Victorian stage actress, Lillie Langtry, appeared at the Royal Theatre sporting precious stones with a value of around £5,000. A Dublin reviewer, who was otherwise unimpressed by her acting abilities, admitted that 'she undoubtedly poses in a magnificent manner, and displays her splendid dresses and diamonds in perfect style'.[35] Yeats and George Moore spent much of the latter part of 1900 unsuccessfully trying to persuade another contemporary stage heroine, Mrs Pat Campbell, to stage a production of their play, *Diarmuid and Grainne* in Dublin.

The Queen's Theatre specialised in patriotic melodramas. Two of its 1900 productions were entitled *A True Son of Erin* and *The Patriot's Wife.* An indefatigable theatregoer who seems to have attended every production on the Dublin stage, Joseph Holloway kept a detailed diary of impressions of the theatrical world. He described *A True Son of Erin*, written by an English actor, James Whitbread, who ran the Queen's Theatre and put on patriotic plays there, as a melodrama that 'knew the pulse of its audience'.[36] Holloway enthused about *The Patriot's Wife* written by Fred Jarman, 'a most exciting, interesting and stirring four-act melodrama' which told of an archetypal tug of love between peasant girl,

Kathleen McGrath, a 1798 rebel, Myles Byrne and his 'black-hearted rival' who was a member of the Wexford Yeomanry.[37] This twisted tale ends with the hero's escape from the gallows and his slaying of the villainous Captain Hunter-Gowan. The performance, in which the English actors apparently made no attempt to put on an Irish accent, included a rousing rendition of the popular ballad about 1798, *The Boys of Wexford.*

The remainder of the theatrical fare on offer was of a kind that was to become the target of D.P. Moran's critical pen as he set out to harry all manifestations of the 'English mind in Ireland'. Theatregoers could choose between pantomime at the Gaiety and the Theatre Royal, a musical entitled *Flirtation* and something called *Danse Electrique Phanto-Gymnast* at the Empire Palace Theatre. At the upper end of the cultural scale, classical opera and Shakespearean plays were frequently produced by touring theatre companies from England. D.P. Moran argued that Ireland could never be a true nation while it was unable to supply even its own theatrical amusements. Imported music hall entertainments were seen by him as 'helping to ruin and sap some of the most honourable and characteristic traits in the national character'.[38]

4. Yeats as Ireland's turn-of-the-century man

There is a real sense in which W.B. Yeats, as an Anglo-Irish exponent of an expansive nationalism, epitomises the Irish dilemma at the turn of the century. He seemed at this time to be in tune with the national mood. His politics had a foot in various nationalist camps and he was on good terms both with the members of the Irish Party and the more advanced nationalists. Yet there were already omens of the difficulties that lay ahead for Yeats' ideas of Ireland's destiny.

Yeats ushered in the year 1900 as the most active and articulate champion of the Irish literary revival. As an embodiment of the literary nationalism of the period, his stance warrants special scrutiny. Throughout the 1890s, he had plunged into polemical arguments in support of an Irish national literature in the English language, and was active in the Irish Literary Society founded in London in 1891 and in the National Literary Society founded in Dublin in 1892. Yeats had discovered the appeal of Irish nationalism in the 1880s under the influence of the old Fenian John O'Leary. Inspired by this new enthusiasm, he set out to create a new literature that would combine national and aesthetic virtues. As he had asked in 1892, 'can we not unite literature to the great passion of patriotism and ennoble both thereby?'[39]

Yeats was a prolific contributor to the newspapers and journals of the day on Irish literary and cultural questions.[40] In his view, nationality and literature were inseparable – 'there is no literature without nationality and no nationality without literature' as he put it in his own declamatory manner. He saw scope for the development of a truly popular national literature in which the imaginative stories possessed by the 'uneducated classes' might be made known to the 'educated classes' and 'so deepen the political passion of the nation that all, artist and poet, craftsman and day labourer, would accept a common design'.

While acutely conscious of the differences of outlook between the Catholic and Protestant traditions in Ireland, Yeats hoped it might be possible to 'bring the halves together if we had a national literature that made Ireland beautiful in the memory, and yet had been freed from provincialism by an exacting criticism, a

European pose'.[41] He wanted to draw on the country's ancient mythology and popular folklore to construct a literary identity for Ireland that would avoid the rampant materialism, and what he termed 'thin cosmopolitanism' of the age, qualities that he and many of his contemporaries disliked about the world of the late-nineteenth century.

Yeats did not fit the conventional nationalist mould for he questioned the literary merits of Thomas Davis, whose poetry written in the 1840s was still viewed with approval in late nineteenth-century Ireland. Indeed, Davis' essays were still being reproduced in the nationalist press in 1900.[42] Yeats styled Davis 'a potent maker of opinion' rather than a true poet and looked for the de-Davisisation of Irish writing in order to expunge all that was merely patriotic and failed to measure up in creative terms. Yeats had clashed with Davis' fellow Young Irelander, Charles Gavan Duffy, about the choice of works to be published by the New Irish Library, a series of cheap editions of Irish books. Duffy favoured popular books of a conventional character while Yeats saw an opportunity to uplift reading standards by making more refined material available to the Irish public.

Around this time, Yeats had become concerned by what he feared was an excessive emphasis being placed by Gaelic revivalists on the claims of the Irish language. He saw the language 'as a fountain of nationality in our midst, but let us not base upon it our hopes of nationhood'. Instead, he argued for the building of a literary tradition 'which shall be nonetheless Irish in spirit from being English in language'.[43] While he shared a good deal of the outlook of the Gaelic revivalists, he inevitably parted company with them on the language question. Some Gaelic

Leaguers were quick to challenge Yeats' Irish literary credentials. In 1899, in a pugnacious contribution to the Gaelic League journal, *An Claidheamh Solais* (The Sword of Light), a young Patrick Pearse dismissed the recently-established Irish Literary Theatre as 'anti-national' and depicted Yeats as:

> a mere English poet of the third or fourth rank, and as such he is harmless. But when he attempts to run an 'Irish' Literary Theatre it is time for him to be crushed.[44]

At the turn of the century, Yeats believed in the Irish literary movement's capacity to capitalise on rising nationalist sentiment without compromising artistic integrity. Yeats hoped the new theatre he set out to create would draw an audience from different classes in Ireland, whose people seemed to him to be more susceptible to genuine artistic impulses:

> The contemplation of great sacrifices for great causes, the memory of rebellions and executions, the reveries of a religious faith, founded on visions and ecstasies, and uncountable old tales told over the fire, have given them imaginative passions and simple and sincere thoughts.[45]

The Irish Literary Theatre was the brainchild of Yeats, Lady Gregory and Edward Martyn, a prosperous Catholic landowner with literary ambitions. The idea was conceived in 1897 with the aim of building up a 'Celtic and Irish school of dramatic literature' which would portray Ireland as 'the home of an ancient idealism'.[46] It attracted support from unionists and nationalists alike. The prospectus for the new theatre proclaimed that 'we will show that Ireland is not the home of buffoonery and easy sentiment', a swipe at the tradition of patriotic melodrama and stage Irishness.

In its first season in May 1899, the new theatre produced *The Countess Cathleen,* together with Edward Martyn's play in the tradition of Ibsen's dramatic realism, *The Heather Field.* It was Yeats' play that attracted unfavourable attention. Though he had previous experience of being at odds with mainstream attitudes, the opposition confronting *The Countess Cathleen* was of a more potent character as religious concerns combined with patriotic qualms about the play. With its supernatural atmosphere and its portrayal of a willingness to sell souls for food in a famine-ridden land, it was inevitable that Yeats' play would stir things up. Cardinal Logue attacked it as an affront to religion and patriotism. Lines such as:

> What is the good of praying? father says.
> God and the Mother of God have dropped asleep.
> What do they care, he says, though the whole land
> Squeal like a rabbit under a weasel's tooth?[47]

were bound to offend the orthodox mind, and it is perhaps surprising that the hostility to a play, described in the nationalist press as 'a hideous caricature of our people's mental and moral character', was comparatively muted. No doubt the haunting evocation of the suffering wrought by the Great Famine appealed to those who might otherwise have disowned the play on religious grounds. The controversy generated was a gentle forerunner of the more serious rifts that arose over Synge's *Playboy of the Western World* when it premièred at the Abbey Theatre in 1907. The *Playboy* controversy engendered in Yeats a profound frustration with aspects of contemporary

Embroidery at the Yeats family home in Dublin.

Ireland that was to persist for the rest of the poet's life and provide material for some memorable poems such as 'September 1913' with its poignant refrain, 'Romantic Ireland's dead and gone, it's with O'Leary in the grave', lamenting the wilting of that bracing spirit of romantic revival that had captivated the Irish nationalist intelligensia at the turn of the century.

The Irish Literary Theatre survived for three seasons before it merged with a local amateur drama group in Dublin to become the Irish National Theatre Society. In 1904, this organisation evolved into the Abbey Theatre. In 1900, the Irish Literary Theatre produced Martyn's play *Maeve*, *The Bending of the Bough*, Martyn's political satire rewritten by George Moore and published under the latter's name, and Alice Milligan's *The Last Feast of the Fianna*. The 1900 season took place in the much larger Gaiety Theatre, thus underlining the relative success of this new venture despite, or perhaps because of, the controversy aroused by its first season.

Neither *Maeve*, which Yeats saw as 'a symbolic expression of Irish and English ideals',[48] nor *The Last Feast of the Fianna* won much approval from the tireless Joseph Holloway, who found in them 'only vague daydreams or fairy pictures to console our craving for something dramatic with human heart in it'.[49] For their characters and storyline, both plays harked back to the legends associated with Ireland's pre-Christian age. Alice Milligan's play told of Oisin's departure for the fabled land of Tír na n-Óg in the company of the fairy princess, Niamh, who had a face 'radiant and beautiful like the dawning day'.[50] For its part, Martyn's play features an Irish girl who departs for Tír na n-Óg, 'the land where my daydreams will come true'[51] rather than marry an Englishman whose money is coveted by her father as a means of restoring the family's faded financial fortunes. It says something about the character of turn-of-the-century Irish literature that two of the three plays produced by the Irish Literary Theatre should have had the mythical, otherworldly land of Tír na n-Óg as their focus.

George Moore's play, with its political theme, was well received on account of its 'brilliant dialogue', while the audience lapped up its allusions to local politics. *The New Ireland Review* shared some of Holloway's hesitations about the new literary theatre which, it was felt, risked 'making our idealism a vain and impotent longing for some fairy land'.[52] The literary theatre was praised by J.M. Synge, in one of his first published pieces,

for its attempt 'to replace the worthless plays now familiar to the public with artistic work'.[53] The *Irish Weekly Independent* was also enthusiastic, praising Martyn and Milligan for their 'beautiful works' and lauding Moore, as someone from a landlord background, for belatedly throwing himself 'heartily into the Irish intellectual movement'.[54] Edward Martyn came in for similar applause for taking a nationalist stand when he announced his resignation as Deputy Lieutenant of Galway County following an altercation at the Kildare Street Club because of Martyn's refusal to permit *God Save the Queen* to be sung on his Galway Estate. In his letter of resignation, Martyn, previously a Catholic unionist, said that while he had been brought up in ignorance of Irish history, he was now determined to resist the effort 'to impose a domination of English ideas in every walk of life'.[55] Martyn later became the first President of Sinn Féin when it was formed by Arthur Griffith in 1905.

While *The Bending of the Bough,* with its wealth of topical political allusion, attracted a fairly good audience, the turn-out was nothing compared with the throng that attended a rival production, *La Poupée.* This musical had a bizarre plot involving a young man who was destined to spend his life in a monastery. As he was set to acquire a fortune upon marriage, a bogus wedding with a specially-made mechanical doll was arranged with a view to securing the young man's inheritance. Perhaps inevitably, the doll-maker's daughter is substituted for the mechanical device and the two live happily ever after. Those who came to the theatre to be titillated by the antics of the mechanical doll in the monastery were disappointed as, to avoid controversy, the monks were transformed into celibate members of a Huguenot brotherhood.

Yeats spent much of 1900 engaged in co-writing a play with Moore entitled *Diarmuid and Grania*, based on the Celtic mythological tale. It was a difficult experience and Yeats' father thought it had been a mistake to team up with Moore in this way.[56] The play was eventually produced in 1901 as part of the Irish Literary Theatre's third and last season, alongside Douglas Hyde's Irish language drama, *Casadh an tSúgáin* (The Twisting of the Rope). Hyde's play, based on a folktale which Hyde worked on with Yeats at Lady Gregory's house in Coole Park, was probably the first Irish language play ever to be professionally staged.

At the start of 1900, when reviewing the literary achievements of the year just ended, *The Irish Times* acknowledged that Yeats had 'done some good work' in 1899. He had published a new edition of his collected poetry, as well as his third major collection, *The Wind Among the Reeds,* which even a not-entirely sympathetic James Joyce praised as 'poetry of the highest order'.[57] Although this latter volume has been regarded by some as 'the high water mark of Yeats' lyricism',[58] many of its poems are vague and obscure. It is true that the collection contains such works as 'The Song of Wandering Aengus' and 'He Wishes for the Cloths of Heaven', which have a sublime lyric power that can equal anything in the Yeats catalogue:

> Though I am old with wandering
> Through hollow lands and hilly lands,
> I will find out where she has gone,
> And kiss her lips and take her hands;
> And walk among long dappled grass,
> And pluck till time and times are done
> The silver apples of the moon,
> The golden apples of the sun.

While the poem's subject matter is mythological, and has some of the qualities of late romantic poetry, it comes across as a work with a modern ring to it. The conversational pitch of the phrase 'I will find out where she has gone', and the use of words like 'hollow lands',[59] evokes something of the characteristic twentieth-century voice. 'He Wishes for the Cloths of Heaven' makes a similar impression with its directness and simplicity:

> But I, being poor, have only my dreams;
> I have spread my dreams under your feet;
> Tread softly because you tread on my dreams.

The impact of other poems in the collection is marred by excessive obscurity and a cloying world-weariness. Its *fin de siècle* spirit is evident in phrases like – 'time drops in decay, like a candle burnt out', 'out-worn heart in a time out-worn', 'dream-heavy land', 'the dew-dropping sky', 'dream-awakened eyes' and 'dove-grey faery lands'. *The Wind Among the Reeds* abounds with the colour grey and with references to twilight. Its longest title, 'He mourns for the change that has come upon him and his beloved, and longs for the end of the world' aptly sums up the mood of gentle despair that pervades a collection full of aching poems of lost love and faded youth. Still living in Paris, Synge's end-of-century poetic efforts exhibit a similar world-weary tone:

> Is my love living to hold my hate
> Or silently searching my soul with the dead.
> Would she forgive me, or fool my fate
> I loathe the living, to death I am wed.[60]

While *The Wind Among the Reeds* provides glimpses of the tougher and more passionate style of the later Yeats, the overall impression conveyed is of a poet running out of inspiration, destined perhaps for the same fate that was to meet the Edwardian poets as they failed to master the transformation brought about by the First World War and the modernist movement in literature that triumphed in its wake. Yeats managed to straddle this gulf in sensibility between the nineteenth and twentieth centuries, and in *The Green Helmet and other poems* (1910) and *Responsibilities* (1914) he is already a decidedly 'modern' poet. Indeed, his first indisputably twentieth-century poem, 'Adam's Curse', appears in the first collection he published in the new century, *In the Seven Woods.* 'Adam's Curse', with its dismissal of 'the noisy set:

> Of bankers, schoolmasters and clergymen
> The martyrs call the world

presages Yeats' subsequent poetic achievements. At the end of the nineteenth century, he needed a new focus to harden his work and found this in turn-of-the-century Ireland where the combination of gaelic nationalism and Catholic conservatism was about to mount a challenge to Yeats the aesthete and, as W.H. Auden saw it, hurt him into poetry. [61]

Yeats' sole 1900 publication was *The Shadowy Waters* which his father read with great enthusiasm and Maud Gonne thought 'perhaps the most beautiful thing you have ever written'.[62] It was more of an extended dramatic poem than a play, its plot being totally lacking in dramatic potential. George Moore was probably closest to the mark when he described *The Shadowy Waters* as a 'storehouse for all the fancies that had crossed his mind' during the seven years Yeats was writing it.[63] Its main character,

Forgael, is pictured sailing the shadowy waters seeking love:

> But of a beautiful unheard-of kind
> That is not in the world.[64]

This misty dreamer is accompanied by Aibric who subscribes to a more pragmatic creed. Their exchanges about the nature of love contain some interesting lines highlighting the tension between the 'real' and the 'ideal' that permeates Yeats' work:

> *Forgael:* But he that gets their love after the
>   fashion
> Loves in brief longing and deceiving hope
> And bodily tenderness, and finds that even
> The bed of love, that in the imagination
> Had seemed to be the giver of all peace,
> Is no more than a wine cup in the tasting,
> And as soon finished.
> *Aibric:* All that ever loved
> Have loved that way – there is no other way.
> *Forgael:* Yet ever have two lovers kissed but they
> Believed there was some other near at hand,
> And almost wept because they could not find it.
> *Aibric:* When they have twenty years; in middle
>   life
> They take a kiss for what a kiss is worth
> And let the dream go by.

The ship's sailors' ideas are earthier still:

> I am so lecherous with abstinence
> I'd give the profit of nine voyages
> For that red Moll that had but the one eye.

As the sailors are plotting to kill Forgael, they come upon a phantom ship which they plunder and take its Queen, Dectora, captive. The action ends with Forgael and Dectora departing together for 'a country at the end of the world'.

The Shadowy Waters is a tale of impossible dreams and unearthly dreamers. While it contains some impressive lines, it is enshrouded in a mystical and melancholic haze. The end result is a far cry from the hard-edged poetry that Yeats created when he found his true theme 'in the foul rag and bone shop of the heart'. On a more inspirational note, if the testimony of the poem itself is to be believed, it was around the turn of the century that Yeats first saw *The Wild Swans at Coole:*

> All suddenly mount
> And scatter wheeling in great broken rings
> Upon their clamorous wings.[65]

The period between Queen Victoria's diamond jubilee in 1897 and her Irish visit in 1900 was rich in opportunities for displays of nationalist enthusiasm. These years marked the high point of Yeats' nationalism. It was the time in his life when he came closest to an overt political stance, partly as a consequence of his ongoing fascination with Maud Gonne, then at the height of her renown as a flamboyant activist, and partly, according to one source, 'out of seeing himself, briefly, in the role of a leader'.[66] Among other activities, Yeats involved himself in plans to commemorate the centenary of the rising of 1798, in arrangements for the erection of a memorial to its leader, Theobald Wolfe Tone, and in the Evicted Tenants' Committee. At the beginning of 1900, his credentials were accepted even by advanced nationalists although it was argued that the new nationality espoused by Irish writers like Yeats 'must get more iron in its soul before it can win people to regard it as genuine'.[67] In October, Yeats was in Dublin to preside at a Gaelic League concert at which he spoke in support of the Irish language.[68] He was among those invited by D.P. Moran to contribute to the first edition of *The Leader,* a journal destined to become the standard bearer of the type of nationalism Yeats grew to disdain and went on to castigate in some of his most animated later poems. Although Yeats quickly came in for dismissive treatment in the pages of *The Leader,* he was reluctant at first to break decisively with Moran and wanted to see 'all our movements of the younger men drifting together and combining to some extent at least'.[69]

There were clouds on the new century's horizon that threatened Yeats' concept of a national literature. Although his status as an advanced nationalist was reinforced by the enthusiastic reception for the production in 1902 of his play, *Kathleen ni Houlihan,* which had Maud Gonne playing the lead role, as early as the following year he was launching into a fierce onslaught on what he saw as the propensity of some nationalists to override intellectual freedom.

> I have listened of late to a kind of thought to which it is customary to give the name obscurantism ... Extreme politics were once the politics of intellectual freedom also, but now ... even extreme politics seem about to unite themselves to a hatred of ideas.[70]

While the seeds of subsequent disenchantment were already present at the turn of the century, the connection between literature and nationalism ran deep in what appeared to be a rich, mutually beneficial vein of creativity. It seemed eminently possible for a serious writer to be both a strong nationalist and a leading creative force.

5. AE the literary/mystical nationalist

Literary nationalism reached its high point as the old century waned. The writers were contributors to 'a new movement of ideas' that was 'observable in contemporary Ireland' in the last years of the nineteenth century.[71] John 'Eglinton', not noted for a nationalist outlook, argued, like George Moore, that the well of creative inspiration was running dry in the more urbanised and industrialised parts of Europe and might be about to migrate to a quiet rural country like Ireland.[72] In the same spirit, Yeats called for literature to make Ireland 'a holy land to her own people'.[73] It was this spiritual dimension that attracted another writer, George Russell. Known as AE, Russell was a visionary poet and painter who, nonetheless, spent much of his career working for Horace Plunkett's Irish Agricultural Organisation Society, first as an organiser of rural co-operative banks and later as editor of the Organisation's journal, *The Irish Homestead*.

Born in Lurgan in 1867, AE struck up a friendship with Yeats while they were both art students in Dublin during the 1880s. Towards the end of the nineteenth century, AE developed an exotic brand of nationalism which he expressed in pamphlets entitled, *The Future of Ireland and the Awakening of the Fires* (1897) and *Ideals in Ireland: priest or hero?* (1899). For AE, ancient Ireland was a land of high ideals which he wanted to see restored. He divined a new intellectual fellowship which could 'in a generation create a national ideal for Ireland'.[74] Though much less of a nationalist activist than Yeats, AE shared his friend's aversion to cosmopolitan influences emanating from England. As he put it:

> to me the imperial ideal seems to threaten the destruction of that national being which has been growing throughout the centuries and I ask myself what can it profit my race if it gain an empire and yet lose its own soul.[75]

Despite his mystical nationalism, AE went on, as commentator and journalist, to produce a body of down-to-earth political analysis which has few rivals in the Irish tradition.

AE looked forward to the twentieth century with an enthusiasm and optimism. He felt that:

> the twentieth century may carry us far from Finn and Oscar and the heroes of their time, far even from the ideals of Tone, Mitchell and Davis, but I hope it will not carry us into contented acceptance of the deadness, the dullness, the commonplace of English national sentiment . . . If the stupefying influence of foreign control is removed, if we had charge of our own national affairs, it would mean the starting up to life of a thousand dormant energies, spiritual, intellectual, artistic, social, economic and human.[76]

In November 1899, AE protested to the United Irish League's newspaper, *The Irish People*, which had criticised him for not taking a sufficiently strong stance against landlordism. The objective of self-government, AE observed:

> would be gained at a cost too great if force and bitter words are the only weapons used and brotherhood and a generous recognition

of the sincerity and good qualities of political opponents are principles to be relegated to oblivion.

For AE, who recoiled from the bitterness and factionalism of practical politics, 'the moral and spiritual aspect of our national life must always be first in importance'.[77]

In 1900, AE took George Moore on a cycling tour of pre-Christian sites with the intention of driving 'Irish mythology and idealism into him'.[78] On the evidence of Moore's writings at the time, this effort seems at least to have succeeded in infusing him with a new passion for Ireland. Throughout the year, AE was engaged in writing his long mythological poem, *The Feast of Age,* a work that was never completed. Fragments from it were published in a 1900 anthology[79] containing selections from the principal Irish poets of the day, including Yeats, Katherine Tynan, Hyde, Lionel Johnson (recruited by Yeats on the strength of his Irish family connections) and Standish O'Grady.

Like the bulk of his poetry, AE's poem, 'Dana', suffers from an airy obscurity that also affected some of Yeats' early work, but lacking the assets of insight and imagery that invariably redeem Yeats' work. AE's verse lacks precision and seems to be at pains to evade any hint of worldliness:

> I can enchant the trees and rocks, and fill
> The dumb brown lips of earth with mystery,
> Make them reveal or hide the god.

Words and phrases like 'dewy eyes', 'unkissed on lovely lips', 'dim caress', and 'twilight dropping hair' are everywhere in his poems bringing with them a nineteenth-century aura from which AE's poetic work rarely escaped. George Moore later summed up the otherworldly character of AE's verse, remarking that it led him away 'into a young world which I recognised at once as the fabled Arcady that had flourished before man discovered gold, and forged this gold into a ring which gave him power to enslave'.[80] This has meant that AE's work has not much appealed to the literary taste of the twentieth century.

AE's most impressive poem in the 1900 anthology, 'Inheritance', recalls the hidden ancient influences on the modern age:

> A thousand ages toiled for thee
> And gave thee harvest of their gain;
> And weary myriads of yore
> Dug out for thee earth's buried ore.

The 'shadowy toilers of old' are described as fighting:

> Blind battles with they knew not what
> And each before he passed away
> Gave clear articulate cries of woe:
> Your pain is theirs of long ago.[81]

'The careless sweetness of your mind' is seen as coming 'from the buried years behind' so that 'wise and filled with sad and gay you pass unto the further day'. 'Inheritance' is a poem with a directness and clarity that still works in a way that many of AE's mystical and mythological efforts do not. Unlike Yeats, AE never unleashed in verse his anger at contemporary developments. Instead, he found a productive outlet for his disappointment with twentieth-century Ireland in the journalism he contributed to *The Irish Homestead*[82] and *The Irish Statesman.*

167

In a letter to Yeats, AE explained his concept of poetry:

> Ideas have a beauty in themselves apart from words in literature or art. I think the aim of the writer should be to afford an avenue to the idea and make the reader forget the words . . . which evoked it.[83]

AE sternly resisted Yeats' promptings for him to redraft some of his poems:

> I find nothing to agree with in your letter . . . in our ideas about art we have little or nothing in common.[84]

In fact, they had quite a lot in common during the 1890s, but Yeats' poetry was acquiring attributes that AE would never be able, nor indeed want, to match.

6. Irish literature and the struggle against modernity

AE was not impressed by Yeats' descent into political controversy over the Royal Visit, taking the view that a literary man should only become involved in public controversy when he had some principle to vindicate.[85] In July 1900, AE took just such a public stand when he objected to a suggestion by the poet 'Fiona MacLeod' that patriotism and nationality were merely race hatred. AE argued that the absence of self-government had resulted in 'the spiritual life of our race' being suppressed. He objected to the fact that 'the songs of the London Music Halls may be heard in places where the music of faery enchanted elder generations'. English life with its pervasive materialism was seen as 'more remote from spirit, more aloof from deity than that led by any people hitherto in the memory of the world' and this made him favour the Irish aspiration to 'a distinct and self-governed nationality' so that the 'moral leprosy' and 'vulgarity of mind' creeping over the country could be usurped.[86] This idea that Ireland had a mission to resist modern vulgarity enjoyed wide currency. Yeats saw the literary movement as a bulwark against 'the vulgar books and vulgar songs that come to us from England'.[87] Maud Gonne hit a similar note when she bemoaned the fact that so much of what is 'beautiful in Ireland has to go and get destroyed in England for the sake of money'.[88]

Like many of his literary contemporaries, AE felt himself out of tune with what he called 'the loud age of imperial ideas and wars and self-intoxication'.[89] In taking this position, he was in step with practically the whole of nationalist Ireland, whose alienation from mainstream British opinion at the end of the nineteenth century was made manifest by the outbreak of the Boer War. Lady Gregory held the view that English poets were obliged to sing of victory and write of 'visible and material things that appeal to a people who have made "The Roast Beef of England" a fetish'. By contrast, Irish poets were believed to sing of defeat, to be inspired by ideals, and to be on the road leading from 'things seen to things unseen'.[90]

There was a consensus amongst the writers of the period that Irish literature had a special spiritual mission. As Yeats put it, 'Ireland, which has always believed in the spiritual life, is creating in English a poetry . . . full of spiritual ardour'.[91] This view was shared by a reviewer in the New Ireland Review for whom 'the spirituality of the Irish people – their revolt from the despotism of fact – is not a symptom of weakness, but of sanity'.[92]

The extended introduction to *A Treasury of Irish Poetry* published in 1900, provides an insight into the tenor of Irish literary thought and taste at that time. Ancient Ireland, and Irish spirituality and mythology, were seen as innately suitable as the basis for a new literature that would contrast with, and be superior to, the main body of writing in English. With its ethos of pride and victory, English literature was seen as contrasting with its Irish counterpart which mirrored a spirit 'unconquered by trouble', and was a literature founded on 'defeat and sorrow and hope'.[93] Nationality was viewed as 'the deepest thing in Ireland'[94] and the prime inspiration for Irish writers. Cultivation of Ireland's distinctive nationality seemed, to sensitive minds, an attractive way of escaping the rampant materialism of the late Victorian era. Belief in Ireland's distinctiveness, in its spiritual superiority, was strong. Anglophobia was rife as England, inextricably associated with the then dominant Imperial outlook, was deemed inimical to artistic activity. These ideas were current at a time when Ireland's separate identity was being enthusiastically rediscovered and promoted as an instrument of radical politics. The artistic espousal of Ireland's separateness and distinctiveness fed into the currents of the new nationalism welling around Ireland in the year 1900.

In literary terms, however, the new Irish writing was far from revolutionary. The writers who participated in the literary revival were not actually attempting to create a new literature at all. Rather, they embraced Irish themes in an effort to give new life to older poetic forms. Irish poetry at the turn of the century was a subsidiary branch of the English mainstream, dressed up with an Irish subject matter. Aesthetically, the spirit of the literary revival would continue to be a conservative one until Irish themes and twentieth century influences, mediated by Yeats, Synge and Joyce, contracted an artistic marriage in the early decades of the new century.

In 1900, an older atmosphere pervaded lines like:

> The kindly room when day is here,
> At night takes ghostly terrors on;
> And every shadow hath its fear
> And every wind its moon

and

> A lovely dawn of dreams doth creep
> Athwart the darkness of her sleep [95]

which broke no new ground. Indeed, perhaps the freshest voice represented in the 1900 anthology was Douglas Hyde with his translations from Irish originals:

> My grief on the sea
> Abandoned, forsaken
> To grief and to care
> Will the sea ever waken
> Relief from despair.[96]

While the Irish literary revival was a child of the 1890s, it was not until the first decade of the twentieth century that Irish literature truly found its distinctive voice. This emerged in the plays of J.M. Synge with their exuberant exploration of rural Ireland; in the modernist novels of James Joyce with early twentieth-century Dublin as their theme; in the portraits of working-class Dublin during the revolutionary period to be found in the plays of Seán O'Casey; and in the mature poems of W.B. Yeats crammed with passionate hopes and furious disenchantments.

7. Literature and the language question

Douglas Hyde had been one of the most successful Irish writers of the 1890s. His *Love Songs of Connaught* introduced literature in the Irish language to a wider English-speaking audience. In 1899 and 1900, *The New Ireland Review* published a series of Hyde's *Religious Songs of Connaught,* a tradition of writing which he maintained was still 'found everywhere in Ireland except in those places where the National Schools have robbed the people of their inheritance'.[97]

In *A Literary History of Ireland,* his major scholarly work, published in 1899, Hyde argued that literature in Irish was 'vastly more ancient and numerous than anything that the rest of Europe has to show'.[98] Hyde's book pointed out that while early Irish literature had produced no great drama, it had excelled in saga and romance, forms that had been neglected by the Greek and Roman traditions. His book traces the history of Irish literature through the mythological, heroic and Fenian cycles, doing so with an obvious concern to establish its ancient pedigree as a rejoinder to those of his contemporaries who disdained the entire Irish tradition. Although himself a graduate of Trinity College, he was scathing about some of its leading staff members for what he saw as their sweeping attack on the Irish language and literature and, by implication, on the entire Irish race.[99] Although Hyde was ostensibly non-political, his history viewed the twelfth-century Norman invasion as having 'almost from its very commencement, thoroughly arrested Irish development, and disintegrated Irish life' and for three centuries

afterwards 'Ireland produced nothing in art, literature or scholarship even faintly comparable to what she had achieved before'.[100] In Hyde's version of Irish literary history, this long period of decay was followed by 'an extraordinary reawakening of the Irish literary spirit' during the seventeenth-century even as the Gaelic political order was coming under what turned out to be a terminal threat.[101] He saw the Irish literature of the seventeenth century as a convincing insight into the political upheavals of the period. In seeing this as a national struggle, Hyde differed from Standish O'Grady, who was inclined to view it as a class conflict between the smaller gentry and the more powerful nobility.

For Hyde, 'the sweetest creation' of all Irish literature came after the break up of the bardic schools 'when poetry became the handmaid of the many, not the mistress of the few' and 'the populace . . . burst forth into the most passionate song'.[102] Hyde's work, with its powerful nationalist overtones, had a major impact on, among others, Patrick Pearse and Maud Gonne, who saw it as an 'inspiration' that provided 'the intellectual background of revolt'.[103] While Hyde remained on good terms with Yeats, his analysis of the Irish literary tradition, with its glorification of the eighteenth-century Gaelic school pointed inexorably towards Daniel Corkery's *Hidden Ireland* and to his ultimate repudiation of the entire Yeatsian legacy in *Synge and Anglo-Irish Literature.* By that time, however, Yeats had come to revere another variant of Ireland's eighteenth century, that of Swift, Goldsmith, Berkeley and Burke. Hyde's literary history provided intellectual fuel for an autarkic view of Ireland, its culture, history and identity. In the early twentieth century, Irish-Ireland ideas, with their blunt uncomplicated appeal, proved more potent than the hybrid definition of nationality espoused by turn-of-the-century writers. The Irish-Ireland identity outdid its rivals because it was the more natural complement to developments in the political domain. The initial triumph of this Irish-Ireland ethos, and its very gradual eclipse in the closing decades of the twentieth century, was perhaps the dominant feature of Ireland's cultural history over the last hundred years.

8. A Catholic writer at the turn of the century: Canon Sheehan

The Irish novels from the turn of the century that have, over the years, attracted the most readers in Ireland had little to do with the literary revival – nor with the Gaelic revival for that matter! These were Canon Sheehan's Catholic novels, *Luke Delmerge,* which first appeared in the *American Ecclesiastical Review* in February 1900, and *My New Curate,* which was first published in book form in 1900, having been serialised during the previous year. A Catholic priest from Cork and a prolific novelist, Sheehan, though now largely neglected, was immensely popular at the time. It has been claimed that 'he defined Ireland "almost entirely in terms of its Catholicism" and summoned his Catholic Ireland "to a mission that is nothing less than warfare against modernity"'.[104]

A clerical epic, *Luke Delmerge* tells the story of an intellectual priest's journey from humble rural origins through Maynooth and on to a parish in England and scholarly contributions to the Catholic periodicals. At the outset, Sheehan outlines his view of the novel:

> all fiction is truth – truth torn up by the roots from bleeding human hearts, and carefully bound with fillets of words to be placed there in its vases of green and gold on your reading desk, on your breakfast table. Horrid? So it is Irreverent? Well a little. But you my dear and the rest of humanity will have nothing else.[105]

The novel highlights the tension between Luke's appreciation of the advantages of imperial Catholicism and the deep Irish resentment of English dominance. Luke believes that Catholic Ireland ought to be prepared to lend a hand in the English Imperial effort:

> to bring all humanity … into the happy circle of civilization and evoke from Afghan and Ashantee the glory of the slumbering godhead.[106]

He took the view that 'the world was to be conquered by the world's weapons – learning, knowledge, light, science, literature, seized by the Church and used with deadly effect against the world'. However, Luke recognised that in Ireland everything was 'quaint, archaic, conservative, medieval'.[107] His fellow Irish priests had no sympathy for the idea of 'breeched and bloated Britain' as an agent of civilisation. They saw it as part of 'a mighty rolling mechanism that is crushing into a dead monotony all the beauty and picturesqueness of the world'. Such sentiments are curiously consistent with the creed of Yeats and his circle even if the inspiration for it is quite different – 'it is our faith that makes us hate and revolt from English methods'.[108]

Though undeniably pious and peopled with predictable characters, *Luke Delmerge* is, in its own way, an impressive novel. The narrative, though ponderous, is not without its charm and, though aimed at a popular audience, the book is not an undemanding read. It illuminates a side of early twentieth-century Ireland, its profoundly Catholic identity which, while not well represented in the work of the literary revival, turned out to be one of its dominant characteristics for much of the hundred years that followed.

Canon Sheehan's novel, *My New Curate*, provides a revealing insight into clerical thinking at the turn of the century. The novel's two main characters are a wise old parish priest and his young curate, who seeks to better the economic lot of his flock by opening a new factory and launching a fishing vessel. The two priests are impressively scholarly figures and the story takes the reader through a year of their lives in rural Ireland, against a backdrop of simple popular piety which affords the clergy a privileged place in society. The book celebrates the special calibre of Irish piety and extols Ireland's oasis-like character in a modern world that had lost the key to virtue. Coupled with this assumption of Ireland's spiritual superiority, there is a strong sense of Irish catholic virtue being under siege from the world outside. The novel's young curate is described as:

> inveighing, in his own tumultuous manner, against the new and sacrilegious ideas that are just now being preached by the modern apostles of free thought in novel and journal. We agreed in thinking that the Christian ideal of marriage was nowhere so happily realized as in Ireland, where, at least until recent times, there was no lurid and volcanic company-keeping before marriage, and no bitter ashes of disappointment after . . . But, reverting to the new phases in the ever-shifting emotionalism of a godless

world . . . he compared the happy queenly life of our Irish mother with that of the victim of fashion, or that of uncatholic lands where a poor girl passes from one state of slavery to another.[109]

In *The Lake*,[110] George Moore's more sceptical pen gives a less glowing account of popular piety but his priest, Father Oliver Gogarty, is, like Canon Sheehan's young curate, heavily engaged in temporal activities for the betterment of his community, in his case pressurising the Board of Works to build a new bridge and attempting to revive local industry.

9. Out of Ireland

Oscar Wilde, who so epitomised the spirit of the 1890s, died in poverty and exile in Paris in November 1900. His nemesis, the Marquis of Queensberry, now best remembered for having codified the rules of boxing, predeceased him by a few months. The trial which led to Wilde's conviction for gross indecency had been one of the sensations of the 1890s. This episode did much to create an image of cosmopolitan decadence against which many in Ireland were determined to turn their backs upon as the twentieth century dawned. There is a suggestion that Edward Carson, who had successfully defended Queensberry against the charge of libel brought against him by Wilde, may have run into the ailing author in Paris during the last months of Wilde's life.[111] What a melancholy encounter that would have been for two Dubliners whose memory lives on a century after Wilde's death. Wilde's new monument in Dublin's Merrion Square reflects Ireland's new pluralism. Carson's monument in Belfast recalls the twentieth century's divided legacy.

Arguably the most memorable 'Irish' character in turn-of-the-century literature was created by someone who was not an Irishman at all. Rudyard Kipling's Indian-born Irish orphan, Kim O'Hara, managed to personify the high imperial sentiments of the late nineteenth century. Kipling finished *Kim* in the summer of 1900 when he was in South Africa as a war correspondent. The English 'spirit of the age' which Kipling embodied was far removed from the outlook exhibited by the Irish writers of the period. This situation mirrored the deep chasm of ideals that divided the two neighbouring islands as the nineteenth century slipped quietly into the twentieth.

CHAPTER 7

Fin de Siècle:
the Turn-of-the-Century World

... we are bound to assume, as the scientific hypothesis on which history has been written, a progress in human affairs.

Cambridge Modern History (1902).[1]

At the opening of the twentieth century the long process whereby the whole globe has been brought under the influence of European civilisation was practically completed; and there had emerged a group of gigantic empires, which in size far surpassed the ancient Empire of Rome; each resting upon, and drawing its strength from, a unified nation-state. In the hands of these empires the political destinies of the world seemed to rest, and the lesser nation-states appeared to be altogether overshadowed by them.

An early twentieth-century view of turn-of-the-century imperialism.[2]

But a day of reckoning . . . was in store for mighty England, despite her power of pelf on account of her crimes. There would be a fall and the greatest fall in history. The Germans and the Japs were going to have their little lookin, he affirmed. The Boers were the beginning of the end. Brummagem England was toppling already and her downfall would be Ireland, her Achilles heel . . . His advice to every Irishman was: stay in the land of your birth and work for Ireland and live for Ireland.

Skin-the-Goat's less positive Irish perspective on imperialism.[3]

Irish history is often written with scant reference to developments elsewhere. No portrait of turn-of-the-century Ireland would, however, be complete without considering its condition with reference to the state of the *fin de siècle* world. To what extent was Ireland set apart from the contemporary European mainstream, charting its own eccentric course into the twentieth century, or was it moulded by the economic and political currents washing the wider world as the century turned? Measured against European norms, Ireland's entire nineteenth-century experience comes across as *sui generis*, bearing little resemblance to the general European pattern of revolutionary upheaval alternating with conservative reaction against a background of economic change fuelled by industrialisation. Instead, Ireland's nineteenth-century history was one of progressive national political awakening against a background of economic decline and demographic catastrophe. The late nineteenth century was a time when the world's foot was on the accelerator of change and contemporaries were conscious of a world altering before their eyes. This chapter seeks to conjure up the essential parameters of a world that seemed so advanced to those who experienced it first hand, but which seems curiously backward to our eyes.

1. An aristocratic marriage

The Countess of Chotek is not a name to ring many bells in late twentieth-century minds. A hundred years ago, in a very different world, she was something of a sensation, who was about to enter into a controversial, celebrity marriage. Even those who watched her rise to prominence at the turn of the century, however, could not have imagined how great an impact this young

woman, from what is now the Czech Republic, would go on to make on the course of the new century. Her violent death, fourteen years later, was to become one of the tragic turning points of modern history, its circumstances firmly etched on the collective memory.

On 1 July 1900, Sophie Chotek von Chotkowa und Wognin married the Archduke Franz Ferdinand, heir to the throne of the Habsburg Empire. Her death, and that of her husband, in Sarajevo on 28 June 1914, at the hands of a Serbian nationalist, Gavrilo Princip, who wanted to detach Bosnia-Herzegovina from the Austro-Hungarian Empire, set in train a series of fateful events that triggered the First World War. It is arguable that the assassination of the Austrian Imperial couple marks the true end of the nineteenth century, as well as the moment when the violent twentieth century began in earnest. The scene of Princip's act, on Appel Quay on the banks of Sarajevo's Miljacka River, went on to become a shrine of Serbian nationalism until the tumult that followed the break-up of Yugoslavia at the end of the Cold War put Serbs out of favour with the late twentieth-century residents of Sarajevo as they squared up to Princip's nationalist successors during the Bosnian war. Princip's monument is no more, but the political passions that drove him to kill a Bohemian countess remain a source of anxiety and potential instability in post-Cold War Europe.

The circumstances surrounding Sophie Chotek's marriage call to mind how different life was on the other side of that deep trench driven through the modern world by the Great War which her death helped bring about. Sophie was born into a Bohemian family, that was aristocratic, but not sufficiently noble to qualify her as a fitting bride for an Imperial heir. She was acting as a lady-in-waiting to an Archduchess when Franz Ferdinand fell in love with her and insisted on going ahead with the marriage in the teeth of objections from the stuffy Habsburg court. In accordance with rigid Imperial protocol, their marriage had to be a morganatic one, and she was obliged to renounce any claim to the throne for herself and her heirs. Neither the groom's uncle, the Emperor Franz Joseph, nor any other member of the Imperial family attended Sophie's wedding to Franz Ferdinand. Until she was awarded the title, Duchess of Hohenberg, strictly speaking Sophie was unable even to sit at her own table at Vienna's Belvedere Palace on formal occasions. Even in death, her coffin could not be placed on the same level as the Archduke's and she was not entitled to be laid to rest in the Imperial burial vaults in Vienna. Instead, side by side with her husband, she was buried at Artstetten near the banks of the Danube, site of the couple's family castle and country estate where their descendants still reside.[4] Such was the stultifying conservatism of Europe's ruling elite that it was even suggested the Emperor Franz Joseph might have been relieved when the couple's death removed the stain from the dynasty caused by his nephew's embarrassing morganatic marriage.[5]

2. A time of empires

Sophie Chotek's story reminds us that Europe at the turn of the century was a continent of four empires, Austro-Hungarian, German, Russian and Turkish, which were in various states of political repair. This period was the pinnacle of European power when its leading States dominated much of the world. The nineteenth century had been a European century. The Great

Powers had largely succeeded in keeping the peace between themselves for a century after the Congress of Vienna brought down the curtain in 1815 on the upheavals of the Napoleonic Wars. This protracted international calm was punctuated by revolutionary episodes and witnessed the gradual evolution of an industrial economy and the hesitant emergence of parliamentary democracy in advanced societies. The century's closing years were marked by a renewed economic spurt and by an astonishing spread of European political influence throughout the world.

In Germany, Otto von Bismarck, who had been responsible for uniting the country under Prussian leadership, had departed from power a decade earlier and the young Emperor, Wilhelm II, Queen Victoria's grandson, who turned out to be the last German Emperor, had taken greater political control into his own hands. There were those, in England and in Germany, who were keen to turn these ties of blood between the two ruling houses into stronger political bonds, building also on the two countries' rivalry with France. During 1900, Britain's Colonial Secretary, Joseph Chamberlain, mooted the possibility of a triple alliance between Britain, the United States and Germany. The English thinker, Houston Stewart Chamberlain, encouraged an only-too-willing German Emperor to believe in Germany's spiritual mission in the modern world and fostered an anti-semitism that would blight the country's twentieth-century history.[6] Already in 1900, there were significant anti-semitic riots in Germany resulting in the destruction of Jewish homes and synagogues.

At the turn of the century, the Turkish Empire was in particularly poor shape, retreating from its erstwhile supremacy in the Balkans, its frailty attracting the attention of other countries eager to cash in on Turkey's gradual eclipse as a European power, or to prevent rivals from doing so. The Habsburg Empire of Austria-Hungary, which did not have any possessions outside of Europe, was to the fore amongst those with ambitions to profit from Turkey's decline, but the Habsburgs too had a precarious hold on great power status. The challenge of keeping together the different parts of its vast and heterogeneous European empire, composed of Germans, Hungarians, Czechs, Slovaks, Roumanians, Serbs, Croats, Slovenes and Bosnians, was proving to be quite a handful, and Vienna was coming to rely more and more on the might of the new German Empire to help prop up Austria's position. At the turn of the century, Czechs and Hungarians were restive, seeking greater scope for the assertion of their national rights. Austria's Franz Joseph, already 70 years of age in 1900, had spent more than half a century as Emperor and turned out to be the last but one in a long line of Habsburgs occupying the Imperial throne in Vienna. His successor took over towards the end of the First World War and went into permanent exile in 1918.

If Germany was undoubtedly the rising star amongst turn-of-the-century empires, Russia was, as it would remain for most of the twentieth century, a country of vast expanse and huge potential but beset by major weaknesses. In 1900, Russia was already under the rule of its last Tsar, the resolutely autocratic Nicholas II, and was belatedly trying to modernise its economy, even if its reform efforts remained half-hearted. Nearly a century later, the ceremonial reburial of the last of the Tsars, together with his wife, Alexandra (who was also a granddaughter of Queen Victoria), his family and members of the Imperial household in the Romanov family Church, the Cathedral of St Peter and St Paul in St Petersburg, brought down a symbolic curtain on Russia's turbulent twentieth-century history. Russia's century began under autocratic rule and went through war, revolution, dictatorship and systematic purges on an unparalleled scale, before ending in a climate of far-reaching economic reform and an attempt at constructing a democracy whose success or otherwise will do much to determine the fate of Europe in the early decades of the new millennium. The killing by the Bolsheviks of the Tsar and his family in Yekaterinburg in 1918 recalled the fate of Louis XVI and Marie Antoinette at the hands of French Revolutionaries more than a century before.[7]

The other most influential turn-of-the-century European states, Britain and France, did not, on account of their broadly democratic systems of government, consider themselves to be empires in quite the same sense as the Habsburgs, the Hohenzollerns, the Romanovs or the Ottomans. While they might be lacking an imperial title, Britain and France were arguably the continent's most successful states. They held sway over vast colonial territories that testified to their greatness as world powers. Following the creation of two significant new states, Germany and Italy, modern European imperialism took off in earnest in the 1870s. The leading European states acquired a raft of new colonial possessions and set about carving up much of the world between them.[8] In the three decades before 1900, Britain added four and a quarter million square miles and 66 million people to her already vast colonial Empire, while France increased the number of its colonial subjects by 26 million.[9] In the decades before the First

World War, virtually the whole of Africa fell into European hands. Only Liberia and Ethiopia managed to maintain a semblance of independence. In Asia, where Britain ruled India and Malaya, and France held much of Indo-China, only Siam and China, Persia and Afghanistan preserved a precarious independence. This age of empire saw the creation of a genuinely global economy with Europe as its focal point.

Colonial expansion was not confined to England and France, those early starters in the race to pick up overseas possessions. With increasing urgency following the departure from power of Bismarck, who had been sceptical about the value of German entanglements outside of Europe, Imperial Germany launched a determined bid to accumulate new territories in Africa and the Pacific, an activity that was considered an essential expression of its great power status. Germany's foreign trade was growing rapidly at the end of the century and, in 1897, the Emperor Wilhelm II declared a new *Weltpolitik* devoted to enhancing Germany's world role.[10] Germany seized the Chinese port of Kiao-Chow, a base from which it could project naval power in the Far East. Expressing sentiments more commonly associated with a later German leader, the Emperor saw the strengthening of his navy as a means by which Germany's black, white and red flag 'would to all eternity at home and abroad maintain the dignity of the Empire'.[11]

Italy, Europe's other newly united country, was also pursuing its colonial mission in Eritrea and Somaliland, although it had suffered a humiliating defeat at the hands of Ethiopia in 1896, a rare experience for a European power in the late nineteenth century. Europe's lesser powers, Portugal, Holland and Belgium, also had extensive overseas possessions. Spain, which had parted with most of its original overseas empire, sought to compensate for these losses by obtaining a new foothold in Morocco. Even a small state like Denmark had a modest territorial stake in the West Indies and a move to sell it to the United States in 1900 was dropped because of opposition from the Danish King and his subjects.

Many contemporaries were proud of the heights of political influence that Europeans had scaled.[12] Since 1900, the words 'Empire' and 'Imperialism' have acquired pejorative connotations and it is difficult from this remove to appreciate how favourably these concepts were viewed by many people a century ago. Even if imperialism already had its detractors, notably J.A. Hobson who published his famous critique in 1902 later to be taken up and put to polemical use by Lenin, the acquisition and retention of overseas possessions was seen in a largely positive light. Public opinion responded favourably to the currents of 'music hall' imperialism and the term jingoism did not then sound quite the ludicrous note it later acquired. Looking back from a vantage point during the Great War, when one might have, at a minimum, expected a certain ambivalence about imperialism given that Europe's empires were then immersed in an orgy of human slaughter in the trenches of Europe, the historian, Ramsay Muir, was anything but apologetic about the fruits of the age of Empire. He still viewed the British Empire, at least, as a wondrous political achievement which:

> if the wisdom of its leaders can solve the riddle of the Sphinx which is being put to them, the Great War will indeed have brought, for a quarter of the world, and not

for that quarter alone, the culmination of modern history.[13]

For its turn-of-the-century admirers, modern imperialism was not seen as merely the application of brute power and a lust for conquest, control and economic aggrandisement. Rather it was thought to consist of 'the enlargement and diffusion, under the shelter of power, of the essentials of Western civilisation: rational law and liberty'.[14] In 1900, *The Nineteenth Century,* a leading English journal with a broadly liberal outlook, was, under the shadow of, at first, the Boer War and then the Boxer Rebellion, hugely preoccupied with imperial issues. Its articles decried the amateurishness of existing British imperial arrangements and urged greater military preparedness in defence of the country's overseas interests. One contributor explained the urge for imperial adventure thus:

> pride in our national achievements, consciousness of national vigour and eagerness to provide it with new outlets, growing perception of the grandeur of the Empire and jealousy of its honour – these are healthy symptoms.[15]

The patriotic challenge posed by the Boer War made another writer 'feel the manhood of our race stirring again in our veins'.[16] The journal favoured an Imperial Federation involving the self-governing colonies and encouraged the Liberal Party to embrace what it saw as a sane imperialism that would be consonant with liberal principles.

While turn-of-the-century Europeans may have justified imperialism on the basis of its alleged capacity to salvage and civilise less successful peoples, the main motive for overseas expansion was national pride coupled with the lure of economic gain. Merchant adventurers like Cecil Rhodes were instrumental in popularising the attractions of colonial expansion. Missionaries and explorers gave it a religious and romantic tinge. Considering the extent of Europe's outward-looking ethos, it is hardly a coincidence that two of the best known turn-of-the-century novels, Conrad's *Lord Jim* and Kipling's *Kim*, have Asian settings. All in all, Imperial ambition was seen as the birthright of the successful, modern nation state as the twentieth century got underway. As one French politician had put it some years earlier, 'to remain a great nation, or to become one, you must colonise'.[17]

With this late nineteenth-century hunger for overseas territories, there inevitably arose new scope for rivalry between the European powers. During this imperial age, new and more assertive expressions of nationalism were making their presence felt. In itself, imperialism was essentially an aggressive form of nationalism, pertinent to those nations large enough to regard territorial expansion as part of their national birthright. The nationalism of hitherto less-prominent peoples rose to challenge existing empires, for example in the Balkans. Right-wing nationalism bred anti-semitism which was

Opposite Top: Contingent of Dublin Fusiliers (83rd Foot Regiment, The Royal Irish Rifles) arriving by train in Springfontein around 1900 during the Boer War. Bottom: Connaught Rangers after the Battle of Colenso in December 1899.

Patrick Street, Cork, in 1901 when Cork also had an electric tram system. The newspaper billboard refers to the Transvaal Crisis.

on the rise at the turn of the century and which encouraged the emergence of Zionism, which, against all odds, became perhaps the most successful nationalism of the twentieth century. Set in a context of rising nationalist passions, turn-of-the-century Irish nationalism presents an unassuming profile, expressing itself primarily through the agency of conventional opposition politics at the Westminster Parliament and through an exploration of Ireland's distinctive cultural heritage.

During the 1890s, the colonial ambitions of France and Britain cut across each other in Africa and their forces came face to face at Fashoda on the Nile in 1898. Outright conflict was narrowly avoided. Such events fuelled arguments favouring greater military preparedness. By 1900, Germany had begun the military build-up that would enable it to take on the other European powers during the Great War. In the autumn of 1899, legislation was pushed through the Reichstag to double the size of the country's navy.[18] At the same time France unveiled ambitious plans for expanding its naval forces. This sense of rising international tension prompted the autocratic Nicholas II to propose the convening of an International Peace Congress which met in the Hague in 1899.[19] In *A Portrait of the Artist as a Young Man,* Joyce's university classmate, Francis Skeffington, or Mac-Cann as he is known in the book, is portrayed collecting signatures in support of the Tsar's peace initiative. Unimpressed by MacCann's crusade for 'general disarmament, arbitration in cases of international disputes . . . the new humanity and the new gospel of life which would make it the business of the community to secure as cheaply as possible the greatest possible happiness of the greatest possible num-

ber', Stephen Dedalus refuses to sign.[20] In 1901, the two young students joined forces to publish Joyce's attack on the Irish literary revival and Skeffington's appeal for equality for women within the university.[21] The Hague Conference, while not the roaring success peace campaigners had hoped for, did lead to the setting up of an international court of arbitration. There were many people at the turn of the century who, like Skeffington, yearned for a climate of international co-operation to supplant the national rivalries that threatened to cloud the bright horizons of the new century. The Nobel Peace Prize, first awarded in 1901, and, in its own way, the Olympic movement, founded in 1896, were the product of this yearning for peaceful and co-operative alternatives to conflict between the world's increasingly well-equipped modern armies.

While the outbreak of the Boer War and the Boxer Rebellion in China, and indeed Britain's decision in 1900 to grant effective independence to Australia, brought intimations of eventual European decline, the influence of its leading powers was still expanding as the new century dawned. In 1900, Germany acquired control over Samoa. Britain took Tonga and was still extending its writ in West Africa where British rule was formally established over the 25 million inhabitants of the area belonging to the Royal Niger Company. Britain and Germany were busy co-operating in Southern Africa, agreeing to build a 400-mile railway between the Cape Colony and German South-West Africa. For its part, France was actively spreading its authority in Algeria and Morocco.

The twentieth century has seen a steady decline in Europe's position in the world. The four European empires were dismantled after the

An early photograph of the Irish Guards Regiment which was established in 1900. This picture was taken at the Tower of London and features Lord Roberts, Commander of British Forces in the Boer War (front centre).

First World War, while the process of decolonisation that took off after the Second World War caused Britain, France, Belgium and Holland to shed their overseas territories in rapid succession. The concluding decade of the twentieth century has seen the collapse of the last European 'empire', with the dissolution of the Soviet Union and the ending of its grip over the countries of Eastern Europe. The final major international crisis of the twentieth century, the war in Bosnia and the civil war in Kosovo, came about when the removal of Cold War restraints enabled rival nationalisms to assert themselves again in the Balkans, just as they had done in the decades prior to the First World War. The tragedies of famine and genocide that have beset Africa in the final decades of the twentieth century were, in part, a by-product of ethnic rivalries that can be traced back to the late nineteenth century 'scramble for Africa'.

Even in the late nineteenth century, Europe's ascendancy did not go completely unchallenged, and non-European powers were already gaining ground. The initial reverses suffered by Britain in the early months of the Boer War underlined the limits of European power in the face of determined local resistance. Britain felt obliged to resort to draconian measures to subdue the Boers. Kitchener's action in herding Boer families into concentration camps offered a foretaste of subsequent twentieth-century horrors. The Boer War provoked much anti-British feeling in continental Europe, where sympathy for the Boer cause was considerable even if European intervention on their side was never on the cards. US President McKinley offered to mediate, but his overtures were firmly rebuffed by the British.

Perceptive Europeans recognised that the fortunes of the older European empires were waning and that new powers were on the move in the world. The Victorian historian of British India, William Wilson Hunter, who died in January 1900, was acutely aware of the spread of Russian influence. The so-called 'Great Game' between Britain and Russia, their rivalry in Central Asia, had been a nineteenth-century British obsession. Hunter nonetheless saw the United States as the key player for the future. Writing in 1898, at the end of a long civil service career and following the American takeover of the Philippines, he enthused about their fitness to carry the torch of western civilisation in Asia:

> America starts her career of Asiatic rule with an amplitude of resources and with a sense of moral responsibility which no previous State of Christendom brought to the work . . . The United States, in the government of their dependencies will represent the political conscience of the nineteenth century. I hail their advent in the East as a new power for good.[22]

The thought that Asia might develop without the guidance of an outside Empire seems not to have crossed his mind.

For much of the nineteenth century, Americans had been preoccupied with their country's political consolidation, its westward expansion and its phenomenal economic development. By the end of the century, however, the American sleeping giant was beginning to stir itself on the international stage. During the 1890s, an effort to expand British Guiana at the expense of Venezuela ran into resistance from Washington, which seemed willing, belatedly, genuinely to apply the Munroe Doctrine[23] and extend a protective arm around Latin America and the

Caribbean. In 1898, the United States took control of the Philippines and acquired Puerto Rico and Hawaii following a war with Spain, which also put paid to Spanish rule in Cuba. Talk of a 'manifest destiny' with regard to America's international role became more common, and more popular, as Kipling urged Americans to fight 'the savage wars of peace'.

> Take up the White Man's burden -
> Send forth the best ye breed -
> Go bind your sons to exile
> To serve your captives' needs;
> To wait in heavy harness
> On fluttered folks and wild –
> Your new caught sullen peoples,
> Half devil and half child.[24]

Delivering an after-dinner speech in New York in April 1900, the US Secretary for War provided a foretaste of future trends when he declared that 'the hour is coming when the American people will be forced to fight for the Munroe Doctrine or abandon it'.[25] Despite the emergence of a more confident and outward-looking America in the 1890s, the appeal of isolationism remained strong; it was destined to exercise a powerful influence over US policy until 1941. The 1900 Presidential Election was fought out between an expansionist in the person of President McKinley and a more isolationist tendency represented by his opponent, William Jennings Bryant, in which Irish-Americans were strong supporters of Bryant. Two years earlier, McKinley's Secretary of State, John Sherman, had resigned his post in protest against the outbreak of the war with Cuba. An opponent of territorial acquisition, Sherman had quickly joined the Anti-Imperialist League.

In September 1901, McKinley succumbed to a bullet from a Polish-American anarchist, Leon Czolgosz and was succeeded by Theodore Roosevelt who, at 42, became the youngest US President in history. Roosevelt's active foreign policy (his personal motto was 'speak softly and carry a big stick') and high public profile set a pattern for twentieth-century American Presidencies. His immense popularity was born of his colourful personality and his exploits in the Spanish-American War of 1898 where, though Assistant Secretary of the Navy, he commanded a cavalry regiment known as the 'Rough Riders' composed of cowboys and aristocrats who scored some high-profile successes in battle which engendered considerable public enthusiasm. His flair for diplomacy and success at defusing international crises made him the first Head of State to be awarded the Nobel Prize in 1906. He became a critic of US neutrality in the First World War.

The enfeebled Chinese Empire was attracting considerable outside attention, and not just from European powers. Despite its political and economic backwardness Russia had, in the latter part of the century, been busily spreading itself across Asia. At the turn of the century, the Trans-Siberian Railway, 5,000 miles of track stretching from Moscow to Vladivostok, was under construction; it was completed in 1902 when the first-class passage cost $119 for a journey that took 17 days.[26] In the early twentieth century, Russia's imperial ambitions in the Far East came into conflict with another ambitious Asian power, Imperial Japan.

By the turn of the century Japan, which had enthusiastically embraced Western models of economic development, was already on the rise as a country with expansionist ambitions to be

187

Dublin Fusiliers and their families at an outing on Killiney Beach near Dublin.

reckoned with. The Sino-Japanese War of 1895 had seen Japan gain control over Formosa (now Taiwan) and Korea. In April 1900, the Japanese navy showed off its fleet under the approving eye of the Emperor at Kobe. This highlighted the rising military power of Japan which, just five years later, would amaze the world with its defeat of Russia. This destabilised the Tsarist regime and paved the way for the first Russian Revolution in 1905 which put an end to centuries of Russian absolutism and set the stage for Lenin's Bolsheviks to seize power in 1917. Japan's victory set that country up to become Asia's first great power in the opening half of the century.

The Boxer Rebellion offered violent evidence of local resistance to the growth of European influence. With quiet support from the Dowager Empress, the Boxers, members of a secret society known as the 'Righteous Harmonious Fists', hemmed foreign diplomats into their compounds in Peking, murdered the German Ambassador, and massacred 1,500 Europeans. Countless Chinese Christians were also set upon as agents of foreign influence. The rebellion inspired an unusual alliance between the European powers who, supported by Japan and the United States, put together an intervention force to suppress the Chinese insurgents and ensure that the country maintained an 'open door' to foreign trade and influence. 1900 witnessed the first in a series of territorial manoeuvres that heralded a century of violent upheaval in Asia. Using the Boxer revolt as a pretext, Russia moved to annex Manchuria.

3. The cult of optimism

Mounting Great Power tensions notwithstanding, the turn of the century was an age of conspicuous optimism when belief in the idea of progress was strong. This *belle époque,* rooted in an expanding world economy, gave Europeans and Americans plenty to be happy about. As one authority puts it:

> the consciousness of living in a new age, a new material context, and a form of society totally different from anything that had ever occurred before was by the turn of the century so widespread as to constitute a genuine and distinctive element in the mental culture of the period.[27]

Those who experienced the birth of the twentieth century faced the future in a positive frame of mind, buoyed by what they saw as the nineteenth-century's impressive track record, founded on the wealth-creating power of an industrial economy. In 1900, middle-class people saw themselves as living in an age of achievement, and were apt to radiate satisfaction at the accomplishments of the century gone by, and to anticipate continued advancement along a straight line plotted by science and prosperity. 'The man of the twentieth century,' gushed one turn-of-the-century commentator, 'will be a hopeful man. He will love the world and the world will love him.'[28] Writing in the first decade of the new century, the historian, Henry Adams, expressed himself astounded by the transformation that had occurred in the previous hundred years. He measured the 'progression of society' as:

> fully a thousand times greater in 1900 than in 1800; - the force had doubled ten times over, and the speed when measured by electrical standards as in telegraphy, approached

infinity, and had annihilated both space and time.[29]

Following the economic difficulties of the 1870s and 1880s, the closing years of the century ushered in a new economic boom. A raft of exciting inventions was breathing new life into the industrial sector. The 1890s had seen the emergence of cinematography, the telephone, the gramophone and wireless telegraphy and, of course, the internal combustion engine, which brought forth the new century's most potent icon, the private motor car. These innovations would all come into their own in the twentieth century, helping to shape its identity by becoming mass products and instruments of a way of life very different from that of the nineteenth century. By 1900, early picture palaces were beginning to spring up in the major cities, and cinema was about to triumph as the premier popular art form of the modern age. In 1900, the Italian inventor, Gugliemo Marconi was finalising plans for the first trans-Atlantic wireless transmission linking England and America.[30] It was in 1900 that Coca-Cola made its first appearance in Europe, the product having crossed the Atlantic from America to begin its conquest of the world.

While the first flight by the Wright Brothers was still some three years in the future, 1900 marked a significant milestone in aviation history when, on the second day of July, Ferdinand von Zeppelin's airship, all of 380 feet in length, took to the air near Lake Constance and stayed aloft for 20 minutes, reaching a height of more than 1,000 feet.[31] Air travel was not the only novel mode of transport being pioneered in 1900. A newspaper report announced a planned voyage from New York to Lisbon by submarine, a technological breakthrough for which an Irish inventor, John P. Holland, could claim credit. While travel through the air remained for some years yet more of a dream than a reality, at the turn of the century even motoring was in its infancy and, what's more, the humble bicycle tyre was no more than ten years old.

While contemporaries were not without some foreboding as to the potentially destructive impact of new technology when applied to conflict between nations, on the whole, the influence of scientific progress was seen as highly positive. When Sir William Turner, President of the British Association, addressed its annual conference in 1900, he exulted in the exploits of 'the universal republic of science'. Recapping on the nineteenth century, he listed the wonders derived from the application of science to society:

> Man has to a large extent overcome time and space; he has studded the oceans with steamships, girdled the earth with electric wire, tunnelled the lofty Alps, spanned the Forth with a bridge of steel, invented machines and founded industries of all kinds for the promotion of his material welfare, elaborated systems of government fitted for the management of great communities, formulated economic principles, obtained an insight into the laws of health, the causes of infectious diseases and the means of preventing them.

Inevitably, this enthusiastic chronicle encouraged the distinguished anatomist to look forward with confidence to the future. The world was in the grip of science and all was, therefore, well. Looking to the future, there was:

an ample guarantee that the march of science is ever onwards, and justifies us in proclaiming for the next century as in the one fast ebbing to a close, that science is great and it will prevail.[32]

By the turn of the century, the United States had become the world's leading economic power, outstripping Britain and Germany which was also advancing its economic position at an impressive rate. Americans were already expressing boundless confidence in their country's economic and political accomplishments, something that would epitomise America's twentieth-century outlook. In his annual address to Congress in 1900, President McKinley highlighted the fact that the new century was being born with 'evidences on every hand of individual and national prosperity and with proof of the growing strength and increasing power for good of Republican institutions'.[33]

4. *Not everyone's* belle époque

In this imposing climate of optimism, there were, of course, dissenting voices. Lady Gregory's cousin and one-time lover, the poet Wilfrid Scawen Blunt, was a noted critic of the cult of national power and military might instilled by imperialism. He was disgusted by the intervention of the Great Powers in China in their bid to quell the Boxer Rebellion, and by other manifestations of European power politics. In December 1900, he inscribed in his diaries a pungent critique of the contemporary scene:

> All the nations of Europe are making the same hell on earth in China, massacring and pillaging and raping in the captured cities as outrageously as in the Middle Ages. The

Emperor of Germany gives the word for slaughter and the Pope looks on and approves. In South Africa our troops are burning farms under Kitchener's command, and the Queen and the two Houses of Parliament, and the bench of bishops thank God publicly and vote money for the work. The Americans are spending fifty millions a year on slaughtering Filipinos; the King of the Belgians has invested his whole fortune on the Congo, where he is brutalizing the negroes to fill his pockets. The French and Italians for the moment are playing a less prominent part in the slaughter, but their inactivity grieves them. The whole white race is revelling openly in violence as though it had never pretended to be Christian. God's equal curses be on them all! So ends the famous nineteenth century into which we were so proud to have been born.[34]

A supporter of the Land League who was imprisoned for inciting disorder in Ireland in 1888, at the turn of the century Blunt was scathing about what he saw as the vulgar materialism of late Victorian England. In his diaries, he bade a sour goodbye to the old century:

> may it rest in peace as it has lived in war. Of the new century, I prophesy nothing except that it will see the decline of the British Empire. Other worse Empires will rise perhaps in its place, but I shall not live to see the day.[35]

The late nineteenth-century world of new inventions and middle-class confidence was also a world of paupers and peasants where conspicuous prosperity existed side by side with a grinding poverty for those at the wrong end of the social ladder. Migration and emigration were an integral part of life as people sought better lives away from their places of birth. In the two decades before the Great War, 30 million Europeans emigrated while 60 million more moved into the continent's rapidly expanding industrial heartlands.[36] This *belle époque,* when the average life expectancy of Americans still stood at just 46 years, was founded on unremitting labour on the part of the working classes. Despite the dramatic nineteenth-century advances in medicine, poor people's lives remained alarmingly short. In turn-of-the-century Paris, the mean age of death in certain areas was astonishingly early at 28 years of age while in urban Holland on average people died at 31 years.[37] Bubonic plague was still a health worry. The year 1900 saw outbreaks in Glasgow, Hong Kong and Rosario in Argentina. Steamships plying the world's oceans could transport infectious disease and the plague spread from South America to Cape Town and deaths were also recorded in Sydney and Melbourne. It did not require a plague epidemic to wreak havoc on vulnerable communities. In 1900, India was in the throes of a major famine which cost two million lives, a forerunner of the succession of largely-preventable human catastrophes that would blight the century ahead.

Working conditions were undergoing a measure of improvement in response to demands from the trade unions which emerged as a significant force during the 1890s. Major strikes posed a threat to social and political stability. 1900 saw a strike at the Taff Vale railway in Britain. The following year, a landmark court judgement against the union involved in the dispute convinced British trade unionists of the need to politicise the labour movement. Workmen's compensation acts were being developed, following the example set by Bismarckian Germany. The first such British act was passed in 1898 at the behest of Joseph Chamberlain who, though an active imperialist and conservative on Irish issues, exerted significant influence within Cabinet in favour of 'progressive' social causes. Newly-won concessions notwithstanding, working conditions were still a long way short of today's standards. In France, a factory law passed in 1900 provided for an eleven-hour working day. Child labour under forbidding conditions was a *fin de siècle* reality captured in poignant prose by the journalist, Robert Sherard:

> The drudgery is eternal. There is no hope of relief. One treads, firmly at first, and then with faltering steps, the millround of one's allotted task, until the end which is the nameless grave. And it was because I read in the clear eyes of these children, the ignorance of this cruel but indisputable postulate of the lives of the very poor, that their very brightness, their cheerfulness filled me with more poignant sorrow than any I had felt till then.[38]

While the demands of workers might remain unsatisfied, there was more than enough evidence of change to disturb the peace of conservative minds. In most parts of Europe the Catholic Church had had a bad nineteenth century besieged, as it perceived itself to be, by a godless secularism. During the 1890s, the papacy devised a strategy for coping with the realities of the modern world. A new social policy encyclical, *Rerum Novarum,* sketched the forbidding shape of the modern world in which the Church would have to confront its foes:

The elements of a conflict are unmistakable; in the growth of industry and the surprising discoveries of science; in the changed relations between masters and workmen; in the enormous fortunes of individuals and the poverty of the masses; in the increased self-reliance and closer mutual combination of the working population; and finally in a general moral deterioration.[39]

Separated from us by the chasm of two world wars which changed the world in fundamental ways, turn-of-the-century society exhibits characteristics strange to modern eyes, notwithstanding all of the modernising optimism that abounded at the time. While growing prosperity was creating a new world of material contentment, primitive traditional practices still persisted. Around 1900, 'the commonest way of disposing of unwanted babies in Germany was to give them to the *Engelmacherin* who, for a price, killed them (made "angels" of them), usually with morphine or alcohol'.[40] Duelling was still allowed within the German Army.

5. Political tensions

Alongside the economic revolution wrought by industrialisation, the nineteenth century had also seen considerable political change as the era of absolute monarchy waned and Europeans searched for an alternative model of government. At the turn of the century, Europe was in a stage of transition between monarchy and parliamentary democracy and it would take the seismic shock of the Great War to make universal suffrage a reality even in a democracy as comparatively advanced as Britain's. The advancement of democratic ideas did not mean that the era of kings and emperors was over; far

from it. Even the newly-created states, Germany, Italy and Serbia, had opted for the monarchical model of government with democratic elements grafted on. By the end of the century, however, with the gradual extension of the right to vote, parliamentary democracy and constitutional monarchies were on the rise, even if only two European states, France and Switzerland, actually styled themselves as republics. Indeed, even in France democracy was not out of the woods. The Second Republic had plenty of right-wing opponents and a populist Boulangist movement, of which Maud Gonne's French lover, Lucien de Millevoye, was a prominent member, had only recently fizzled out, but royalists and extreme nationalists remained doggedly opposed to republican institutions.

This was a time when the edifice of middle-class contentment was beginning to show some cracks. Europe's traditional rulers did not have it all their own way. Radical anti-establishment forces were on the rise. Working-class movements were moving to challenge the bourgeois ascendancy that had fuelled a century of economic and political change. In Britain, 1900 saw the foundation of the Labour Representation Committee which brought together representatives of the trades union and socialist societies in a bid to maximise the impact of the voice of Labour in parliament. The Socialist International held its fifth congress during 1900 and working-class issues were steadily forcing themselves onto the political agenda. Even in the politically-backward Russian Empire, radical forces for political change were stirring. Josef Dzuhugashvili, known to the twentieth century as Stalin, addressed a May Day meeting in the Russian province of Georgia in 1900 while another Russian radical, Vladimar Illich Ulyanov, went into exile in Switzerland where, in December 1900, on behalf of the tiny Russian Social Democratic Labour Party, he produced the first edition of a magazine called *Iskra* (The Spark), an unlikely ignition for an unlikely twentieth-century revolution.

Anarchism, with its intense yearning for a new social order devoid of authority and inequality, underwent a violent flourishing in the years before and after 1900 to the great alarm of those with a stake in the established order. There were four major political assassinations between 1897 and 1901.[41] The most famous victim of this spate of assassinations was the Archduke Franz Ferdinand's aunt, the Empress Elizabeth, better known to the nineteenth century as 'Sisi', who, in September 1898, was stabbed to death on Montblanc Quay in Geneva by a young Italian anarchist named Luccheni. The Empress had been one of the most-admired women of the nineteenth century and had, in her later years, travelled incessantly around the continent. An enthusiastic horsewoman and foxhunter, the Empress had visited Ireland twice, in 1879 and 1880 where, as a representative of a great Catholic power, she engendered a warm public response wherever she went. While in Ireland she stayed at Summerhill in County Meath in the company of her favoured English companion, Captain 'Bay' Middleton who had acted as ADC to Lord Spencer, when he was Viceroy of Ireland some years before.[42] Spencer was one of the few English peers to espouse the cause of Home Rule. Diana, Princess of Wales, a woman whose life was not without parallels with that of the Empress 'Sisi', was a descendant of Lord Spencer's.

In July 1900, King Umberto of Italy was cut down at Monza near Milan by an Italian-American anarchist, Gaetano Bresci, while another anarchist tried to kill the Shah of Persia in Paris. French President Loubet had invited all the crowned heads of Europe to join him at the Universal Exhibition in Paris but, such was the extent of security fears, that only the Shah and the King of Sweden made the journey to France. In Brussels, a sixteen year-old anarchist, Jean-Baptiste Sipido, made an unsuccessful attempt on the life of Britain's Prince of Wales, coincidentally on the very day when his mother, Queen Victoria, was setting foot in Ireland.

6. A Universal Exhibition for a new century

France kicked off the new century with a Universal Exhibition in Paris which continued for six months and attracted 50 million visitors. The exhibition gloried in the achievements of the nineteenth century. Its technological wonders astounded those who visited the 547-acre site along the banks of the Seine containing imposing exhibition palaces where the major nations of the world showed off their national accomplishments. In all, 40 nations were represented among the 83,000 exhibitors. More of an entertainment spectacle and an expression of national pride than a trade fair in the modern sense, the Paris exhibition was the eleventh in a series that began with the Great Exhibition of 1851 in London, and the most mammoth in scale. An on-site Palace of Electricity generated enough power to light the exhibits in lavish fashion and to drive its attractions, which included a 106-metre-high Ferris wheel, an electric train and a moving footpath that circled its grounds.[43] There was also a giant cinema and a meticulous recreation of medieval Paris. The Paris Metro, with its distinctive art nouveau decor, was opened in 1900 and those Parisian landmarks, the Grand Palais and Petit Palais, were built for the Exhibition. Not to be outdone, Cork organised its own international exhibition in 1902 with displays from various parts of the globe. The main Irish exhibitor was the Department of Agriculture and Technical Instruction which viewed exhibitions of this kind as a means of stimulating interest in Irish industry.

One observer remarked that the Paris Exhibition proved that 'the triumph of the modern world is purely mechanical'.[44] In keeping with its rustic turn-of-the-century image, Ireland was represented by something that was a far cry from the mechanical – a full-size wax figure robed in Irish lace. In the Transvaal Pavilion, some Irish visitors had laid a bouquet at the statue of President Kruger denouncing 'England's Robber War'.[45] The exhibition did not go on without its hitches. A wooden and concrete bridge built for the occasion gave way under the weight of people using it and eight exhibition visitors died in the accident.

The Paris Exhibition diverted French opinion from the traumas of the Dreyfus affair[46] which had caused deep divisions in French society and exposed the prejudices that existed beneath the surface of the Second Republic. Alfred Dreyfus, an Alsatian jew, had been charged in 1894 with high treason for allegedly passing on military secrets to the German Embassy in Paris. Convicted, Dreyfus was sentenced to imprisonment on the penal sanctuary of Devil's Island in French Guiana. After five years of bitter incarceration the Dreyfus case, which had become something of a *cause célèbre* in France, having attracted the attention of, among others the novelist Émile Zola, was reopened in 1899. The case had prompted Zola to compose *J'accuse*, his celebrated denunciation of contemporary France as a result of which,

fearing prosecution, he was forced to flee into exile in Britain.

The Dreyfus case epitomised the right-left fault line that cut across European societies which was to be at the root of so much conflict during the twentieth century. Right-wing nationalists suspected Dreyfus of being supported by a cabal of Jewish financiers. Dreyfus's second trial sparked bitter dissensions in France where right wingers saw the attempt to free him as an affront to the patriotism of the French military who were being accused of willfully convicting an innocent officer. For the left, the case provided an opportunity to confront right-wing xenophobia and anti-Semitism. The second Dreyfus trial evoked considerable international interest, and it seemed as if it was France itself that was on trial. Foreign governments sent representatives to Rennes for the occasion. A distinguished Irishman, Lord Russell of Killowen, acted as the British Government's observer. Russell, who died in 1900, was Lord Chief Justice of England at the time of his death, the first Catholic to occupy this post since the Reformation. In Ireland, however, he was best remembered for his court room exploits a decade earlier when he had defended Parnell at his trial in 1889. His cross-examination of the forger, Piggot, had helped to clear Parnell's name.[47] While the 1899 trial verdict went against Dreyfus, developments in the political arena worked in his favour. Republicans, many of whom were supporters of Dreyfus, had come to power and, in September 1899, the recently-elected President Émile Loubet, a man with a liberal political background who was keen to draw a line under a damaging controversy, granted Dreyfus a pardon. Seven years later, Dreyfus was completely rehabilitated and restored to his position in the French Army.

7. A Place Apart

The turn-of-the-century world was full of paradoxes. It abounded in confidence but was unable to cope with itself. The behaviour of the Great Powers was getting out of hand. Within advanced societies, fear of rising working-class demands was rife. In a perceptive analysis of Europe at this time, one source suggests it was 'living in a fog of national arrogance covering a vast sea of individual and social despair. While Europe presented a calm front, underneath it was quivering with fear of the future.'[48]

Judged alongside the international currents of imperialism and an optimism born of economic and scientific success, Ireland certainly was a place apart – and there were very many who wanted it kept that way. Referring to this period, Margaret Cousins remarked on 'the very little influence that was felt by my mind from events that were happening outside Ireland and appeared to be regarded as of importance elsewhere'.[49] She felt that things were pending 'in the inner life of a section of the people of Ireland who were conscious and articulate', but that 'the era of parliamentary juggling' was likely to prove futile.

Meanwhile, in the wider European arena, the Great Powers were pursuing a traditional brand of power politics that would reap a harvest of disaster for Europe. Across the world, the twentieth century has been a mixed bag, an age of stark contrasts. The century's historical record shows deep troughs of war and inhuman oppression cohabiting with unequalled peaks of human achievement, particularly in science, technology and medicine. It was a century that dragged the world through two cataclysmic wars, a genocidal holocaust and, under the shadow of nuclear weapons, edged humanity towards the precipice of annihilation. The new ideas articulated by right-wing thinkers, essentially fearful reactions to the modern world, would have their tawdry ascendancy during the 1930s and 1940s. The new radicalism of turn-of-the-century socialists found dark expression in the Eastern portion of Europe during much of the second half of the century, but also contributed to improved working conditions and social security provisions in advanced economies. Seen in this light, the romantic nationalism of turn-of-the-century Ireland, even its narrower offshoots, was a comparatively tender creation. The century's big political ideologies, derived loosely from Marx and Nietzsche, were tried and found disastrously wanting. Older concepts of democracy and liberty have fared better as underpinning principles of a political system that, in western societies, amounts to a clash between mild forms of social democracy and liberal conservatism.

CHAPTER 8

Then and Now:
Another Century Ends

Ireland separates herself from the rejoicings of her Imperial oppressors and stands apart in rightful discontent and disaffection.

A resolution passed by the Irish Party on the day of the coronation of King Edward the Seventh in 1902.[1]

The British and Irish Governments... wishing to develop still further the unique relationship between their peoples and the close cooperation between their countries as friendly neighbours and as partners in the European Union . . . have agreed as follows:

Prologue to the British–Irish Agreement of 10 April 1998.

1. Turn of the century idylls

Michael MacDonagh was a turn-of-the-century Irish journalist based in London. He was a figure of some substance in the world of parliamentary nationalism, who subsequently produced a biography of Daniel O'Connell and a history of the Home Rule movement. Unlike the creative writers of the period, whose works are still celebrated, MacDonagh is the kind of figure whose writings you now have to stumble upon by accident. In 1900 he published an article in the leading London journal, *The Nineteenth Century,* which examined the condition of rural Ireland at that time and outlined his hopes for the new century. This was how he sketched his vision of the country's future:

> What I should like to see is the cabins of Ireland full of contentment and quiet happiness; the country retaining its pastoral characteristics, its touch of perpetual spring ever young and fresh and bright and reposeful – a land of sweet thoughts and quiet breathings; the home of happy agricultural communities tilling their fields and tending their flocks and herds, and the towns few and far apart, astir with a quiet but prosperous trade. This, I hope is the good fortune that time has in store for Ireland.[2]

This sketch of 'contentment and quiet happiness' bears more than a passing resemblance to a much later image of a twentieth-century Irish idyll voiced by a far more prominent Irishman, Eamon de Valera, who was part of the generation that was coming of age at the turn of the century.

De Valera's portrait of a land of 'cosy homesteads' is worth quoting, both because it is so often misunderstood and because it illustrates how ideas that became current at the turn of the century had a very long shelf life in spite, or perhaps because, of the great political changes that separated the year 1900 from the wartime broadcast during which de Valera made his famous remarks. Speaking on St Patrick's Day 1943, this is what de Valera had to say:

> that Ireland which we dreamed of would be the home of a people who valued material wealth only as a basis of right living, of a people who were satisfied with frugal comfort and devoted their leisure to the things of the spirit; a land whose countryside would be bright with cosy homesteads, whose fields and villages would be joyous with sounds of industry, the romping of sturdy children, the contests of athletic youths, the laughter of comely maidens; whose firesides would be the forums of the wisdom of serene old age.[3]

These words, forming perhaps the best-known passage of modern Irish political rhetoric, reverberated down the decades that followed and came, albeit perhaps unfairly, to epitomise the conservative spirit of independent Ireland.

I suspect that de Valera's words were on the quaint side even in 1943, yet they were evidently still acceptable as an expression of a national ideal on the part of a leading politician. Forty years earlier, when the century was in its infancy, such sentiments filled the minds of Gaelic Leaguers, literary revivalists, agricultural co-operators and Irish Irelanders. A land that eschewed materialism was just the kind of Ireland that was widely dreamed of the last time a century turned. It is highly unlikely that any late twentieth-century politician would choose to sketch an ideal Ireland in such pastoral terms as those employed by Michael MacDonagh in 1900 or by Eamon de Valera in 1943. That is one important measure of the gulf between then and now.

For a further indication of how Irish attitudes have altered since 1900, we return to another little known turn-of-the-century source. Charles Johnston, son of the late nineteenth-century Orange leader and Ulster Unionist MP known as Johnston of Ballykillbeg, was in many ways a characteristic product of *fin de siècle* Ireland. His father was no stereotyped Ulster conservative, combining, as he did, strong views on temperance matters with staunch support for the still-radical cause of votes for women. With his school friend, W.B. Yeats, the younger Johnston founded the mystical Hermetic Society in Dublin during the 1880s. Later, having met the Russian mystic, Madame Blavatsky, in London, and married her niece, Johnston returned to Ireland to establish a theosophical lodge. His journey from conventional religion to Eastern mysticism was by no means uncommon in the late Victorian era. Following a spell in the Indian Civil Service, another great late nineteenth-century refuge for middle class ambition, Johnston emigrated to the United States in 1896. Six years later, under the title, *Ireland: historic and picturesque,* he produced a glowing account of the country's history and natural beauty, heavily influenced by his own personal mysticism.

Notwithstanding his family background steeped in the Orange tradition, Johnston's account of Ireland's past evinced strong affinities with the emerging nationalist perspectives of the period. He took the view that Ireland, sustained by its mystical heritage, had emerged comparatively unscathed from the sorrows and vicissitudes of its history:

> stronger at the end in genius, in spiritual and
> moral power, than at the beginning, richer
> in vital force, clearer in understanding, in
> every way more mature and humane.[4]

In the 1990s, in a confident Ireland experiencing a remarkable surge of economic success, it would be difficult to find a match for such ebullient sentiments as those articulated by Johnston. He was not without qualms about the future, but these related to prospective developments in the wider world rather than to any uncertainty about Ireland's prospects. Johnston's mixed emotions about the world's future are oddly prophetic of difficulties ahead.

> The new age now dawning before us carries
> many promises of good for all humanity; not
> less it has its dangers grave and full of men-
> ace; threatening, if left to work unchecked,
> to bring lasting evil to our life . . . The
> opportunities of well being are increased;
> the opportunities of exclusive luxury are
> increased in equal measure; exclusion may
> bring resentment; resentment may call forth
> oppression, armed with new weapons, guid-
> ed by wider understanding, but prompted by
> the same corrupt spirit as of old.[5]

The world might be in for a bumpy ride, but the land of his birth was perceived by him as a place apart. With his clear recollection of wrongs endured and his insistence on Ireland's uniqueness, Johnston is representative of the characteristic Irish mindset of this period. As he

The Cork Exhibition of 1902, which was organised by the Department of Agriculture and Technical Instruction in order to encourage industrial development in Ireland.

Eyre Square, Galway. The poster on the railings advertises fares from Galway to New York for £3 16s.

saw it, Ireland was fitted for a future greatness founded on spiritual virtues rather than on material achievement. In his enthusiasm for all things Irish, Johnston's outlook was not far removed from the Irish Ireland philosophy of D.P. Moran. For Johnston, the modern Irish were a race 'full of clean vigour' promising 'no offering of earthly wealth, but rather a gift to the soul of man; not for Ireland only but for all of mankind'. These were heady claims for any country at any time, but they were not uncommon amongst turn-of-the-century nationalists, nor indeed amongst the leading figures of the literary revival. They tended to view Ireland as a place apart from the troublesome currents of the modern world and what's more they wanted it to remain that way.

2. *The legacy of the turn of the century*

The turn of the century was a remarkably creative period in Irish history and it is no accident it left such a powerful legacy. It was not just Irish writers who were productive, but the country's visual artists as well. The clash of political ideas – Home Rule, advanced nationalism, Gaelic revivalism, and constructive unionism – ensured a lively intellectual atmosphere, one that sustained a number of impressive journals – among them *The United Irishman*, *The Leader*, *An Claidheamh Solais*, *The New Ireland Review*, *The All Ireland Review*, *The Workers Republic*, and *The Irish Homestead*. This ferment of ideas inspired a national awakening to greet the new century, representing a fresh phase of national consciousness with a stronger emphasis on the country's cultural, and hence political, distinctiveness. Previous chapters have explored the atmosphere of revival that permeated the period. It justifies the description of the years around 1900 as an age of revival. Twentieth-century Ireland has been shaped substantially by the successes and failures of that revival.

The political tradition spawned by this national awakening took a certain direction in the first decades of the century, the gist of which, I think, is best captured by the phrase 'Irish Ireland', with its now seemingly superfluous coupling of adjective and noun. These two words are now seldom found as companions. A century ago they jointly expressed an aspiration that enjoyed widespread support, even if its various adherents understood its import in quite different ways. Joyce might pour scorn on the Irish Ireland attitudes of his friend Davin whose mind stood armed against English influence 'in obedience to a password',[6] but he saw more clearly than most that such attitudes had wide currency in the land from which he chose to exile himself. Irish Ireland ideas took a firm hold as the century came of age and shaped the contours of Irish public life for the greater part of the last hundred years.

In June 1998, almost a century after Michael MacDonagh, Charles Johnston, D.P. Moran and others of their contemporaries were grappling with the realities of their day and envisioning an ideal Irish future, I noticed a letter in the *Irish Independent* under a headline that might easily have leapt from the pages of *The Leader* in 1900. 'Tearing the fabric that makes Ireland Irish' was what the headline said. The writer objected to views expressed about abortion in an earlier edition of the same paper and accused the media and 'the sheepish Irish public' of pursuing a:

> morbid fascination with a death-and-cheap-life culture. Let's see just how far Ireland can go without tearing completely the fabric

that makes Ireland Irish – perhaps a little prostitution, a small amount of euthanasia, greater availability of pornography, legalise some drugs and throw in some abortion . . . I have seen advocates of all these nihilist pursuits being championed in the Irish media in recent times. Shocking, and very sad really, if you ever stop to think about it.[7]

This made me realise that the issues preoccupying turn-of-the-century Ireland, and which will be familiar to any reader of James Joyce's novel *A Portrait of the Artist as a Young Man*, have not lost all relevance. The sentiments expressed in the 1998 letter raise important questions about pluralist Ireland and its place in the modern world. Is there, in the late twentieth century, any such thing as a 'fabric that makes Ireland Irish'? If there is, what does it consist of, is it really under threat and how can it be safeguarded? These are questions that ought to be of wide concern as we approach the major chronological watershed of the millennium. It is not easy to find modern equivalents of the many publications in which issues of identity and national destiny were thrashed out with such impressive gusto a century ago.

There were many people around the year 1900 who feared that 'the fabric that makes Ireland Irish' was being roughly treated. It was the impact of anglicisation that caused most concern. English influence was held responsible for a legion of evils including materialism, immoral literature and popular journalism, all of which seemed intent on destroying the authentic fabric of traditional Ireland. For many nationalists, the antidote to anglicisation was for the country to turn in on itself, exploring and nurturing its indigenous strengths. The Gaelic League saw the revival of the Irish language as the best road to national salvation. Gaelic League thinkers feared that, with the loss of the language, other precious assets embedded in the Irish way of life were being unwisely discarded. Revival of the language would, it was argued, unleash the native genius to the betterment of the entire nation. It would insulate Ireland from the otherwise all-consuming vulgarity of the modern world. Liberal Unionists like Horace Plunkett prescribed their own brand of self-reliance with an emphasis on economic advancement. Plunkett saw his co-operative movement as a part of a wider climate of national revival whose various elements could be mutually reinforcing. Literary men like W.B. Yeats and George Moore wanted Ireland, through the cultivation of a national literature, to become an oasis of artistic integrity in an increasingly Philistine world.

Turn-of-the-century Catholic church leaders were anxious about the potentially baleful influence of the modern world on Irish piety. While Irish Catholicism had made massive advances during the nineteenth century, the omens for the future were not unreservedly encouraging. Elsewhere in Europe, a decline in religious affiliation had usually gone hand in hand with the modernising march of industrialisation and the advance of material prosperity. Irreligious influences appeared abundant in the world outside Ireland as the new century dawned, with immoral literature causing particular concern. It was a threat the Church was determined to meet head on. The Catholic Truth Society of Ireland was founded in 1899 to combat the dangers seen to be lurking on the new century's horizon. Churchmen were determined that Ireland should be properly insulated against these dangers, a stance that reinforced the inward-looking proclivities of those who saw national salvation in the creation of an Irish Ireland.

D.P. Moran's crusade for an Irish Ireland represented the most vigorous rejoinder to all that appeared to threaten 'the fabric that makes Ireland Irish'. For Moran, the way to avoid the pitfalls lying in wait in the new century was relentlessly to cultivate all things Irish. Self-reliance was his basic yardstick and Catholicism, the Irish language and the development of Irish industry were his chosen instruments. Outright dismissal of all things English was an essential part of his formula for national success although he was happy to employ the English language in his crusade against English influence in Ireland.

The outbreak of the Boer War in 1899 played a vital role in reinforcing nationalist Ireland's intractability at a time when reform-minded unionism was striving to build bridges across the country's political divide. A turn-of-the-century police report observed with some surprise 'the very large class of respectable merchants, tradesmen, farmers and labourers' publicly supporting the Boers and feared that this phenomenon had reversed progress towards 'content and settlement' under the 1898 Local Government Act.[8] While police sources tended to deride pro-Boer sentiment as 'a mere cheap and harmless form of patriotism'[9] it was more significant than that. The Boer War reinforced an anti-imperialist outlook amongst nationalists at a time of high imperial fervour in Britain and, indeed, within the Irish unionist community. It helped prevent the emergence of an empire-minded nationalism in Ireland akin to Australia and New Zealand where the British cause in South Africa enjoyed solid backing. John Redmond envisaged that, offered similar treatment to Australia, which acquired effective independence in 1900, Ireland would

happily follow the antipodean example of contentment within the Empire. This ambition also motivated the modernising unionism of George Wyndham, Horace Plunkett and the Earl of Dunraven. With the outbreak of the Boer War, even moderate Irish parliamentarians turned fiercely anti-imperialist. Michael Davitt's book on the Boer War[10] expresses a deep loathing of what he saw as the moral bankruptcy of Britain's imperial culture, a fate he was determined modern Ireland would escape.

Much of Ireland's twentieth-century experience was shaped by the triumph of the inward-looking political ethos incubated at the turn of the century. Only in recent decades has there been a gradual but perceptible turning aside from this introspective tradition, together with a search for alternative models of national development. While Arthur Griffith was inspired by the success of the Hungarians in shaking themselves free from Austrian domination, Sinn Féin, as its 'ourselves alone' name implied, looked to resolve the Irish question within an exclusively domestic context. They sought to disavow the opportunities for advancing the nationalist cause within the wider setting of British politics, which parliamentary nationalism had dedicated itself to exploiting. An introspective nationalism, with an accent on Ireland's uniqueness and self-sufficiency, set apart from the main currents of European history, became the preponderant Irish political outlook for at least the first half of the twentieth century.

In 1914, the first great schism in twentieth-century Irish nationalism sundered those Irish volunteers who were willing to participate in the Great War from a minority who viewed the conflict in the same terms as many nationalists had seen the Boer War, namely as a chance to advance Ireland's bid for political freedom by exploiting Britain's external difficulties. Those who remained at home were not prepared to divert their energies from Ireland's struggle by participating in a wider international conflict. The Easter Rising of 1916, which occurred at a time when Europe was in the thick of a titanic struggle between the Great Powers, served to underline how exceptional Ireland's situation was in European terms. Whereas elsewhere in Europe revolution followed in the wake of wartime defeat or national exhaustion, the Easter Rising represented an outrageous act of defiance that was contemptuous of the realities of the Great War. Indeed, until recent times there has been a reluctance within nationalist Ireland to afford any official acknowledgement of Irish involvement in the war. Those who fought for Ireland's cause at home rather than on the battle fields of the Great War monopolised public approval. The decision to establish a joint memorial on the Western Front to all the Irish who died in the Great War, and its inauguration in November 1998 by President McAleese and Queen Elizabeth, represented a striking departure from this erstwhile habit of ignoring nationalist Ireland's contribution to that terrible twentieth century conflict.

The Irish Civil War broke out because those who opposed the Treaty were unable to accept the curtailment of republican sovereignty represented by the oath of allegiance to a foreign monarch. In republican eyes, the Easter Rising and Sinn Féin's subsequent electoral triumph had established a separate Irish polity which owed no allegiance to anything beyond the island. For their part, the pro-Treaty side saw the British links retained by the Treaty as an unavoidable reality and were willing to operate, at least temporarily, within a British Imperial framework.

During the 1920s, demands for the prohibition of indecent literature paved the way for the Censorship of Publications Act of 1929. Its origins can be traced back to the campaigns of the Catholic Truth Society of Ireland that commenced at the turn of the century,[11] and a desire to cut Ireland off from malign outside influences. The idea of nationalism within an Imperial setting retained an appeal for the first Irish Free State government as it worked with the other Dominions to secure the 1931 Statute of Westminster that reshaped the British Empire. With the change of government in 1932, which brought Eamon de Valera to power, came a shift of attitude. The consolidation and constitutional completion of independence became the paramount aim. An independent profile within an increasingly flawed and enfeebled League of Nations, rather than the creation of a national space within a restructured British Empire, had become the State's external priority. The 'economic war' with Britain represented a decisive turning away from the path of co-operation within the Empire. The adoption of economic protectionism and the promulgation of the 1937 Constitution were part of the prevailing go-it-alone mentality. When the Second World War broke out, there was no repeat of the differences that split the Irish Volunteers in 1914. In 1939 there was virtual unanimity about the desirability of non-belligerence. One of the few dissenting voices was that of James Dillon whose family history was steeped in the traditions of nineteenth-century Irish nationalism.

In a sense, neutrality amounted to an ultimate expression of separatism. Experience during 'the Emergency' seemed to confirm the viability of the traditional 'ourselves alone' approach. Self-sufficiency worked for wartime Ireland and neutrality proved sufficiently popular to become, after the war's end, a seemingly immoveable pillar of Irish political culture. De Valera's 1943 speech, quoted at the beginning of this chapter, extolled the country's defiance of the pattern of secular materialism that was believed to prevail beyond Ireland's shores. Viewed from a vantage point in the last years of the twentieth century, de Valera's remarks could be considered as something of an end-of-term eulogy on that phase of Ireland's modern history that was devoted to breaking the constitutional link with Britain. This was a time when nationalist figures were apt to contrast an Ireland of spiritual values with a mythical England that was seen to prize material advancement above all else. The dream of cosy homesteads was a useful antidote to the reality of economic under achievement.

3. A century of two halves

With the declaration of a Republic, accomplished under the leadership of the Fine Gael party which had hitherto manifested less attachment to republican symbols, the historic project of securing political independence was complete. The year was 1949, just short of halfway through a century that had begun with full independence still a radical optimist's dream. Even as they stood aside from, or had been by-passed by, the torrent that swept Europe through two world wars, Irish nationalists were the first to succeed in breaking free from the rule of a European Great Power and effectively blazed a trail that Africans and Asians would follow in their independence struggles. This reversed the nineteenth-century pattern when Irish nationalism

had imported its inspiration from continental European sources, whether the French revolutionary republicanism of the United Irishmen, the European romantic outlook of Young Ireland or the parliamentary liberalism of Daniel O'Connell. There was nothing inevitable about the path to national independence plotted in the twentieth century. When the century opened, the European powers were still in thrall to dreams of Empire and were, South African Boers and Chinese Boxers notwithstanding, still busily projecting their power and expanding their influence around the world. On the day Lord Roberts arrived in Cape Town in January 1900 to command the British forces in South Africa, the first ever railway train arrived in Khartoum from Cairo.[12] Far from planning any retreat from Empire, imperial enthusiasts were eager to carve a railway line all the way to the Cape. Germany was planning a huge naval fleet to further its imperial ambitions. It was not for want of commitment on the part of the Great Powers that the twentieth century failed to match the nineteenth in terms of European imperial success.

The second half of Ireland's twentieth century has been marked by an increasing emphasis on the search for prosperity to complement, and fulfil the potential of, political freedom. Much of the introspective ethos of earlier decades has been dispensed with as the country has become progressively more open to, even enthusiastic about, outside influences. It was the return of mass emigration in the 1950s that provided the catalyst for change. Influential elements in the Irish polity concluded that a radical policy shift was needed to stimulate sufficient economic activity to stem the outflow of people and provide hope of a better life at home.

It should be said that those who pioneered this new direction in economic policy during the 1950s and 1960s were de Valera's political heirs in the Fianna Fáil party. Opening up the Irish economy to inward investment meant recognising that self-sufficiency was an inadequate recipe for national prosperity. Protectionism, the economic underpinning of an Irish Ireland, was gradually shelved and foreign trade adopted as the prime purveyor of national prosperity. Membership of the United Nations in 1955 opened up possibilities for Irish troops to serve in an international cause for the first time since Irish regiments fought in the British Army on the Great War battlefields of the Somme. UN involvement also allowed for a more active engagement in world affairs, especially as Ireland was one of the few European countries to remain formally aloof from the Cold War stand-off that dominated the international arena for 40 years after the defeat of Germany and Japan.

During the 1960s, the protective walls of book censorship were progressively dismantled and, in the decades that followed, social legislation was haltingly liberalised. Arguments about the pros and cons of a more liberal society remained part of the mainstream political debate into the 1990s. As the century draws to a close, the strange birth of liberal Ireland appears to have run its course and it is difficult to predict what route the next phase of national development is set to take. The achievement of political agreement about the future of Northern Ireland in April 1998 has every appearance of a genuine watershed even if the Agreement's implementation remains fraught with difficulties stemming from past divisions and suspicions. A generation of violence in Northern Ireland cast a sorry shadow across the last third of the century as

independent Ireland strove to come to terms with the modern world and find the economic fulfilment that eluded it during the early decades of independence. Membership of the European Union has revolutionised traditional notions of sovereignty and facilitated an unprecedented rise of prosperity and material well-being. Gradually, but steadily, Ireland's British problem has lost much of its political salience as new concerns about the country's place in Europe supplanted earlier preoccupations.

4.   *Whatever happened to Irish Ireland?*

James Joyce named the Irish nets that impeded his artistic development around the turn of the century as those of language, religion and nationality. Nationalist, rural, Gaelic and Catholic were adjectives that, for most of the century, purported to delineate what made Ireland Irish. This descriptive matrix is part of the legacy of the period explored in this book. How have these four horsemen of Irish identity fared during the last hundred years?

Whatever about its record across Europe as a whole, nationalism had a conspicuously successful twentieth-century innings in Ireland. Since the turn of the last century, the greater part of Ireland has moved forward to a largely nationalist tune as the country progressed from being a discontented corner of Queen Victoria's realm to an independent sovereign State linking itself more and more with the countries of the European mainland. This was no straightforward advance along a pre-ordained path, but a torturous route marked by changing contours: the pursuit of a relatively modest measure of Home Rule; a decade of revolutionary upheaval; the political partition of the island; a generation of national assertion when the boundaries of independence were progressively pushed out; and, as the century entered its last quarter, an increasing emphasis on the quest for material prosperity to accompany the political reality of sovereignty.

Home Rule nationalism, still the dominant force in 1900, was perhaps the century's biggest casualty. The reputations of its turn-of-the-century leaders, Redmond, O'Brien, Healy and Dillon, were eclipsed for much of the period that followed by the legacy of Pearse, Connolly, Collins and Griffith. Inevitably, the passage of the decades has also dimmed the light of the revolutionary generation. Names from 1916 that 'stilled my childish play' no longer ring the same patriotic bells. After a generation of historical revisionism, it may be time to reassess their achievements and give them their just place as historical figures no longer encumbered by an association with contemporary controversies. One feels that Redmond and his cohorts might, for their part, be more at home in the Ireland of the 1990s than at any time since independence. Their labours as representatives of Irish interests in Westminster mirror the activities of contemporary political leaders pursuing national interests in European fora. The constitutional nationalism of the Home Rule parliamentarians finds a present-day echo in the Good Friday Agreement's consent principle, not to mention its overt commitment to enhancing further the complex relationship between Ireland and its nearest neighbour.

The Irish unionist tradition, once politically ascendant throughout the island, is now, with the exception of Ulster, no longer a force. Yet, the dawning of a less vexed and more well-rounded relationship between Britain and Ireland as part of the Good Friday Agreement,

together with the new willingness within nationalist Ireland to remember the sacrifices made by tens of thousands of Irishmen in the Great War, would, no doubt, please the likes of Horace Plunkett, the Earl of Dunraven and T.W. Russell who ploughed what turned out to be a lonely furrow for liberal unionism a century ago.

The six northeastern counties of Ulster present a notable deviation from the general assessment of the twentieth century as an era of quite fundamental change. In Ulster, the clash between unionism and nationalism which, in its modern guise, came to a head throughout the island in the 1880s and early 1890s, persisted for much of the century, its contours substantially unaltered by the passage of time. The liberal unionism of T.W. Russell, and the radical working-class strand in Ulster unionist politics, that flowered in the early years of the century, faded swiftly and the crisis that dominated the century's second decade put conservative unionists in seemingly permanent charge of Ulster's political destiny until the upheavals of the early 1970s swept that establishment aside. Portadown was the scene of sectarian confrontation in 1900 just as it was to be again in the 1990s. The Good Friday Agreement, alongside the emergence of a brand of unionism prepared, like constructive unionists at the turn of the century, to enter into a pragmatic compromise with constitutional nationalism, offer the enticing prospect that the Ulster exception to the late twentieth-century Irish pattern of rapid, modernising change may soon no longer apply.

As the twentieth century opened, rural Ireland was in crisis. The land question continued to generate intense passion and retained the potential for violent conflict between competing interests. The landlord class felt besieged by tenant demands. They were described by a sympathiser as:

> a despondent class . . . sullen, angry, sore. Men who have been betrayed, wounded in the house of their friends, deserted by those whose battles they fought, naturally smart under a sense of wrong.[13]

Despite this strong sense of disenchantment amongst landlords, land reform measures passed in the last decades of the nineteenth century had done little to blunt the indignation of tenant farmers. Nationalists and unionist reformers were at one in urging compulsory purchase as a remedy for the country's ills. Rural Ireland was transformed by the Wyndham Land Act of 1903 and subsequent legislation passed during the first decade of the new century. It succeeded in settling the long-running Irish feud between those who owned the land and those who worked it. Thus an economic revolution was completed years before the final push for political independence got underway. Rural Ireland experienced decades of stability (or stagnation, as some would see it) until European Community membership remade the face of Irish agriculture by offering new markets for Irish produce, backed by an attractive system of price and income support for farmers.

As in other advanced countries, technology-based industries and services have lately grown to predominance. The viability of family farming is being called into question as the pressures of international competition and the commercialisation of agriculture hit home. The small, owner-occupied family farm bequeathed by the 1903 Act is coming under threat from international market forces. On the other hand, rural Ireland no longer has the same reliance as before on farming for its survival. The spread of industry and the services sector means that many small rural towns now possess an economic *raison d'être* other than food production. In the process, Ireland has become a post-rural society, one that has been able to embrace the new economic opportunities of the 1990s without the burdens of an urban/industrial past.

While the ending of British rule captured the imagination more than any other event in Ireland's twentieth century, it seems that the century's greatest transformation has been an economic one. Living conditions in both rural and urban areas have undergone dramatic improvement. Late nineteenth-century Ireland was an economic mess. It had been by-passed by the fortunes of the *belle époque* and was notorious for its deep, depressing poverty. Overseas visitors were invariably appalled by what they saw, especially in the west of Ireland. While admiring the character of the people, and the beauty of the landscape, visitors commonly viewed the country as unfit for the rigours of the modern world. Emigration seemed to be steadily draining Irish society's life blood and commentators puzzled over how this blight might be ended. The deprivation and chronic under-achievement that made turn-of-the-century Ireland a byword for hopeless poverty have, as the twentieth century draws to a close, given way to a notable level of prosperity founded on a modern industrial base rather than on the country's traditional economic vocation as a food producer. Economically, Ireland is no longer a place apart, but possesses a successful mixed economy plugged into the European mainstream.

One can argue the case for 1973, when Ireland joined what was then the European

Economic Community, rather than 1916 or 1921 as the most significant date in Ireland's twentieth-century history, although such an argument inevitably begs a myriad of unanswerable questions about how things might have developed in the absence of the dramatic events of the Easter Rising and the war of independence. I take the view that it is the disappearance of the squalid urban tenements and rural mud cabins of the late nineteenth century, as well as the ending of the scourge of mass emigration, rather than the belated fulfilment of the patriots' dream of independence, that represents the crowning achievement of the last hundred years. The fact that illegal immigration and the handling of asylum seekers has become a source of debate in the Ireland of the 1990s highlights the extent to which economic realities have been transformed in the course of the century.

The big ideal that inspired nationalist Ireland one hundred years ago was the revival of the Irish language. On the threshold of the new century, loss of national identity seemed a distinct possibility. The day was saved by an extraordinary surge of Gaelic romanticism which sparked off a literary renaissance and a passionate crusade to restore the fortunes of the Irish language. Without the efforts of the Gaelic League, modern Ireland would have been a very different place, its independence struggle would have lacked an essential ingredient which drew so many of the 1916 leaders into the field of revolutionary politics. In a sense, the Gaelic revival that straddled the late nineteenth and early twentieth centuries did succeed in reviving the Irish language, but primarily as a political tool rather than as a living entity. While the language has not been restored to its early nineteenth-century position, such a radical restoration was

always beyond the bounds of realistic ambition. Nonetheless, the Irish language does survive as an important component of national identity and modern Ireland would be poorer in its absence.

That other great product of late nineteenth-century revivalism, the Gaelic Athletic Association, thrives in the late twentieth century, adding a unique sporting dimension to modern Irish life. The remarkable strength of Gaelic games is without parallel in contemporary Europe where sport has acquired a thoroughly international flavour. The survival of national sporting traditions is matched in the field of music. The *Feis Ceoil*, first held in 1897 as part of the revival of interest in all things Irish and with support from Catholic and Protestant bishops, nationalist MPs, Gaelic League branches, and even the conservative unionist, Lord Ardilaun, left its mark in the form of today's living heritage of traditional music, more vibrant than in any other European country. Early performers at the *Feis Ceoil* included the future singing legend, John MacCormack, and the young James Joyce. These elements, while they might not measure up to turn-of-the-century ideas of an Irish Ireland, provide today's Ireland with a distinctive contemporary identity.

The Roman Catholic Church entered the new century on a rising curve and, for much of the intervening period, wielded substantial influence in a State with an overwhelmingly Catholic population whose historical struggle had been heavily bound up with the assertion of religious identity. Long the most formidable institution in Irish life, the Catholic Church has, of late, entered difficult terrain, its influence waning in the preponderantly secular climate of the late twentieth century. Its standing has been dented by a series of controversies that coincided with the emergence of a less deferential public attitude towards Churchmen. A sharp decline in vocations has reduced the influx of fresh recruits equipped to handle the challenges of a rapidly changing society. Despite recent vicissitudes, however, Church attendance remains high by European standards and a broadly Catholic ethos remains an influential component of the modern Irish identity.

The Irish Ireland identity fashioned in the first quarter of the century is, as a description of contemporary reality, now outmoded. That period in our history has, however, bequeathed a singular way of life and a culture that has defied the expectations of those – and they were many at the turn of the last century – who believed that cosmopolitan influences must inevitably decimate national identity. Without the influence of Irish Ireland attitudes, Ireland, with its possession of English, the world's most powerful language, and the carrier of Hollywood culture, might well have lost much of its individuality. This has not happened. Rather a distinctive Irish niche has been found in the Anglo-American cultural empire. Yeats' 'indomitable Irishry' survives – so far, at least! The pious, conservative Ireland that flourished for the first 50 years after independence is no more, and the debate about its successor, if there is to be one, has hardly even begun. Demands for an Irish Ireland are no longer much heard. Why should they be? There is no need to aspire to an Irish Ireland, for Ireland is Irish, plain and simple. It may not be the kind of Ireland that was dreamed of in 1900 or even in 1943, but what matter?

Modern Ireland has broken through the nets of religion, language and nationality that troubled James Joyce and conditioned much of his life's work. The creative mind cannot endure such nets. Escape from them is an essential part of any artistic flight. The case of a nation is different. It may require this kind of netting as a collective reference point, but national horizons cannot remain unaltered in a world of perpetual change. The last hundred years have reconfigured Irish society from a largely rural entity, set apart from the advanced, urbanised parts of Western Europe, into one by and large as diverse as other contemporary Western European society, albeit with its own distinctive features. For good or ill, Irish society now largely mirrors the mores of the late twentieth-century world. In squeezing through the nets woven at the turn of the century, some of their fabric has brushed off, enough, perhaps, to build new nets for the uncertain waters of a new century? What then is the fabric that makes Ireland Irish? It is a rich fabric woven by its history, by the country's physical and cultural patrimony, by economic circumstances and by the shifting beliefs and aspirations of its population. This fabric does not need Joyce's nets to act as a description. Any effort to describe an Irish identity in terms borrowed from another time will inevitably fall down. National identity is not something that can be imposed or conceived in abstract terms, at least not in the late-twentieth century. The nets that Joyce sought to fly served their purpose in the circumstances of a century ago which called for a vigorous expression of national identity that could mobilise large numbers of people. For Irish society, learning, by trial and error, to fly those nets has been a troubling but essential experience. Those particular nets have now been cast!

5. *Another Troy?*

George Moore recalls walking across Trafalgar Square during the Boer War and musing that

'no one in a hundred years will be concerned to know how any one of the men who sat deliberating the fate of a continent lived and died . . . I can think of no other reason except that the traffic of Ministers is with this world whereas dreams and visions and aspirations come from beyond the world . . . we remember a nation for its art rather than for its colonies.'[14]

Time has confirmed the wisdom of Moore's observation as the 'monuments of unaging intellect' composed by those turn-of-the-century figures, Joyce, Yeats, Synge, O'Casey and such later figures as Samuel Beckett, retain an interest that stone memorials, whether to Lord Roberts in London, or to the Dublin Fusiliers in St Stephen's Green, cannot hope to match.

The turn of the century was a time when dreamers and their dreams were in plentiful supply. There is not much talk of dreams anywhere at the end of the twentieth century. It is debatable if we now dream much about our collective destiny at all. Do we now possess any shared vision of Ireland for the twenty-first century akin to the ones in which turn-of-the-century writers were wont to revel? Alternatively, with political independence firmly established and material prosperity on the rise, is there any need for such dreams and fancies? As Robert Emmet's epitaph has long since been written in the script of the twentieth-century's second and third decades, is there a place in today's orbit for people like Yeats, Arthur Griffith, Douglas Hyde, Horace Plunkett and D.P. Moran with their restless, competing imaginings about Ireland's future? There is no late twentieth-century consensus about the issues of identity that were being hotly debated a century ago. There is no current equivalent of the Gaelic League, of radical journalists like Arthur Griffith, nor, indeed, unionist figures like Horace Plunkett, to spur on the kind of debate about our identity that, as the new century unfolds, we may regret not having had.

For what it's worth, my own view is that the key to national success for Ireland in the new millennium will rest with the cultivation of its distinctiveness, rather than in a search for conformity with international norms. It is to be hoped that the Irish of the twenty-first century will seek to explore and develop their Irishness, as their predecessors sought to do a century ago, while leaving behind the introspective attitudes bequeathed by the Irish Ireland movement. Such an approach was understandable, even desirable, for the development of a nation demoralised by its traumatic nineteenth century experience. There is no longer any need to be fearful of outside influences as many turn-of-the century figures were.

The debate about national identity that raged at the turn of the last century saw to it that the twentieth century would represent the dawn of a new era for Ireland. It has proved to be an era when the Irish nation came into its own in the shape of political independence, literary and cultural achievements out of all proportion to population size and, latterly, a thriving economy. As we witness the sunrise of a new millennium, which brings the prospect of another new day dawning, this is a good time to reflect, as this work has tried to do, on the distance that has been travelled since the sun set on Ireland's tempestuous nineteenth century.

Perhaps it is sufficient for contemporary Ireland to aspire to a slightly improved version of what it already possesses? It may be that vision and lofty aspiration are by-products of the culture of the late nineteenth century, largely redundant in a society whose principal ambitions have either been achieved or debunked. Is it the case that, in the twentieth-century graveyard of idealism, the very idea of a collective national aspiration, as opposed to personal ambition, now presents an outmoded appearance? Late twentieth-century Ireland may have reached a plateau of relative contentment where there is no longer the strong yearning that so many Irish people felt a hundred years ago to change the country's political and economic condition. As it approaches the millennium, Ireland, home a century ago to many would-be revolutionaries who rejected the smugness and arrogance of Imperial Britain, seems, uncertainties in Northern Ireland notwithstanding, a far less turbulent, and dare I say it, complacent place. Contemporary Ireland is not without its serious problems and imposing challenges, but there is now much to hold on to and fewer great grievances to rage against than was the case when the twentieth century dawned on an island of apprehensive landlords, resentful tenants, impoverished tenement dwellers, Gaelic revivalists, Home Rulers, advanced nationalists and a deprived working class increasingly conscious of the inequities it endured. In today's climate of economic revival and comparative satisfaction, as W.B. Yeats might ask, is there another Troy for us to burn?

ABBREVIATIONS

The following abbreviations are employed in the footnotes. References to published works are given with the author's or editor's name and the publication date. The details are supplied in the Bibliography.

AELetters	*Typescript of Letters from AE (National Library of Ireland)*
AIR	*All-Ireland Review*
AR	*The Annual Register: a review of public events at home and abroad for the year 1900*
BN	*The Belfast Newsletter*
CE	*The Cork Examiner*
CL	*The Collected Letters of W.B. Yeats, Vol. 2, 1896–1900*
CP	*Collected Plays of W.B. Yeats*
CS	*An Claidheamh Soluis*
DATI	*The Department of Agriculture and Technical Instruction of Ireland*
DDE	*The Dublin Daily Express*
FJ	*The Freeman's Journal*
GYL	*Anna MacBride White, and A. Norman Jeffares, (eds.), Always your Friend: The Gonne-Yeats Letters 1893–1938*
Holloway	*Joseph Holloway, Impressions of a Playgoer (MS 1798), National Library of Ireland*
IC	*The Irish Catholic*
IDI	*The Irish Daily Independent*
IF	*The Irish Figaro*
IH	*The Irish Homestead*
IHS	*Irish Historical Studies*
IP	*The Irish People*
IT	*The Irish Times*
IW	*The Irish Wheelman*
IWI	*The Irish Weekly Independent*
IWIN	*The Irish Weekly Independent and Nation*
IWUE	*The Irish Weekly and Ulster Examiner*
NAI	*National Archives of Ireland*
NIR	*New Ireland Review*
NLI	*National Library of Ireland*
NC	*The Nineteenth Century*
LQV	*The Letters of Queen Victoria, third series, Vol. 3*
NW	*The Northern Whig*
UI	*The United Irishman*
WF	*The Weekly Freeman*
WN	*The Weekly Nation*

FOOTNOTES

Chapter One

1 Yeats, *Autobiographies*, p. 199.
2 MacDonagh, 1920, p. 244-5, who witnessed the events of the period as a journalist covering the Westminster Parliament.
3 Canon Sheehan's book, *My New Curate,* was published in book form in 1900.
4 There is no major modern biography of Redmond. Bew, 1996, provides a brief overview.
5 For an analysis of 'revisionism', see Brady, 1994.
6 Healy is the subject of a recent biography, Callanan, 1996.
7 Briggs and Snowman, 1996, p. 1, point out that it was not until the nineteenth century that the term *fin de siècle* was first used.
8 Davies, 1996, p. 1. The author recalls a senior historian who wrote books on the Munich crisis (1938-9) and the last week of peace. 'His colleagues waited in vain for a crowning volume to be called *One Minute to Midnight.'*
9 Hobsbawm, 1994.
10 David Harkness, *Twentieth-Century Ireland* is the exception. Murphy, 1975, Fanning, 1983, Lee, 1989 and Keogh, 1994 all begin their narratives well into the century. Boyce, 1990, stretches the nineteenth-century history to 1923 while Travers, 1988, concludes a year earlier.
11 Pethica, 1996, p. 226.

Chapter Two

1 Quoted in Tuchman, 1980, p. 268.
2 Skidelsky, 1983, p. 90, fn.
3 *LQV*, p. 456.
4 'The Queen's After-Dinner Speech', in De Burgh Daly, 1962, pp. 55-8.
5 'The Queen's Advice to Lord Zetland before Starting for Ireland' in *Ibid.*, pp. 53-4.
6 Curran, 1970, p. 65.
7 Letter from Salisbury to Balfour, 7 March 1900, quoted in Curtis, 1963, p. 419.
8 *LQV*, p. 501.
9 DMP Crime Special Branch memorandum 20996 S on the Dublin Municipal Elections, 24/1/1900 (NAI).
10 *IDI*, 19 March 1900.
11 *IDI*, 2 April 1900.
12 *NW*, 17 March 1900.
13 The views of Redmond and O'Brien are quoted in Boyce, 1982, p. 268.
14 *WF*, 24 March 1900.

15 *IDI*, 3 April 1900. For Yeats' claim to have written the resolution, see CL, Vol 2, p. 510.
16 Quoted in Foster, 1997, p. 228. Other biographical sources for Yeats' life during this period include Jeffares, 1988, pp. 103-131 and Ellmann, 1961, pp 102-137.
17 Letter to the *FJ*, 20 March 1900, in CL Vol 2, p. 503.
18 From an article in *UI*, April 1900, reproduced in Frayne, 1975, p. 212.
19 *IDI*, 5 April 1900.
20 *IDI*, 4 April 1900.
21 *IDI*, 5 April 1900.
22 Gaughan, 1986, p. 31.
23 *NW*, 4 April 1900.
24 *IDI*, 5 April 1900.
25 *WF*, 6 January 1900. Roberts' local connections are recalled by a large Victorian clock that still stands in the lobby of the Granville Hotel in Waterford. It was given to him by Waterford Corporation in 1893 and Roberts left it behind reputedly with a dismissive remark, 'not another clock!'
26 Information supplied by Mr Patrick Cooke, Curator of Kilmainham Jail.
27 Curran, 1970, p. 67.
28 *NW*, 5 April 1900.
29 *NW*, 6 April 1900.
30 *NW*, 5 April 1900.
31 *IWI*, 7 July 1900.
32 Maud Gonne's piece, a translation of an article in a French magazine, *Irlande Libre*, is reprinted in Ward, 1995, pp. 10-13. See also Cardozo, 1990, pp. 181-209.
33 See letter 74 (19 April 1900) in MacBride White and Jeffares, 1993, pp. 122-3.
34 *Ibid.*, p. 482.
35 For his account of these events, see Colles, 1911, pp. 48-56.
36 For Mallon's career, see Bussy, 1910.
37 *WN*, 12 May 1900.
38 Colles, 1911, p. 56.
39 From the Irish-American newspaper, *The Irish World*, quoted in Davis, 1974, p. 14.
40 See Gonne, 1994, pp. 266-77.
41 An anti-recruitment poster quoted in Denman, 1994, p. 213.
42 Bartlett and Jeffery, 1996, p. 337.
43 Wiggin, 1902, pp. 41-3.
44 *AR*, 1900, p. 82.
45 Strachey, 1969: first published in 1921, p. 252.
46 *IF*, 14 April 1900.
47 Horgan, 1948, p. 87.
48 Curran, 1970, p. 67.

49 *LQV*, p. 522.
50 Royal Irish Constabulary, 1902, p. 23.
51 Connolly, 1998, p. 126.
52 Royal Irish Constabulary, Evidence taken before the Committee of Inquiry, 1902, p. 136.
53 *WF*, 8 September 1900.
54 *WF*, 15 September 1900.
55 *WN*, 26 May 1900.
56 From a report published in 1899 and quoted in Horn, 1975, p. 17.
57 1901 Census returns (NAI).
58 Burke, 1993, p. 35 and p. 61.
59 Tannenbaum, 1976, p. 83.
60 Oldham, 1900, p. 9.
61 This figure is given in Cullen, 1972, p. 166.
62 Vaughan, 1996, p. 322.
63 *BN*, 1 September 1900.
64 See Waldron, 1992.
65 Lyons, 1978, pp. 390–422.
66 *IWI*, 15 September 1900.
67 *WF*, 15 September 1900.
68 The witticism, attributed to a James Montgomery, is recorded in Vivian Mercier's book, *The Irish Comic Tradition* and quoted in Craig, 1998, p. 35.
69 *WF*, 22 September 1900.
70 *IWI*, 20 October 1900.
71 Costello, 1992, pp. 168–9.
72 'Irishman's Diary', *IT*, 17 December 1997.
73 *WF*, 8 September 1900.
74 *WF*, 1 September 1900.
75 *WF*, 24 November 1900.
76 Maddox, 1988, pp. 37–8.
77 *WN*, 14 July 1900.
78 Poor Law Reform Commission, 1906, p. 42.
79 IWUE, 13 January 1900.
80 *IWI*, 20 October 1900.
81 Register of Prisoners, 1901 (NAI).
82 *IWI*, 7 July 1900.
83 *IF*, 29 December 1900, p. 857.
84 *IWI*, 14 July 1900.
85 *IWI*, 3 March 1900.
86 *IWI*, 14 July 1900.
87 *WF*, 15 September 1900.
88 *IWI*, 9 June 1900.
89 *WF*, 27 October 1900.
90 *WF*, 6 October 1900.
91 *WF*, 10 February 1900.
92 IWIN, 15 September 1900.
93 *WF*, 22 September 1900.
94 *IWI*, 28 April 1900.
95 *WF*, 27 January 1900.
96 *WF*, 27 January 1900.
97 *IWI*, 27 January 1900.
98 *WF*, 27 January 1900.
99 *IWI*, 9 June 1900.
100 *FJ*, 20 June 1900.
101 *IWI*, 28 April 1900.
102 *IWI*, 3 February 1900.
103 *IWI*, 10 February 1900.
104 *FJ*, 30 July 1900.
105 *FJ*, 8 August 1900.
106 Callanan, 1996, pp. 439–440 and *IWI*, 29 September 1900.
107 Murphy had recently purchased *The Irish Daily Independent* and *The Irish Weekly Independent*, both originally Parnellite papers.
108 Callanan, 1996, p. 441.
109 *IWI*, 24 February 1900.
110 *IWI*, 3 March 1900.
111 Jackson, 1989, pp. 377–95.
112 *IWI*, 13 October 1900.

Chapter Three

1 Sutherland, 1909, p. 37.
2 Johnson, 1901, p. 140.
3 Wiggin, 1902, pp. 234–5. Mrs Wiggin visited in 1900.
4 *IWUE*, 6 January 1900. At the time, Russell was a junior Minister in the Salisbury Government.
5 *BN*, 3 July 1900. There were 95 deaths of children under one and 96 of people over 60.
6 Ó Gráda, 1994, p. 242, puts life expectancy at 50 years in the 1870s and at 58 years in the 1920s.
7 Census, 1901, General Report, p. 20.
8 Dunraven, 1905, p. 3.
9 McCarthy, 1903, p. 22.
10 Longworth, 1900, p. 12.
11 Micks, 1925.
12 Material for this section is drawn from Census of Ireland for the year 1901: Part 2; General Report.
13 Lynd, 1909, p. 48.
14 Pim, 1899.
15 Ó Gráda, 1994, p. 215.
16 *IWI*, 28 July 1900.
17 Pim, 1899.
18 See Tannenbaum, 1976, p. 72.
19 *IWUE*, 17 February 1900.
20 Burke, 1993, p. 13.
21 *The Leader, Vol 1, No. 1*, 1 September 1900, p. 1.
22 *WF*, 3 March 1900.
23 Johnson, 1901, p. 50.
24 *WF*, 13 October 1900.
25 *WF*, 1 September 1900.
26 *WF*, 15 September 1900.
27 *IWI*, 9 June 1900.
28 Ó Gráda, 1994, p. 233.
29 Gwynn, 1903, pp. 99–103.
30 McDonagh, 1900, pp. 76–77.

31 Census 1901, p. 11.

32 Johnson, 1901, pp. 2–3.

33 Sutherland, 1909, pp. 4–5. These impressions were recorded during a visit in 1902.

34 *Ibid.*, pp. 73 and 80.

35 *Ibid.*, p. 60.

36 Wiggin, 1902, p. 235.

37 Cooper, p. 208.

38 Gedney, 1896, p. 77.

39 *Ibid.*, pp. 77–8.

40 Paul-Dubois, 1908, p. 298.

41 *Ibid.*, p. 301.

42 *Ibid.*, pp. 302–3.

43 'An Irish Cottage', in *IH* (29 April 1899), and reproduced in Summerfield, 1978, pp. 49–50.

44 Lynd, 1909, p. 190.

45 Roche, 1900, p. 4.

46 Report of the Commissioners of National Education in Ireland for the year 1900, p. 1.

47 *Ibid.*, p. 16.

48 Report of the Intermediate Education Board for Ireland for the Year 1900, p. vi.

49 Report of the Vice-Regal Commission on Poor Law Reform in Ireland, Vol 1, 1906, p. 2.

50 Mackail and Wyndham, Vol 2, pp. 408–9.

51 *DATI, Ireland: Agricultural and Industrial*, 1901, p. 151.

52 Advertisement in *CS*, 8 July 1899.

53 DATI, *Ireland: Agricultural and Industrial*, 1901, p. 152.

54 *Ibid.*, p. 153.

55 Quoted in H.D. Gribbon, 'Economic and Social History, 1850–1921' in Vaughan, 1996, p. 283.

56 Tenth Report of the Congested Districts Board for Ireland for the year ending 31st March 1900, p. 18.

57 Gwynn, 1903, p. 104.

58 *Ibid.*, p. 200.

59 Lynd, 1909, p. 19.

60 See Aalen and Whelan 1992, pp. 251–304 and Aalen, 1990, p. 7.

61 Austin, 1900, p. 3.

62 Wiggin, 1902, p. 18.

63 Daly, 1985, pp. 77–8.

64 Dawson, 1901, pp. 52–3.

65 *WF*, 10 March 1900.

66 *IWI*, 7 July 1900.

67 Anonymous pamphlet entitled 'Boundaries or Bankruptcy: address to the Ratepayers and Residents of Rathmines and Rathgar Urban District', 1900.

68 Irish Republican Socialist Party Handbill on 'The Royal Visit' 1900 (NLI, LO P 109).

69 O'Casey, 1971, p. 197.

70 Cameron, 1904, p. 3.

71 Advertisement in *IF*, 6 January 1900.

72 Advertisements in *CS*, 22 April 1899.

73 The story appears in *Dubliners*.

74 Job advertisement in *CS*, 24 March 1900.

75 D.G. Boyce, 'Edward Carson and Irish Unionism', in Brady, 1989, p. 145.

76 Dawson, 1899, p. 10.

77 Daly, 1985, p. 79.

78 Cameron, 1904, p. 1.

79 O'Casey, 1971, p. 144.

80 *WF*, 10 November 1900.

81 Gwynn, 1903.

82 Supplement to the Twenty-Ninth Annual Report of the Local Government Board for Ireland for 1900–1901.

83 MacCarthy, 1903, p. 116.

84 See James Killen, 'Transport in Dublin: Past, Present and Future', in Aalen and Whelan, 1992, pp. 305–25.

85 Murray's *Handbook for Travellers in Ireland*, p. 5 and *WN*, 17 February 1900.

86 *Ulysses*, p. 116.

87 *BN*, 17 March and 9 July 1900.

88 *IWIN*, 1 December 1900. For a history of Dublin trams, see Kilroy, 1997, pp. 42–7.

89 *IWI*, 2 June 1900.

90 *IWI*, 26 May 1900.

91 *BN*, 17 March 1900.

92 See Hobsbawm, 1987, p. 50.

93 *AR* for 1900, p. 255.

94 See 'The shipbuilding industry of Belfast' in DATI, *Ireland: Industrial and Agricultural*, pp. 279–81.

95 First Annual General Report of the Department of Agriculture and Technical Instruction for Ireland, 1900–1, p. 23.

96 DATI, 1903, p. 24.

97 DATI, *Journal, Vol 1, No. 1*, p. 4.

98 DATI, *Ireland: Industrial and Agricultural*, 1901, pp. 178–200.

99 See Burke, 1993, pp. 16–22 which highlights this general rise in rural prosperity between 1890 and 1914.

100 Royal Commission on the Poor Laws and Relief of Distress, 1909, p. 34.

101 Sutherland, 1909, p. 28.

102 Paul-Dubois, 1908, p. 299.

103 *FJ*, 10 May 1900.

104 T.W. Russell, quoted in Sutherland, 1909, p. 12.

105 T.W. Russell, 1901, pp. 48–9.

106 See The Irish Landowners' Convention, 1899 and 1901.

107 The Irish Landowners' Convention, 1901, pp. 6–7.

108 Austin, 1900, p. 41.

109 *WN*, 21 April 1900.

110 *WF*, 3 March 1900.

111 *WN*, 3 March 1900.

112 Report on the Present Condition of Tenant Purchasers under the Land Purchase Acts, quoted in Ford, 1969, p. 405.

118 Poor Law Reform Commission (Ireland), 1906, p. 65.

119 Census 1901, p. 8.

120 Dawson, 1901, pp. 52–3.

121 *IWI*, 28 July 1900.

122 Poor Law Reform Commission (Ireland), 1906, p. 36.

123 Royal Commission on the Poor Laws and Relief of Distress, 1909, p. 36.

124 *Ibid.*, p. 46.

125 *WF*, 20 October 1900.

126 Poor Law Reform Commission (Ireland), 1906, p. 16.

127 Cameron, 1904, p. 1.

128 Dublin Sanitary Association, 1900, p. 16.

129 Cullen, 1972, pp. 165–6.

130 *IT*, 4 January 1900.

131 Dublin Sanitary Association, 1900, p. 20.

132 Report of the Committee appointed by the Local Government Board of Ireland to inquire into the Public Health of the City of Dublin, 1900.

133 Cameron, 1904, p. 1.

134 Poor Law Reform Commission (Ireland), 1906, p. 23.

135 *Thom's Directory*, 1900.

136 Report of the Committee appointed by the Local Government Board of Ireland to inquire into the Public Health of the City of Dublin, 1900, p. 10.

137 Supplement to the Twenty-Ninth Annual Report of the Local Government Board for Ireland for 1900–1901.

138 *WN*, 20 January 1900.

139 O'Casey, 1971, p. 92.

140 Quoted in Briggs and Snowman, 1996, p. 190.

141 Cameron, 1904, p. 11.

142 Cameron, 1904, p. 13.

143 Report of the Committee appointed by the Local Government Board of Ireland to inquire into the Public Health of the City of Dublin, 1900, p. 16.

144 *BN*, 3 July 1900.

145 Report on Typhoid Fever in Limerick quoted in Ford, 1969, p. 419.

146 Advertisements from *WF* for January and February 1900 where medical advertisements consume a significant portion of the advertising space.

147 *The Leader, Vol 1 No. 11*, p. 163.

148 Brodie, 1980, pp. 1–6 and 178.

149 *IWI*, 10 February 1900.

150 See W.F. Mandle, 'The GAA and popular culture, 1884–1924' in MacDonagh, Mandle and Travers, 1983, p. 112.

151 *Irish Tourist, Vol 4, No. 1*, May 1897, pp. 1–2 & 10.

152 *IW, Vol XIII, No. 7*, 2 May 1899, p. 311.

153 *IW, Vol XIII, No. 2*, 28 March 1899, p. 169.

154 Montgomery, 1997.

155 *Irish Tourist, Vol 7, No. 3*, July 1901, p. 50.

156 'After the Race' in Joyce, 1915.

157 Blunt, 1932, p. 371.

158 *Irish Tourist, Vol 8, No. 5*, August 1901, p. 17.

159 *AR* for 1900, p. 264.

160 *WF*, 1 September 1900.

161 Wiggin, 1902, p. 30.

162 *Irish Tourist, Vol 1, No. 1*, June 1894, p. 1.

163 Cooke, 1902, p. 9.

164 Wiggin, 1902.

165 Cooke, 1902, p. 12.

166 Cooper, p. 191.

167 Austin, 1900, p. 8.

168 *Irish Tourist, Vol 4, No. 7*, October 1897, pp. 122–3.

Chapter Four

1 *WF*, 1 September 1900.

2 Quoted in Colum, 1959, p. 51.

3 Bennett, 1994, p. 196.

4 See F.H.A. Aalen, 1990, p. 9.

5 Horgan, 1948, p. 87.

6 In a letter to *The Leader, Vol 1, No. 1*, 1 September 1900, p. 13.

7 *UI*, 5 January 1901. This piece would have been written either by Arthur Griffith or by his close friend, William Rooney, who died young in 1901.

8 Lyons, 1979, p. 55.

9 A concept coined by the editor of *The Leader*, D.P. Moran.

10 Lynch, 1924, p. 224.

11 McCarthy, 1891.

12 Lyons, 1951, p. 38, makes the point that the decline of the Irish Party sprang less from divisions over Parnell than from 'the somewhat sordid struggle for power' waged within the anti-Parnellite majority.

13 O'Connor, 1981, pp. 118–28.

14 For a comprehensive account of Dillon's life, see Lyons, 1968.

15 See Bew, 1996, p. 19.

16 See Michael Laffan, 'John Redmond and Home Rule' in Brady, 1989, p. 133–42.

17 Redmond was speaking in 1895 and is quoted in Rolleston, 1900, p. 2.

18 See O'Brien, 1898.

19 For the details of the moves that preceded the Party's 1900 reunion, see Lyons, 1951, pp. 67–89.

20 See Murphy, 1989, pp. 14–15.

21 See Crossman, 1994, pp. 91–7.

22 *IWUE*, 6 January 1900.

23 Foster, 1988, p. 433.

24 File No. CBS/IGCI/20125/S, Monthly Confidential Report of the Inspector General of the RIC for September 1899 (NAI).

25 'Kerry locals say they don't need Kitchener', *The Sunday Times* (Irish Edition), 15 February 1998.

26 Doyle, 1900.

27 See Inglis, 1974, pp. 53–5.

28 *BN*, 17 March 1900.

29 Quoted in Holroyd, 1989, p. 42.

30   *AR* for the year 1900, p. 1.
31   *Ibid.*, p. 246.
32   Quoted in Lyons, 1968, pp. 216–17.
33   *IWUE*, 17 February 1900.
34   Gonne, 1994, pp. 276–7.
35   Joyce, *Ulysses*, pp. 162–63.
36   Pearl, 1969, p. 14.
37   *IWIN*, 15 September 1900.
38   Quoted in Sheehy-Skeffington, 1967, p. 166.
39   Davitt's letter of 4 November 1900 is reproduced in Finneran, Mills Harper and Murphy, 1977, pp. 67–8.
40   Davitt, 1902, p. 589.
41   *IDI*, 20 October 1899.
42   *CE*, 14 October 1899.
43   Mandle, 1987, p. 120.
44   *FJ*, 23 July 1900.
45   File No. CBS/IGCI/20411/S, Monthly Confidential Report of the Inspector General of the RIC for October 1899 (NAI).
46   O'Casey, 1971, p. 198.
47   *IP*, 21 October 1899.
48   *FJ*, 13 October 1900.
49   From T.W. Rolleston's pamphlet, 'Ireland, the Empire and the War' as quoted in *IF*, 24 March 1900, p. 177.
50   Gwynn, 1903, p. xi.
51   *IT*, 4 January 1900 and *IWI*, 6 January 1900.
52   *IDI*, 4 January 1900.
53   *IT*, 31 January 1900.
54   McCracken, 1989.
55   *FJ*, 10 May 1900.
56   See David Fitzpatrick, 'Militarism in Ireland, 1900–1921', in Bartlett and Jeffery, 1996, p. 380.
57   *FJ*, 7 May 1900.
58   *FJ*, 6 June 1900.
59   Quoted in Kee, 1972, p. 446.
60   *DDE*, 19 October 1899.
61   Fenlon, 1900, p. 337.
62   McCracken, 1989, p. 123.
63   *WN*, 10 March 1900.
64   Patterson, 1980, p. 42.
65   *NW*, 1 March 1900.
66   *WF*, 17 February 1900.
67   *IWI*, 12 May 1900.
68   *WN*, 3 February 1900.
69   *WN*, 17 March 1900.
70   Quoted in *WN*, 21 April 1900.
71   *FJ*, 28 July 1900.
72   *WF*, 20 January 1900.
73   O'Brien, 1898, p. 31.
74   Foster, 1995, p. 266.
75   For an account of O'Brien's eventful political career, see Warwick-Haller, 1990.
76   Quoted in Foster, 1995, p. 266.

77   Garvin, 1981, p. 93.
78   Quoted in Bew, 1987, p. 43.
79   See File No. CBS/IGCI/20125/S, Monthly Confidential Report of the Inspector General of the RIC for September 1899 (NAI).
80   Monthly Confidential Reports of the Inspector General of the Royal Irish Constabulary for 1899 and 1900 in the NAI.
81   United Irish League, 1900.
82   Garvin, 1981, pp. 100–1.
83   See Breandán Mac Aodha, 'Was this a social revolution' in Ó Tuama, 1972, pp. 20–30.
84   Hyde, 1967, p. 630. Hyde's book was first published in 1899.
85   *Ibid.*, pp. 633–4.
86   *IWI*, 21 July 1900.
87   *IWI*, 28 July 1900.
88   *UI*, 30 December 1899.
89   Dunleavy and Dunleavy, 1991, pp. 210–11.
90   Fahy, Cathecism, p. 1.
91   *Ibid.*, p. 3.
92   Fahy, 1901, p. 13.
93   *Ibid.*, p. 14.
94   For an account of MacNeill's role in the Gaelic League and of his Irish Ireland outlook, see Donal MacCartney, 'MacNeill and Irish Ireland' in Martin and Byrne, 1973, pp. 75–97.
95   Quoted in Kevin B. Nowlan, 'The Gaelic League and other national movements' in *Ibid.*, p. 43.
96   *AIR, Vol 1, No. 1*, 6 January 1900.
97   Moran, 1900, pp. 271–2.
98   Plunkett, 1983, p. 153. Plunkett's book was first published in 1904.
99   *FJ*, 12 May 1900.
100 *FJ*, 21 July 1900.
101 See Edwards, 1977, pp. 26–44.
102 *FJ*, 25 July 1900.
103 O'Hickey, 1899, pp. 2–3.
104 *CL*, Vol 2, p. 563.
105 For an account of Moran's influential career, see Maume, 1995.
106 Brian Inglis, 'Moran and Ryan', in O'Brien, 1960, p. 112.
107 *The Leader, Vol 1 No. 1*, 1 September 1900, p. 5.
108 *Ibid.*, p. 8.
109 Cited in Kee, 1972, p. 438.
110 Russell (AE), 1904, pp, 6–7.
111 Moran quoted in *Ibid.*, pp. 8 and 11.
112 Moran quoted in *Ibid.*, p. 12.
113 *WF*, 6 January 1900.
114 *WF*, 20 October 1900.
115 *IC*, 6 January 1900.
116 *IWI*, 6 October 1900.
117 The Archbishop of Armagh quoted in *IWI*, 3 March 1900.
118 See Moody, 1958, pp. 90–108.

119 *IWI*, 6 October 1900.

120 *IC*, 3 February 1900.

121 *IC*, 6 October 1900.

122 *IWIN*, 1 December 1900.

123 *IC*, 6 October 1900.

124 *IWI*, 6 October 1900.

125 Catholic Truth Society of Ireland, *First Fifty Years, 1899–1949* (Dublin, Veritas, 1949), p. 11.

126 *WN*, 28 April 1900.

127 *IC*, 6 October 1900.

128 *IC*, 6 October 1900.

129 *IC*, 6 October 1900.

130 For an account of Griffith's life pre-Sinn Féin, see Davis, 1974, pp 3–16.

131 Quoted in Colum, 1959, p. 57.

132 Davis, 1974, p. 17.

133 Gonne, 1984, pp. 306–7.

134 Foster, 1995, p. 273.

135 See Ward, 1995, pp. 14 and 19.

136 See Mitchell, 1974, pp. 18–20 and O'Connor, 1992, pp. 61–4.

137 Garvin, 1981, p. 91.

138 See O'Halpin, 1987, p. 15.

139 De Burca, 1980, p. 82. For a detailed account of the GAA's nationalist origins, see Mandle, 1987.

140 Dublin Women's Suffrage and Local Government Association, 1901, p. 7.

141 See Dublin Women's Suffrage and Local Government Association, *Suggestions for intending women working under the Local Government Act* (Dublin, 1901).

142 Dublin Women's Suffrage and Local Government Association, 1900, p. 3.

143 Dublin Women's Suffrage and Local Government Association, 1901.

144 Haslam, 1906, p. 4.

145 Moody, 1958, pp. 89–109.

146 *IDI*, 4 April 1900.

147 See Morris, 1979, p. 48.

Chapter Five

1 Quoted in Mackail and Wyndham, Vol 1, 1925, p. 86.

2 Dunraven, 190, p. 237.

3 Plunkett, 1983, p. 5.

4 Dowden, 1904, p. 3.

5 See Thom, 1900.

6 For a positive assessment of Salisbury, see Taylor, 1976, pp. 122–8 who is critical of his opposition to Home Rule which, while *it* gave the Conservatives 20 years in power, he believed made him 'the prisoner of all the violent men prepared to resist Home Rule'.

7 Tuchman, 1980, p. 3.

8 Shannon, 1988, pp. 33–81.

9 Pakenham, 1991, p. 557, tells of how Lansdowne had to travel from his shooting lodge in Co. Kerry to attend a crucial British Cabinet meeting on the Boer War.

10 For the split in Gladstone's Liberal Party, see Jenkins, 1995, pp. 520–62.

11 See Jalland, 1980, pp. 19–49 and Boyce, 1996, pp. 18–48.

12 *IDI*, 30 June 1900.

13 Wiggin, 1902, pp. 49–50.

14 For a description of the British administrative system in nineteenth-century Ireland, see McDowell, 1964.

15 Robinson, 1923, p. 138. A significant administrative force in pre-Treaty Ireland, Robinson was Vice-President of the Irish Local Government Board from 1898 until 1922.

16 *IDI*, 2 January 1900.

17 Papers from the Chief Secretary's Office are held in the NAI.

18 See F.S.L. Lyons, 'The aftermath of Parnell 1891–1903' in Vaughan 1996, p. 89.

19 *The Times*, 25 September 1900, quoted in Gailey, 1987, p. 26.

20 Tynan, 1916, p. 223.

21 Leslie, 1937, p. 187.

22 See Elizabeth, Countess of Fingall, 1937, p. 270.

23 Healy, Vol 2, 1928, p. 447.

24 Robinson, 1923, p. 144.

25 Horace Plunkett quoted in Gailey, 1987, p. 240.

26 Mackail and Wyndham, Vol 2, 1925, pp. 407–8.

27 Dowden, 1904, p. 3.

28 Quoted in O'Brien, 1912, p. 10.

29 See Crossman, 1996, pp. 187–8.

30 For an account of the administration of Ireland at the turn of the century, see O'Halpin, 1987, pp. 5–23.

31 Herlihy, 1997.

32 See United Irish League of Great Britain, Leaflet No. 1, n.d. and Leaflet No. 2, 1902.

33 Dooley, 1998, pp. 33–9. Roberts' father, Lt. Colonel Abraham Roberts, was commander of the 1st Bengal European Regiment, which later became part of the Royal Munster Fusiliers.

34 Quoted in Igoe, 1994, p. 136.

35 For an account of the Boer War, see Pakenham, 1979. Roberts' career in British India is covered in Hopkirk, 1994, pp. 386–450.

36 *LQV*, p. 440.

37 *IP*, 21 October 1899.

38 *LQV*, p. 446.

39 Buckland, 1972, p. 2.

40 'Escopette', 1900, p. 1.

41 *BN*, 7 July 1900.

42 Langtoft, p. 53.

43 *Ibid.*, p. 54.

44 *BN*, 7 July 1900.

45 *IT*, 4 September 1900.

46 Walker 1978, pp. 151–6.
47 Gailey, 1996, p. 67. For an account of Carson's legal and political career, see Montgomery Hyde, 1974.
48 *IWI*, 19 May 1900.
49 *FJ*, 1 August 1900.
50 *IWI*, 19 May 1900.
51 *IF*, 28 July 1900, p. 486.
52 Nicholas Mansergh, 'The Unionist Party and the Union', in Edwards and Pyle, 1968.
53 For an analysis of constructive unionism, see Shannon, 1988, pp. 82–135.
54 *BN*, 16 March 1900.
55 Plunkett, 1983, p. 6.
56 *Ibid.*, p. 9.
57 *Ibid.*, p. 10.
58 For Plunkett's political career, see West, 1986, pp. 36–59.
59 Plunkett, 1900, p. 903.
60 James Joyce, *Ulysses*, p. 79.
61 *IT*, 4 September 1900.
62 Letter of 26 November 1900, quoted in Jackson, 1989, p. 377.
63 Quoted in Plunkett, 1900, p. 898.
64 *IWIN*, 15 September.
65 West, 1986, p. 58.
66 Quoted in Asa Briggs, 'The 1890s Past, Present and Future Headlines', in Briggs and Snowman, 1996, p. 192.
67 See Lynch, 1924.
68 Montgomery Hyde, 1974, pp. 170–7.
69 Dunraven, Vol 2, 1922, p. 2.
70 For an account of the devolution crisis, see F.S.L. Lyons, 'The aftermath of Parnell', in Vaughan, 1996, pp. 101–3.
71 'Irish Reform Association's Programme', in Dunraven, 1907, pp. 271–9.
72 Irish Unionist Alliance, 1905, p. 12.
73 Quoted in *Ibid.*, p. 13.
74 Dunraven, Vol 2, 1922, p. 14.
75 Dunraven, Vol 1, 1922, p. 32.
76 For an analysis of southern unionism, see Beckett, 1976, pp. 211–30 and Buckland, 1972.
77 Buckland, 1973, p. 22.
78 See Graham Walker, 'Thomas Sinclair, Presbyterian Liberal Unionist' in English and Walker, 1996, p. 30.
79 T.W. Russell, *Ireland and the Empire*, 1901, p. 129.
80 *Ibid.*, p. viii.
81 Quoted in Jackson, 1989.
82 T.W. Russell, 1902, p. 30.
83 T.W. Russell, *Ireland and the Empire*, 1901, p. viii.
84 *IDI*, 27 June 1900. While regretting Russell's change of heart, the paper conceded that he had earned the respect of all classes of Irishman. A difficult meeting of Russell's constituency association is reported in *BN*, 9 July 1900.
85 *BN*, 24 March 1900.
86 See T.W. Russell, *Ireland and the Empire*, 1901.
87 T.W. Russell, 1902, p. 31.
88 T.W. Russell, *Compulsory Purchase in Ireland*, 1901, p. 57.
89 T.W. Russell, 1900, p. 4.
90 See David Burnett, 'The Modernisation of Unionism, 1892–1914?', in English and Walker, 1996, pp. 46–47.
91 Lucas, 1908, p. 298.
92 See Jackson, 1995, p. 137.
93 McMinn, 1982, pp. 17–29 and Jackson, 1987, pp. 376–404.
94 See Bardon, 1992, pp. 415–7 and election leaflets in National Library of Ireland, L.O.P. 114.
95 Quoted in Dunraven, Vol 1, 1922, p. 24.

Chapter Six

1 *CL, Vol 2*, p. 537.
2 Joyce, 1901, p. 15.
3 Census of Ireland for the year 1901, General Report, p. 7 and 1901 Census forms (NAI).
4 McDonagh, August 1900, p. 299.
5 See McDonagh, July 1900, pp. 75–88.
6 Moore's book, which comes in three parts, *Ave, Salve and Vale*, was first published in 1911. It gives an account of his time in Dublin as a participant in the literary revival.
7 *Stephen Hero* was not published until 1944, but was probably written between 1904 and 1906.
8 Moore, 1976, pp. 215–16.
9 *Ibid.*, pp. 220–2.
10 Moore, 1936, p. 193. The novel was first published in 1905.
11 *IDI*, 17 March 1900.
12 Moore 'Literature and the Irish language', in Gregory, 1901, p. 46.
13 Moore, 1900, p. vii.
14 Moore, 'Literature and the Irish Language', in Gregory, 1901, p. 49.
15 Moore, 1900, pp. viii–xi.
16 Seanad Éireann, 11 June 1925, Cols. 427–82. Colonel Moore accused Yeats of 'an absolute sectarian view' on divorce.
17 Joyce, 1901, p. 17.
18 Joyce, 1977, footnote 2, p. 52.
19 *Ibid.*, p. 59.
20 Costello, 1980, pp. 20–1.
21 Letter dated March 1901 in Gilbert, 1957, p. 52.
22 Ellmann, 1966, p. 69.
23 Quoted in *Ibid.*, p. 74.
24 Joyce, 1901. See also Manganiello, 1980, p. 28.
25 Kohfeldt, 1984, p. 93.
26 Gregory, 1900.
27 Pethica, 1996, p. 249.
28 *AIR, Vol 1, No. 1*, 6 January 1900, p. 1.
29 Moran, 'The Battle of two Civilisations' in Gregory, 1901, p. 39.
30 Brooke and Rolleston, 1900, p. viii.
31 *IWI*, 3 March 1900.

32 This play was based on Gerald Griffin's novel, *The Collegians*, which was published in 1829 and has been described as 'one of the most powerful Irish novels ever written'. (Cleeve, 1966, p. 55).

33 *IDI*, 2 January 1900. Boucicault's character later surfaced in a very different literary guise as the pen name used by Brian O'Nolan for his legendary satirical column in *The Irish Times*. See Myles na Gopaleen, *The Best of Myles: a selection from 'Cruiskeen Lawn'*, (London, Picador, 1977). Seán O'Casey's first dramatic venture was as an actor in 1896 in an amateur performance of another Boucicault play, *The Shaughran*.

34 *UI*, 6 January 1900.

35 *WF*, 13 October 1900.

36 Entry for 11 January 1900 in Holloway.

37 Entry for 27 February in Holloway.

38 *The Leader, Vol 1, No. 1*, p. 3.

39 Yeats, 'The Irish National Literary Society' in Jeffares, 1976, p. 18.

40 For an idea of how busy Yeats was as a propagandist for the Irish literary revival, see Frayne, 1970 and 1975.

41 From 'Reveries over Childhood and Youth' in Jeffares, 1976, p. 39.

42 *IWI* carried a series of Davis essays in the early months of 1900, for example 'Ethnology of the Irish Race' on 17 February 1900.

43 Frayne, 1975, p. 250.

44 Published in May 1899 and quoted in Dudley-Edwards, 1977, p. 30.

45 Letter to the Editor of the *Daily Chronicle*, 27 January 1899 reproduced in *CL, Vol 2*, p. 351.

46 From the theatre's prospectus quoted in Fallis, 1978, p. 88.

47 CP, 1952, p. 4.

48 CL, Vol 2, p. 483.

49 Entry for 19 February in Holloway.

50 Milligan, 1900, p. 17.

51 Martyn, 1917, p. 44.

52 NIR, March 1900, p. 51.

53 'A Celtic Theatre' in *FJ*, 22 March 1900.

54 *IWI*, 24 February 1900.

55 *IWI*, 31 March 1900.

56 Hone, 1983, p. 66.

57 Joyce, 1901, p. 16.

58 Joseph Hone quoted in Kiely, 1994, p. 41.

59 It may be Yeats' poem gave Eliot the idea for the title of his quintessentially modern poem, 'The Hollow Men'.

60 Synge, 1982, p. 23.

61 W.H. Auden, 'In Memory of W.B. Yeats' in Pritchard 1972, pp. 143–5.

62 Letter 96 (December 1900) in GYL, p. 138.

63 Moore, 1976, p. 187.

64 Yeats, 1913, p. 141. My own copy of this book, bought in New Delhi in the early 1980s from an Indian lady whose father had known Yeats, is inscribed in the poet's own hand with the words 'for wisdom is a butterfly and not a stormy bird of prey'.

65 Moore, 1976, pp. 190–1.

66 Jeffares, 1988, p. 102.

67 *UI*, 6 January 1900.

68 Foster, 1997, p. 235.

69 *CL*, Vol 2, p. 585.

70 Frayne, 1975, p. 306.

71 Editor's preface to *Literary Ideals in Ireland*. The editor was probably T.P. Gill who, in 1900, became Horace Plunkett's controversial choice as his deputy at the new Agriculture Department.

72 'What should be the subjects of National Drama?' in *Literary Ideals in Ireland*, p. 11.

73 *Ibid.*, p. 19.

74 *Ibid.*, p. 83.

75 Gregory, 1901, p. 16.

76 *Ibid.*, pp. 18–20.

77 Letter 75a (10 November 1899) in AE Letters (NLI).

78 Quoted in Summerfield, 1975, p. 106.

79 Brooke and Rolleston, 1900.

80 Moore, 1976, p. 140.

81 This poem can be found in Russell (AE), 1926, pp. 141–2.

82 AE's journalistic output is collected in Summerfield, 1978.

83 Letter 80 of late May 1900 in AE Letters.

84 Letter 80 in AELetters.

85 Letter 77 of 22 April 1900 in AE Letters.

86 'Irish ideals and Fiona MacLeod' in *AIR*, 21 July 1900.

87 'The literary movement in Ireland' in Gregory, 1901.

88 Letter 94 (12 December 1900) in GYL, p. 137.

89 Letter 86 (4 February 1901) in AE Letters.

90 Gregory, 1900, pp. 622–34.

91 Introduction to Lionel Johnson's work in Brooke and Rolleston, 1900.

92 NIR, March 1900, p. 51.

93 Brooke and Rolleston, 1900, p. xx.

94 *Ibid.*, p. xix.

95 Katharine Tynan and Alice Furlong in Brooke and Rolleston, 1900, pp. 417 and 427.

96 *Ibid.*, p. 457.

97 NIR, September 1899, p. 61.

98 Hyde, 1967, p. 263.

99 NIR, December 1899, p. 193.

100 Hyde, 1967, p. 453.

101 *Ibid.*, p. 514.

102 *Ibid.*, p. 542.

103 Quoted in Dunleavy and Dunleavy, 1991, p. 208.

104 Vivian Mercier, 'Literature in English, 1891–1921' in Vaughan, 1996, pp. 363–4.

105 Sheehan, 1941, p. 4. This novel was first published in 1900.

106 *Ibid.*, p. 243.

107 *Ibid.*, p. 245.

FOOTNOTES

108 *Ibid.*, pp. 243–4.
109 Sheehan, 1942, p. 276. This novel was first published in 1899.
110 Moore, 1936.
111 Ellmann, 1987. For an account of Carson's involvement in Wilde's case, see Montgomery Hyde, 1974, pp. 126–44.

Chapter Seven

1   Quoted in Pollard, 1971, p. 149.
2   Muir, 1917, p. 190.
3   Joyce, *Ulysses*, p. 624.
4   See Crankshaw, 1963, chapters 17–19 and Hofmann, 1988, pp. 155–6.
5   See Taylor, 1985, p. 249.
6   In 1901, Chamberlain met the German Kaiser who had been intrigued by his book, *The Foundations of the Nineteenth Century.* Emperor and thinker exchanged warm letters which are reproduced in Röhl, 1970, pp. 39–48.
7   'Yeltsin speaks of shame and Russia's atonement', *IT*, 18 July 1998.
8   See Hobsbawm, 1987 and Keylor, 1984, pp. 3–40.
9   See Thomson, 1957, chapter 20.
10 Keylor, 1984, p. 9.
11 *AR* for 1900, p. 284.
12 The competition for colonial possessions is documented in Pakenham, 1991, Hobsbawm, 1987, pp. 56–83 and Davidson, 1974, pp. 258–75.
13 Muir, 1917, pp. 234–5.
14 Muir, 1917, p. 4.
15 G.S. Clarke, 'The Defence of Empire and the Militia Ballot' in NC, Vol XLVII (January 1900), p. 5.
16 NC, Vol XLVII (January 1900), p. 171.
17 French statesman, Leon Gambetta, quoted in Joll, 1976, p. 81.
18 See Pakenham, 1979, p. 250.
19 See Tuchman, 1980.
20 *The Essential James Joyce*, p. 206.
21 Joyce, 1901.
22 Wilson Hunter, 1899, pp. 15–16.
23 The Munroe Doctrine, first promulgated in the early nineteenth century, declared the United States to have a special interest in the Americas.
24 Quoted in Wilson, 1979, p. 275.
25 *AR* for 1900, chronicle of the year, p. 12.
26 100 years later, the railway was in economic difficulties. See 'Sorry for this delay of 100 years' in *The Economist*, 27 June 1998.
27 Harris, 1993, p. 32.
28 From David Starr Jordan, 'The Call of the Twentieth Century', quoted in Schlesinger Jr., 1997, p. 2.
29 Quoted in *Ibid.*, p. 6.
30 On the turn-of-the-century's fecundity in new technological developments, see Romein, 1976, pp. 309–23.

31 Romein, 1976, p. 309.
32 Turner's eulogy on scientific progress is quoted from *BN*, 6 September 1900.
33 Bryan, 1987, p. 82.
34 Quoted in Romein, 1976, p. 17.
35 Blunt, pp. 376–7.
36 Tannenbaum, 1976, p. 82.
37 Ferrin Weber, 1899, p. 346.
38 Keating, 1976, p. 188.
39 Quoted in Joll, p. 47. *Rerum Novarum* was published in 1891.
40 Tanenbaum, 1976, p. 116.
41 See Woodcock, 1975, pp. 325–6 and Tuchman, 1980, pp. 63–113.
42 For details of the life and death of the Empress, see Haslip, 1965. Her visits to Ireland are described on pp. 300–15.
43 For an account of the Paris Exhibition and its significance, see Romein, 1976, pp. 296–308.
44 Quoted in Tuchman, 1980, p. 270.
45 Horgan, 1948, p. 98.
46 For an full account of the Dreyfus affair, see Burns, 1992.
47 *IWI*, 18 August.
48 Romein, 1976, p. 111.
49 Cousins, 1950, pp. 68–9. Margaret Cousins moved to India where she founded the All-India Women's Conference.

Chapter Eight

1   Quoted from United Irish League of Great Britain, 1902.
2   MacDonagh, August 1900, p. 87.
3   Quoted in Craig, 1998, p. 13.
4   Johnston, 1902, pp. 383–4.
5   Johnston, 1902, pp. 384–5.
6   Joyce, 1963, p. 193.
7   *II*, 1 June 1998.
8   Inspector General's Monthly Confidential Report for October 1899 (NAI).
9   Inspector General's Monthly Confidential Report for September 1899 (NAI).
10 Davitt, 1903.
11 See Adams, 1968.
12 See *AR*, 1900.
13 Langtoft, p. 18.
14 Moore, 1900, pp. ix–x.

Bibliography

1. Turn-of-the-Century Material

A. Newspapers and Periodicals

All Ireland Review
The Belfast Newsletter
An Claidheamh Soluis
The Cork Examiner
The Cornhill Magazine
The Dublin Daily Express
Fáinne an Lae
The Freeman's Journal
The Irish Catholic
The Irish Cyclist
The Irish Daily Independent
The Irish Figaro
The Irish Homestead
The Irish Independent
The Irish People

The Irish Times
The Irish Tourist
The Irish Weekly Independent
The Irish Weekly and Ulster Examiner
The Irish Weekly Independent and Nation
The Irish Wheelman
The Irish World
The Leader
The New Ireland Review
The Northern Whig
The Times
The United Irishman
The Weekly Freeman
The Weekly Freeman, National Press and Irish Agriculturist
The Weekly Nation

B. Official Publications

Census of Ireland for the year 1901: Part 2; General Report (Dublin, Stationery Office, 1902).

Congested Districts Board, *Tenth Report of the Congested Districts Board for Ireland for the year ending 31st March 1900* (Dublin, Stationery Office, 1900).

Department of Agriculture and Technical Instruction for Ireland, *First Annual General Report of the Department 1900–01* (Dublin, Stationery Office, 1901).

Department of Agriculture and Technical Instruction for Ireland, *Ireland: Industrial and Agricultural* (Handbook for the Irish Pavilion, Glasgow International Exhibition, 1901).

Department of Agriculture and Technical Instruction for Ireland, *Organisation and Policy of the Department* (Dublin, Stationery Office, 1903).

Local Government Board for Ireland, *Supplement to the Twenty-Ninth Annual Report of the Local Government Board for Ireland for 1900–1901: report on the sanitary circumstances of towns and cities* (Dublin, HMSO, 1902).

Poor Law Reform Commission (Ireland), *Report of the Vice-Regal Commission on Poor Law Reform in Ireland* Vol. 1 (Dublin, Stationery Office, 1906).

Report of the Committee appointed by the Local Government Board of Ireland to inquire into the Public Health of the City of Dublin (Dublin, Stationery Office, 1900).

Royal Commission on the Poor Laws and Relief of Distress, *Report on Ireland* (London, HMSO, 1909).

The Royal Irish Constabulary Manual, or Guide to your Police Duties. Fifth Edition (Dublin, Stationery Office, 1898).

Royal Irish Constabulary, *Report of the Committee of Inquiry, 1901* (Dublin, Stationery Office, 1902).

Royal Irish Constabulary, *Evidence Taken before the Committee of Inquiry, 1901* (Dublin, Stationery Office, 1902).

BIBLIOGRAPHY

C. Archival Material

National Library of Ireland.
Typescript of Letters from AE.
Joseph Holloway, *Impressions of a Playgoer* (MS1798).

National Archives of Ireland.
Census returns for 1901.
Chief Secretary's Office Registered Papers.
Crime Branch Special files.

D.   Books, Pamphlets and Articles

The Annual Register: a review of public events at home and abroad for the year 1900 (London, Longmans Green, 1901).
Anon., *Ireland as it is and as it would be Under Home Rule: Sixty-Two Letters written by the Special Commissioner of the Birmingham Daily Gazette* (Birmingham, Birmingham Daily Gazette, 1893).
Anon., *Boundaries or Bankruptcy: address to the Ratepayers and Residents of Rathmines and Rathgar Urban District* (Dublin, 1900).
Austin, Alfred, *Spring and Autumn in Ireland* (London, William Blackwood, 1900).
Blunt, Wilfrid Scawen, *My Diaries: being a personal narrative of events, 1888–1914* (London, Martin Secker, 1932).
Brooke, Stopford A., and Rolleston, T.W. (eds), *A Treasury of Irish Poetry in the English Tongue* (London, Smith Elder, 1900).
Bulfin, William, *Rambles in Eirinn* (Dublin, 1907).
Bussy, Frederick Moir, *Irish Conspiracies: recollections of John Mallon and other conspiracies* (London, Everett, 1910).
Cameron, Charles, *How the Poor Live* (Dublin, 1904).
Colles, Ramsay, *In Castle and Court House: being reminiscences of thirty years in Ireland* (London, T. Werner Laurie, 1911).
Conan Doyle, Arthur, *The Great Boer War* (London, Smith Elder, 1900).
Cooke, John (ed.), *Murray's Handbook for Travellers in Ireland, Sixth Edition* (London, Edward Stanford, 1902).
Cooper, Rev. A.N., *The Tramps of 'The Walking Parson'* (London, Walter Scott, n.d.).
Cousins, James H. and Margaret E., *We Two Together* (Madras, Ganesh, 1950).
Crawford, Lyndsay, *The Problem of Ulster* (New York, Protestant Friends of Irleand, n.d.).
Davitt, Michael, *The Boer Fight for Freedom* (New York, Funk and Wagnalls, 1902).
Dawson, Charles, *Greater Dublin: extension of municipal boundaries* (Dublin, Sealy, Bryers and Walker, 1899).
Dawson, Charles, 'The Housing of the People' in *Journal of the Statistical and Social Inquiry Society of Ireland,* Vol. 11, Part 81 (1901).
De Burgh Daly, Mrs (ed.), *Prose, Poems and Parodies of Percy French* (Dublin, Talbot Press, 1962).
Dowden, Edward, *Irish Unionists and the Present Administration* (Dublin, Irish Unionist Alliance, 1904).
Dublin Sanitary Association, *Report of the Council of the Dublin Sanitary Association for the year ending 3l December 1899* (Dublin 1900).
Dublin Women's Suffrage and Local Government Association, *Report of the Executive Committee of the Dublin Women's Suffrage and Local Government Association for 1899* (Dublin 1900).
Dublin Women's Suffrage and Local Government Association, *Report of the Executive Committee of the Dublin Women's Suffrage and Local Government Association for 1900* (Dublin, 1901).
Dublin Women's Suffrage and Local Government Association, *Suggestions for intending women working under the Local Government Act* (Dublin, 1901).
Dunraven, the Earl of, *Past Times and Pastimes Vols 1 & 2* (London, Hodder and Stoughton, 1922).
Dunraven, the Earl of, *The Crisis in Ireland* (Dublin, Hodges Figgis, 1905).
Dunraven, the Earl of, *The Outlook in Ireland: the case for devolution and conciliation* (Dublin, Hodges Figgis, 1907).
Elizabeth, Countess of Fingall, *Seventy Years Young: Memories of Elizabeth, Countess of Fingall told to Pamela Hinkson.*
'Escopette', *'Dreyfusing' a Class* (Dublin, Hodges Figgis, 1900).
Fahy, Francis A., *A Gaelic League Cathecism* (The Gaelic League of London, n.d.).
Fahy, Francis A., *The Irish Language Movement* (The Gaelic League of London, 1901).

Fenlon, J., 'Ireland and the Boers' in *The New Ireland Review* (February 1900).

Gaelic League, *The Irish Language and the New Intermediate Scheme* (Dublin, Gaelic League, 1900).

Gedney, C.W., *Angling Holidays in Search of Salmon, Trout and Pike* (Bromley, Kent, Telegraph Printing Works, 1896).

Gilbert, Stuart (ed.), *The Letters of James Joyce* (London, Faber and Faber, 1957).

Gonne, Maud, *A Servant of the Queen; Reminiscences by Maud Gonne MacBride,* edited by A. Norman Jeffares and Anna MacBride White (Gerrard's Cross, Colin Smythe, 1994).

Gould, Warwick, Kelly, John, and Toomey, Deidre, (eds), *The Collected Letters of W.B. Yeats Vol.2, 1896–1900* (Oxford, Clarendon Press, 1997).

Gregory, Lady Augusta, 'Felons of our Land' in *The Cornhill Magazine* (May 1900).

Gregory, Lady Augusta, *Ideals in Ireland* (London, Unicorn, 1901).

Gwynn, Stephen, *Today and Tomorrow in Ireland: essays on Irish subjects* (Dublin, Hodges Figgis, 1903).

Gwynn, Stephen, *The Fair Hills of Ireland* (Dublin, Maunsel, 1906).

Haslam Thomas, *Women's Suffrage from a masculine standpoint* (Dublin 1906).

Healy, T.M., *Letters and Leaders of my Day Vol 2* (London, Thornton Butterworth, 1928).

Hyde, Douglas, *A Literary History of Ireland* (London, Ernest Been, 1967); first published in 1899.

Irish Landowners' Convention, *The Irish Land Purchase Question* (Dublin, 1901).

Irish Landowners' Convention, *Irish Land Purchase Legislation: a memorandum on current land purchase proposals* (Dublin, Hodges Figgis, 1901).

Irish Unionist Alliance, *Speeches on Devolution by the Right Hon. Lord Atkinson of Glenwilliam* (Dublin, Irish Unionist Alliance, 1905).

Johnson, Clifton, *The Isle of the Shamrock* (London, Macmillan, 1901).

Johnston, Charles, *Ireland: historic and picturesque* (Philadelphia, Henry T. Coates, 1902).

Joyce, James, *A Portrait of the Artist as a Young Man* (London, 1916).

Joyce, James, *Dubliners* (Dublin, Richards, 1915).

Joyce, James, *Stephen Hero* (St Albans, Triad, 1977). First published in 1944.

Joyce, James, 'The Day of the Rabblement' in F.J.C. Skeffington and James A. Joyce, *Two Essays* (Dublin, 1901).

Joyce, James, *Ulysses* (New York, Random House, 1961).

Keating, Peter (ed.), *Into Unknown England, 1866–1913: selections from the social explorers* (Glasgow, Fontana Collins, 1976).

Langtoft, Geoffrey, *In and About Ireland: to the English people on the wrongs and woes of Ireland* (London 1901).

Langtoft, Geoffrey, *The Situation in Ireland* (London, n.d.).

Literary Ideals in Ireland (Dublin, Daily Express, 1899).

Longworth, Ernest Victor, *The Present State of Ireland* (Dublin, University Press, 1900).

Lucas, Reginald, *Colonel Saunderson, M.P.: a memoir* (London, John Murray, 1908).

Lynch, Arthur, *My Life Story* (London, John Long, 1924).

Lynd, Robert, *Home Life in Ireland (*London, Mills and Boon, 1909).

Mackail, J.W., and Wyndham, Guy (eds), *Life and Letters of George Wyndham, Vols 1&2* (London, Hutchinson, 1925).

McCann, James, *The Irish Problem: some pleas for the preservation of the Irish peasantry* (Dublin, Browne and Nolan, 1902).

McCarthy, Justin, *A Short History of Our Own Times* (London: Chatto and Windus, 1891).

McCarthy, Michael J.F., *Five Years in Ireland, 1895–1900,* Tenth Edition (Dublin, Hodges Figgis, 1903).

MacDonagh, Michael, 'In the bye-ways of rural Ireland, Parts 1&2', in *The Nineteenth Century*, Vol. XLVIII (July & August 1900).

MacDonagh, Michael, *The Home Rule Movement* (Dublin, Talbot Press, 1920).

Martyn, Edward, *Maeve* (London, Duckworth, 1917).

Micks, W.L., *A History of the Congested Districts Board* (Dublin, Eason, 1925).

Milligan, Alice, *The Last Feast of the Fianna* (London, David Nutt, 1900).

Moore, George, *Hail and Farewell,* (Gerrard's Cross, Colin Smythe, 1976). This book was first published in 1911.

Moore, George, 'Literature and the Irish language' in Gregory (ed.), *Ideals in Ireland* (London, Unicorn, 1901).

Moore, George, *The Bending of the Bough* (London, Fisher Unwin, 1900).

Moore, George, *The Lake* (London, William Heinemann, 1936). This book was first published in 1905.

Moore, George, *The Untilled Field* (London, Unwin, 1903).

Moran, D.P., 'The Gaelic Revival' in *New Ireland Review* (January 1900).

Moran, D.P., *The Philosophy of Irish Ireland* (Dublin, 1905).

Mulhall, M.G., *The Dictionary of Statistics*: Fourth Edition, revised to November 1898 (London, George Routledge, 1899).

O'Brien, R. Barry, *Dublin Castle and the Irish People*, Second Edition (London, Kegan Paul, 1912).

O'Brien, William, *Who Fears to Speak of Ninety-Eight?* (Dublin, Sealy, Bryers and Walker, 1898).

O'Casey, Seán, *Autobiographies, Vol.2: Pictures in the Hallway* (London, Pan Books, 1971).

O'Hickey, Rev. M.P., *The True National Idea* (Dublin, Gaelic League Pamphlet No. 1, 1899).

Oldham, C.H., *Economic Development in Ireland* (Dublin, Social and Statistical Inquiry Society of Ireland, 1900).

Paul-Dubois, Louis, *Contemporary Ireland* (Dublin, Maunsel, 1908).

Pethica, James (ed.), *Lady Gregory's Diaries, 1892–1902* (Gerrard's Cross, Colin Smythe, 1996).

Pim, Joseph Todhunter, *A Review of the Economic and Social Condition of Ireland* (Dublin, Thom, 1899).

Plunkett, Horace, 'Balfourian Amelioration in Ireland' in *The Nineteenth Century*, Vol. XLVIII (November 1900).

Plunkett, Horace, *Ireland in the New Century* (Dublin, Irish Academic Press, 1983).

Robinson, Henry A., *Memories: wise and otherwise* (London, Cassell, 1923).

Roche, Anthony, *The Sanitary Condition of Irish Schools* (Dublin, Sealy, Bryers and Walker, 1900).

Rolleston, T.W., *Ireland, the Empire and the War* (Dublin, Sealy, Bryers and Walker, 1900).

Russell, George (AE), *Controversy in Ireland: an appeal to Irish journalists* (Dublin, O'Donoghue, 1904).

Russell, George (AE), *Cooperation and Nationality* (Dublin, 1912).

Russell, George (AE), *The National Being: some thoughts on Irish polity* (Dublin, 1916).

Russell, T.W., *Compulsory Purchase in Ireland; five speeches made by T.W. Russell* (Dublin, Hodges Figgis, 1901).

Russell, T.W., *Ireland and the Empire* (London 1901).

Russell, T.W., *The Irish Land Question* (London 1902).

Russell, T.W. *The Irish Land Question Up-to-Date* (London, Swan, Sonnenschein, 1902).

Russell, T.W., *The Land Question and Compulsory Sale* (Belfast, The Northern Whig, 1900).

Sheehan, Canon, *Luke Delmerge* (London, Longmans, 1941).

Sheehan, Canon, *My New Curate* (Dublin, Talbot Press, 1942).

Skeffington, F.J.C. and Joyce, James A., *Two Essays* (Dublin, 1901).

Summerfield, Henry (ed.), *Selections from the contributions to the Irish Homestead by G.W. Russell (AE), Vol. 1* (Gerrard's Cross, Colin Smythe, 1978).

Sutherland, Hugh, *Ireland Yesterday and Today* (Philadelphia, The North American, 1909).

Thom's Official Directory of the United Kingdom of Great Britain and Ireland for the Year 1900 (Dublin, Thom Alex., 1900).

Tynan, Katharine, *Ireland* (Adam and Charles Black, 1909).

Tynan, Katharine, *The Middle Years* (London, Hutchinson, 1916).

Tynan, Katharine, *Twenty-Five Years: reminiscences* (London, Smith Elder, 1913).

United Irish League, *Constitution and Rules adopted by the Irish National Convention, 19–20 June 1900* (Dublin, United Irish League, 1900).

United Irish League of Great Britain, *Coercion in Ireland: what it means* (London, UIL of Great Britain Leaflet No. 4, n.d.).

United Irish League of Great Britain, *Ireland and the Coronation: why Ireland is discontented* (London, UIL of Great Britain Leaflet No. 2, 1902).

United Irish League of Great Britain, *Who is Sheridan?* (London, UIL of Great Britain Leaflet No. 1, n.d.).

Ulster Tenants' Defence Association, *Report of the Special Committee of the Ulster Tenants' Defence Association on the Report of the Fry Commission on the Working of the Irish Land Acts* (Belfast, 1898).

Victoria, Queen of England, *The Letters of Queen Victoria, Third series*, Vol. 3 (London, Murray, 1932).

Webb, Alfred, *The Humours of Law and Order in Ireland* (Dublin, Eason, 1902).

Weber, Adna Ferrin, *The Growth of Cities in the Nineteenth Century: a study in statistics* (New York, Macmillan, 1899).

Wiggin, Kate Douglas, *Penelope's Irish Experiences* (London, Gay and Bird, 1902).

Wilson Hunter, William, *A History of British India, Volumes 1 & 2* (London, Longmans Green, 1899 & 1900).

Yeats, W.B., *Autobiographies* (London, Bracken, 1955).

Yeats, W.B., *Plays for an Irish Theatre* (London, Bullen, 1913).

Yeats, W.B., *The Collected Plays of W.B. Yeats;* Second Edition (London, Macmillan, 1952).

Yeats, W.B., *The Collected Poems of W.B. Yeats;* Second Edition (London, Macmillan, 1950).

2. Later Works

A. Ireland at the Turn of the Century

Aalen, F.H.A., *The Iveagh Trust; the first hundred years, 1890–1990* (Dublin, Iveagh Trust, 1990).

Aalen, F.H.A., and Whelan, Kevin (eds), *Dublin City and County: from prehistory to the present* (Dublin, Geography Publications, 1992).

Adams, Michael, *Censorship: the Irish experience* (University of Alabama Press, 1968).

Bannon, Michael J. (ed.), *The Emergence of Irish Planning, 1880–1920* (Dublin, Turoe Press, 1985).

Bardon, Jonathan, *A History of Ulster* (Belfast, Blackstaff Press, 1992).

Bartlett, Thomas and Jeffery, Keith (eds), *A Military History of Ireland* (Cambridge University Press, 1996).

Beckett, J.C., *The Anglo-Irish Tradition* (London, Faber and Faber, 1976).

Bennett, Douglas, *Encyclopaedia of Dublin* (Dublin, Gill and Macmillan, 1994).

Bew, Paul, *Conflict and Conciliation in Ireland, 1890–1910: Parnellites and radical agrarians* (Oxford, Clarendon Press, 1987).

Bew, Paul, *John Redmond* (Dublin, Historical Association of Ireland, 1996).

Boyce, D. George, *Nationalism in Ireland,* (London, Croom Helm, 1982).

Boyce, D. George, *The Irish Question and British Politics, 1868–1996 Second Edition* (London, Macmillan, 1996).

Brady, Ciaran (ed.), *Worsted in the Game: losers in Irish history* (Dublin, Lilliput Press, 1989).

Brodie, Malcolm, *100 Years of Irish Football* (Belfast, Blackstaff Press, 1980).

Buckland, Patrick, *Irish Unionism 1: The Anglo-Irish and the New Ireland 1885–1922* (Dublin, Gill and Macmillan, 1972).

Buckland, Patrick, *Irish Unionism 2: Ulster Unionism and the origins of Northern Ireland 1886 to 1922* (Dublin, Gill and Macmillan, 1973).

Bull, Philip, *Land Politics and Nationalism: a study of the Irish land question* (Dublin, Gill and Macmillan, 1996).

Burke, Joanna, *Husbandry to Housewifery: women, economic change and housework in Ireland, 1890–1914* (Oxford, Clarendon Press, 1993).

Callanan, Frank, *T.M. Healy* (Cork, Cork University Press, 1996).

Campbell, Flann, *The Dissenting Voice; Protestant Democracy in Ulster from Plantation to Partition* (Belfast, The Blackstaff Press, 1991).

Cardozo, Nancy, *Maud Gonne* (New York, New Amsterdam Books, 1990).

Catholic Truth Society of Ireland, *First Fifty Years, 1899–1949* (Dublin, Veritas, 1949).

Cleeve, Brian *Dictionary of Irish Writers: first series* (Cork, Mercier Press, 1966).

Colum, Padraic, *Arthur Griffith* (Dublin, Browne and Nolan, 1959).

Connolly, S.J., (ed.), *The Oxford Companion to Irish History* (Oxford University Press, 1998).

Costello, Peter, *James Joyce* (Dublin, Gill and Macmillan, 1980).

Costello, Peter, *James Joyce: the years of growth, 1882–1915* (London, Kyle Cathie, 1992).

Craig, Patricia (ed.), *The Oxford Book of Ireland* (Oxford University Press, 1998)

Crossman, Virginia, *Politics, Law and Order in Nineteenth Century Ireland* (Dublin, Gill and Macmillan, 1996).

Cullen, L.M., *An Economic History of Ireland since 1660* (London, Batsford, 1972).

Curran, C.P., *Under the Receding Wave* (Dublin, Gill and Macmillan, 1970).

Curtis, L.P., Jr, *Coercion and Conciliation in Ireland 1880–1892: a study of conservative unionism* (Princeton University Press, 1963).

Daly, Mary E., 'Housing Conditions and the Genesis of Housing Reform in Dublin, 1880–1920' in Bannon, Michael, *The Emergence of Irish Planning, 1880–1920* (Dublin, Turoe Press, 1985).

Davis, Richard P., *Arthur Griffith and Non-Violent Sinn Féin* (Dublin, Anvil Books, 1974).

de Burca, Marcus, *The GAA: a history* (Dublin, Gaelic Athletic Association, 1980).

BIBLIOGRAPHY

Denman, Terence, 'The red livery of shame: the campaign against army recruitment in Ireland, 1899–1914' in *IHS*, No. 114 (November 1994).

Digby, Margaret, *Horace Plunkett: an Anglo-American Irishman* (Oxford, Basil Blackwell, 1949).

Dooley, Tom, 'The Royal Munster Fusiliers' in *History Ireland, Vol.6 No. 1*, (Spring 1998).

Dudley-Edwards, Ruth, *Patrick Pearse: the triumph of failure* (London, Victor Gollancz, 1977).

Dunleavy, Janet Egleston and Dunleavy, Gareth W., *Douglas Hyde: a maker of modern Ireland* (Berkeley, University of California Press, 1991).

Dunne, Seán, (ed.), *The Ireland Anthology* (Dublin, Gill and Macmillan, 1997).

Edwards, O.D., and Pyle, Fergus (eds), *1916: The Easter Rising* (London, MacGibbon and Kee, 1968).

Ellmann, Richard, *James Joyce* (Oxford University Press, 1966).

Ellmann, Richard, *Oscar Wilde* (London, Hamish Hamilton, 1987).

Ellmann, Richard, *W.B. Yeats: the man and the masks* (London, Faber and Faber, 1961).

English, Richard and Walker, Graham (eds), *Unionism in Modern Ireland: new perspective on politics and culture* (Dublin, Gill and Macmillan, 1996).

Fallis, Richard, *The Irish Renaissance: an introduction to Anglo-Irish literature* (Dublin, Gill and Macmillan, 1978).

Finneran, Richard, J., Mills Harper, George, and Murphy, William M. (eds), *Letters to W.B. Yeats* Volume 1 (London, Macmillan, 1977).

Ford, P and G., *A Breviate of Parliamentary Papers, 1900–1916* (Shannon, Irish University Press, 1969).

Foster, R.F., *Modern Ireland 1600–1972* (London, Allen Lane, 1988).

Foster, R.F., *Paddy and Mr Punch* (London, Penguin Books, 1995).

Foster, R.F., *W.B. Yeats: a life, Volume 1: the apprentice mage* (Oxford University Press, 1997).

Frayne, John P. (ed.), *Uncollected Prose by W.B. Yeats Vols. 1 and 2* (London, Macmillan, 1970 and 1975).

Gailey, Andrew, *Ireland and the Death of Kindness: the experience of constructive unionism, 1890–1905* (Cork University Press, 1987).

Gailey, Andrew, 'King Carson: an essay on the invention of leadership' in *Irish Historical Studies*, No. 117 (May 1996).

Garvin, Tom, *The Evolution of Irish Nationalist Politics* (Dublin, Gill and Macmillan, 1981).

Gaughan, J. Anthony, *Alfred O'Rahilly; 1: Academic* (Dublin, Kingdom Books, 1986).

Gorham, Maurice, *Dublin Yesterday* (London, B.T. Batsford, 1972).

Herlihy, Jim, *The Royal Irish Constabulary: a short history and genealogical guide* (Dublin, Four Courts Press, 1997).

Holroyd, Michael, *Bernard Shaw, Volume 2, 1898–1918: the pursuit of power* (London, Chatt & Windus, 1989).

Hone, Joseph (ed.), *J.B. Yeats: letters to his son, W.B. Yeats and others, 1869–1922* (London, Secker & Warburg, 1983).

Horgan, John J., *Parnell to Pearse: some recollections and reflections* (Dublin, Browne and Nolan, 1948).

Horn, Pamela, *The Rise and Fall of the Victorian Servant* (Dublin, Gill and Macmillan, 1975).

Igoe, Vivien, *A Literary Guide to Dublin* (London, Metheun, 1994).

Inglis, Brian, *Roger Casement* (London, Coronet, 1974).

Jackson, Alvin, *Colonel Edward Saunderson: Land and Loyalty in Victorian Ireland.* (Oxford University Press, 1995).

Jackson, Alvin, 'Irish Unionism and the Russelite threat, 1894–1906' in *Irish Historical Studies, No. 100* (November 1987).

Jackson, Alvin, 'The failure of unionism in Dublin, 1900' in *Irish Historical Studies*, No. 104 (November 1989).

Jackson, Alvin, *The Ulster Party; Irish unionists in the House of Commons, 1884–1911.* (Oxford University Press, 1989).

Jalland, Patricia, *The Liberals and Ireland; the Ulster question in British politics to 1914* (Brighton, The Harvester Press, 1980).

Jeffares, A. Norman (ed.), *W.B. Yeats Selected Criticism* (London, Pan Books, 1976).

Jeffares, A. Norman, *W.B. Yeats* (London, Hutchinson, 1988).

Kee, Robert, *The Green Flag: a history of Irish nationalism* (London, Weidenfeld and Nicholson, 1972).

Kiely, Benedict, *Yeats' Ireland: an illustrated anthology* (London, Tiger Books, 1994).

Kilroy, Jim, 'Galleon of the Streets - Irish Trams', in *History Ireland, Vol. 5 No. 2* (Summer 1997).

Kohfeldt, Mary Lou, *Lady Gregory: the woman behind the Irish renaissance* (London, Andre Deutsch, 1984).

Leslie, Shane, *Men Were Different: five studies in late Victorian biography* (London, Michael Joseph, 1937).

Lyons, F.S.L., *Charles Stewart Parnell* (London, Fontana, 1978).

Lyons, F.S.L., *Culture and Anarchy in Ireland 1890–1939* (Oxford, Clarendon Press, 1979).

Lyons, F.S.L., *John Dillon; a biography* (London, Routledge & Kegan Paul, 1968).

BIBLIOGRAPHY

Lyons, F.S.L., *The Irish Parliamentary Party 1890–1910* (London, Faber and Faber, 1951).

Maltby, Arthur and Maltby, Jean, *Ireland in the Nineteenth Century; a Breviate of Official Publications* (Oxford, Pergamon, 1979).

Manganiello, Dominic, *Joyce's Politics* (London, Routledge and Kegan Paul, 1980).

MacAodha, Brendan, 'Was this a social revolution' in Sean O Tuama (ed.), *The Gaelic League Idea* (Cork, Mercier Press, 1972).

MacBride White, Anna and Jeffares, A. Norman (eds), *Always your Friend: The Gonne-Yeats Letters 1893–1938* (London, Pimlico, 1993).

MacDonagh, Oliver, Mandle, W.F. and Travers, Pauric (eds), *Irish Culture and Nationalism 1750–1950* (London, Macmillan, 1983).

McMinn, J.R.B., 'Liberalism in North Antrim' in *Irish Historical Studies, No. 89* (May 1982).

Martin, F.X. and Byrne, F.J.(eds), *The Scholar Revolutionary: Eoin MacNeill, 1867– 1945* (Shannon, Irish University Press, 1973).

McCracken, Donal, *The Irish Pro-Boers* (Johannesburg, Perskor, 1989).

McDowell, R.B., *The Irish Administration 1801–1914* (London, Routledge & Kegan Paul, 1964).

Maddox, Brenda, *Nora: a biography of Nora Joyce* (London, Hamish Hamilton, 1988).

Mandle, W.F., *The Gaelic Athletic Association and Irish Nationalist Politics, 1884–1924* (London, Christopher Helm, 1987).

Maume, Patrick, *D.P. Moran* (Dublin, Historical Association of Ireland, 1995).

Mitchell, Arthur, *Labour in Irish Politics, 1890–1930* (Dublin, Irish University Press, 1974).

Montgomery, Bob, *An Irish Roadside Camera; Ireland's earliest motorists and their automobiles, 1896–1906* (Dublin, Marino Books, 1997).

Montgomery Hyde, H., *Carson: The Life of Sir Edward Carson, Lord Carson of Duncairn* (London, Constable, 1974).

Moody, T.W., 'The Irish University Question of the Nineteenth Century' in *History*, Vol. XLIII, No. 148 (June 1958).

Murphy, Cliona, *The Women's Suffrage Movement and Irish Society in the Early Twentieth Century* (New York, Harvester Wheatsheaf, 1989).

O'Brien, Conor Cruise (ed.), *The Shaping of Modern Ireland* (London, Routledge and Kegan Paul, 1960).

O'Connor, Emmet, *A Labour History of Ireland, 1824–1960* (Dublin, Gill and Macmillan, 1992).

O'Connor, Frank, *The Cornet Player Who Betrayed Ireland* (Dublin, Poolbeg Press, 1981).

O'Grada, Cormac, *Ireland: a new economic history, 1780–1939* (Oxford, Clarendon Press, 1994).

O'Halpin, Eunan, *The Decline of the Union: British Government in Ireland 1892–1920* (Dublin, Gill and Macmillan, 1987).

O'Nolan, Brian (Flann O'Brien), *The Best of Myles: a selection from 'Cruiskeen Lawn'* (London, Picador, 1977).

Ó Tuama, Sean (ed.), *The Gaelic League Idea* (Cork, Mercier Press, 1972).

Patterson, Henry, *Class Conflict and Sectarianism: the Protestant working class and the Belfast labour movement, 1868–1920* (Belfast, Blackstaff Press, 1980).

Pearl, Cyril, *Dublin in Bloomtime: the city James Joyce knew* (London, Angus and Robertson, 1969).

Pritchard, William H. (ed.), *W.B. Yeats: a critical anthology* (Harmondsworth, Penguin, 1972).

Shannon, Catherine B., *Arthur Balfour and Ireland 1874–1922* (Washington D.C., The Catholic University of America Press, 1988).

Sheehy-Skeffington, F., *Michael Davitt: revolutionary agitator and labour leader.* (London, Macgibbon & Kee, 1967).

Summerfield, Henry, *That Myriad Minded Man: a biography of George Russell.* (Gerrard's Cross, Colin Smythe, 1975).

Synge, J.M., *Collected Works, Volume 1: Poems* (Gerrard's Cross, Colin Smythe, 1982).

Thompson, William Irwin, *The Imagination of an Insurrection: Dublin, Easter 1916* (Oxford University Press, 1967).

Vaughan, W.E., (ed.), *A New History of Ireland VI: Ireland under the Union II, 1870– 1921* (Oxford, Clarendon Press, 1996).

Waldron, Jarlath, *Maamtrasna, the murder and the mystery* (Dublin, Edmund Burke, 1992).

Walker, B.M. (ed.), *Parliamentary Elections in Ireland 1801–1922* (Dublin, Royal Irish Academy, 1978).

Ward, Margaret, *In Their Own Voice: women and Irish nationalism* (Dublin, Attic Press, 1995).

Warwick-Haller, Sally, *William O'Brien and the Irish Land War* (Dublin, Irish Academic Press, 1990).

Welch, Robert, (ed.), *The Oxford Companion to Irish Literature* (Oxford, Clarendon Press, 1996).

West, Trevor, *Horace Plunkett, Co-operation and Politics: an Irish Biography.* (Washington, Catholic University of America Press, 1986).

BIBLIOGRAPHY

B.   The turn-of-the-century world

Briggs, Asa, and Snowman, Daniel (eds), *Fin de Siècle: how centuries end, 1400–2000* (New Haven, Yale University Press, 1996).

Bryan, C.D.B., *The National Geographic Society; one hundred years of adventure and discovery* (Oxford, Phaidon, 1987).

Burns, Michael, *Dreyfus: a family affair, 1789–1945* (London, Chatto and Windus, 1992).

Crankshaw, Edward, *The Fall of the House of Habsburg* (London, Longmans Green, 1963).

Davidson, Basil, *Africa in History: themes and outlines* (London, Granada, 1974).

Davies, Norman, *Europe: a history.* (Oxford University Press, 1996).

Gilbert, Martin, *A History of the Twentieth Century: Vol. 1, 1900–1933* (London, Harper Collins, 1997).

Harris, Jose, *Private Lives, Public Spirit: a social history of Britain 1870–1914.* (Oxford University Press, 1993).

Haslip, Joan, *The Lonely Empress; a biography of Elizabeth of Austria* (London, George Weidenfeld and Nicholson, 1965).

Hobsbawm, E.R., *The Age of Empire, 1875–1914* (London, Weidenfeld and Nicholson, 1987).

Hobsbawm, E.R., *The Age of Extremes: the short twentieth century, 1914–1991.* (London, Michael Joseph, 1994).

Hofmann, Paul, *The Viennese; splendor, twilight and exile* (New York, Doubleday, 1988).

Hopkirk, Peter, *The Great Game: the struggle for Empire in Central Asia.* (New York, Kodansha, 1994).

Jenkins, Roy, *Gladstone* (London, Macmillan, 1995).

Joll, James, *Europe Since 1870; an international history* (Harmondsworth, Pelican, 1976).

Keylor, William R., *The Twentieth Century World: an international history* (Oxford University Press, 1984).

Morris, James, *Farewell the Trumpets: an Imperial Retreat* (Harmondsworth, Penguin, 1979).

Muir, Ramsay, *The Expansion of Europe; the culmination of modern history* (London, Constable, 1917).

O'Farrell, Patrick, *The Irish in Australia* (New South Wales University Press, 1987).

Pakenham, Thomas, *The Boer War* (George Weidenfeld & Nicholson, 1979).

Pakenham, Thomas, *The Scramble for Africa* (London, Weidenfeld and Nicolson, London, 1991).

Pollard, Sydney, *The Idea of Progress; history and society* (Harmondsworth, Pelican, 1971).

Röhl, J.C.G., *From Bismarck to Hitler; the problem of continuity in German history* (London, Longman, 1970).

Romein, Jan, *Watershed of Two Eras: Europe in 1900* (Middletown Connecticut, Wesleyan University Press, 1976).

Schlesinger, Jr, Arthur, 'Has Democracy a Future' in *Foreign Affairs, Vol. 76, No. 5* (September/October 1997).

Skidelsky John, *John Maynard Keynes: hopes betrayed, 1883–1920* (London, Macmillan, 1983).

Strachey, Lytton, *Queen Victoria* (London, Chatto and Windus, 1969: first published in 1921).

Tannenbaum, Edward R., *1900: the generation before the Great War* (New York, Doubleday, 1976).

Taylor, A.J.P., *Essays in English History* (Harmondsworth, Pelican, 1976).

Taylor, A.J.P., *The Habsburg Monarchy, 1809–1918: a history of the Austrian Empire and Austro-Hungary* (Harmondsworth, Penguin, 1985).

Thomson, David, *Europe Since Napoleon* (London, Longmans, 1957).

Tuchman, Barbara, *The Proud Tower; a portrait of the world before the war, 1895–1914.* (London, Macmillan, 1980).

Wilson, Angus, *The Strange Ride of Rudyard Kipling; his life and works* (London, Granada, 1979).

Woodcock, George, *Anarchism: a history of libertarian ideas and movements* (Harmondsworth, Pelican, 1975).

Index

A

Act, of Union, 5, 14, 22, 68, 125, 152
Adams, Henry, 189–190
Africa, 179, 183
Agriculture, 64–65, 209
Allen, Fred, 22
All Ireland Review, 109, 202
Anarchism, 194
Ancient Order of Hibernians, 117
Anglo-Irish Treaty, 1921, 14, 205
Antrim, County, 49, 60, 124
Ardilaun, Lord, 88, 138, 210
Asia, 186
Association Football, 74–75
Atkinson Robert, 108
Auden, W.H., 164
Austin, Alfred, 57–58, 68, 84
Australia, 50–51, 102, 204
Austro-Hungarian Empire, 176–178

B

Balfour, Arthur, 119–120, 125, 127, 138
Balfour, Gerald, 110, 127, 134, 138, 141.
Barnacle, Nora, 34
Battle of the Boyne, 14
Beckett, Samuel, 212
Belfast, 44, 49, 59–60, 64, 70, 142
Belfast Newsletter, The, 103, 143
Birth rates, 46
Bismarck, Otto von, 177
Blackrock College, Dublin, 24, 26
Blunt, Wilfrid Scawen, 80, 191
Boer War, 4, 8, 18–19, 21, 26, 49, 58, 68, 88–89, 91, 96–105, 114, 118–119, 125, 131, 138–139, 151, 180, 186, 204, 212
    Irish unionist attitude towards, 103–104
    pro-Boer sentiment in Ireland, 22, 26, 40, 96, 98–101, 106, 204
Boucicault, Dion, 157–158
Bould Thady Quill, The, 64

Boxer Rebellion, 180, 188
British Army, 29, 88, 102–103
British Empire, 5, 9, 87, 93, 98, 101–102, 114, 120, 125–126, 175, 178–179, 183, 204–206, 213
Bryant, William Jennings, 187
Buller, Redvers, 131
Byrne, J.F., 149

C

Cadogan, Earl of, 19, 126
Campbell, Mrs Pat, 158
Canada, 102
Carson, Edward, 59, 119, 134, 172
Casement, Roger, 97
Catholic Church, 9, 36, 60, 64, 106, 113–116, 192–193, 203–204, 210–211
Catholic Truth Society of Ireland, 115, 148, 203, 205
Censorship, 150, 205
Census of Population of 1901, 31, 46, 51
Chamberlain, Houston Stewart, 177
Chamberlain, Joseph, 97–98, 177, 192
Childers, Erskine, 97
China, 179, 187, 189
Chotek, Sophie, 176–177
Churchill, Winston, 97
Church of Ireland, 9
Claidheamh Soluis, An, 107, 155, 160, 202
Clancy, George, 149
Clonmacnoise, County Offaly, 82
Coleraine, County Derry, 137
Colles, Ramsay, 27–28
Collins, Michael, 208
Colonialism, 177–189
Congested Districts Board, The, 46, 54–55, 62, 129
Connaught, Arthur, Duke of, 131
Connaught Rangers, 104, 180–181
Connolly, James, 27, 97–98, 117, 208

Conservative unionism, 15, 133–135, 138
Constructive unionism, 8–9, 15, 46, 124, 135, 137–141
Cooper, Rev. A.N., 84
Cork, 52, 64, 72, 84, 182, 195, 200
Corkery, Daniel, 170
Cousins, Margaret, 196
Craig, James, 97
Crime, 27, 30–37
Crossley, F.W., 81
Cultural nationalism, 8, 92, 112–131, 166–170
Cumann na nGaedheal, 30, 116
Curragh Mutiny, 131
Cycling, 77–78

D

Daily Mail, The, 79, 139
Daily Nation, The, 39
Davies, Norman, 13–14
Davis, Thomas, 159
Davitt, Michael, 40, 87, 100, 119, 139–140, 204
    Boer Fight for Freedom, The, 100
Delgany, County Wicklow, 76
Department of Agriculture and Technical Instruction, 8, 44, 51, 60, 64, 129, 135, 144, 195, 200
Derrycreagh, County Cork, 111
De Valera, Eamon, 198–199, 205–207
Diarmuid and Grania (George Moore and W.B. Yeats), 152 155, 158, 163
Dillon, James, 205
Dillon, John, 12, 23, 51, 93, 98, 139–140, 208
Disease, 72–74, 192
Dodder River, 31
Domestic servants, 31–35
Dowden, Edward, 138
Down, County, 49, 60, 124
Doyle, Arthur Conan, 97

Dreyfus, Alfred, 132, 195–196
Dublin, 49, 55, 58, 60, 69–70, 73, 88
Dublin Castle, 12, 22, 28, 30, 38, 98, 101, 106, 117, 127
Dublin Corporation, 2, 22, 49, 73, 117–118
Dublin Daily Express, The, 18–19, 89, 138
Dublin Metropolitan Police, 27, 31, 33, 36
Dunraven, Earl of, 123, 139–141, 204, 208

E
Easter Rising of 1916, 8, 14, 27, 205, 210
Economic conditions, 44, 46, 64
Economic war, 205
Education, 54, 107–108, 110, 114
Egan, James, 26
'Eglinton', John, 166
Elizabeth, Empress of Austria, 194
Elizabeth II, Queen, 205
Emigration, 49–52, 192, 209
Emmet, Robert, 212
European Union, 207, 209–210

F
Fahy, Francis A., 108–109
Farrell, 'Digger', 27
Feis Ceoil, 88, 210
Fianna Fáil Party, 106, 207
Fine Gael Party, 206
Fingall, Countess of, 127
Finlay, Fr Thomas, 112
Fishing industry, 46–47
Flower, Henry, 31–34
Flying of nationalist flags, 22, 96
Ford, Henry, 80–81
Fortnightly Review, The, 153
Foster, R.F., 96
France, 5, 178–179, 183, 193–196
Franz Ferdinand, Archduke, 176–177
Franz Joseph, Emperor of Austria, 177–178
Freeman's Journal, The, 39, 100, 153
French, Percy, 19, 23–24, 26, 29
French Revolution, 14, 178

G
Gaelic Athletic Association, 8, 75, 101, 117–118, 210

Gaelic football, 75
Gaelic League, 8–9, 107–112, 118, 120, 150, 165, 203, 210, 212
Galway, 201
Gandhi, Mahatma, 97
Gannon, Bridget, 31–34
Gavan Duffy, Charles, 159
General Election of 1900, 41, 143
Germany, 5, 177–179, 183, 193, 206–207
Giant's Causeway, County Antrim, 83
Gill, T.P., 138
Gladstone, William Ewart, 8, 68, 124–125, 132, 134–135
Glasgow, 64, 73, 192
Gogarty, Oliver St John, 100
Golf, 75–77
Gonne, Maud, 13, 17, 26–28, 98, 106, 116–117, 152, 165, 168, 170, 193
Good Friday Agreement of 1998, 197, 207–208
Gorey, County Wexford, 6
Government of Ireland Act of 1920, 14
Grafton Street, Dublin, 4, 88
Grand Parade, Cork, 11
Great Famine, 13, 46, 64, 160
Great War, 14, 64, 85, 88, 96, 139, 204–205, 207
Gregory, Lady Augusta, 109, 150, 154, 163, 168
Griffith, Arthur, 27, 30, 40, 87, 97–98, 116, 124, 162, 204, 208, 212
Gweedore, County Donegal, 48
Gwynn, Stephen, 55, 102

H
Hague Conference, 1899, 183
Harrel, David, 128
Harrington, Timothy, 12, 32–33, 40, 139
Haslam, Thomas, 119
Health standards, 69–74
Healy, Tim, 13, 22, 38–39, 93, 98, 208
Hicks-Beach, Michael, 125
Hobsbawm, Eric, 14
Hobson, J.A., 179
Holland, John P., 190
Holloway, Joseph, 158, 162
Holy Year, 1900, 9, 113–114

Home Rule, 8, 15, 87, 89, 91, 93, 119, 132, 154, 207–208
Home Rule Bill, 1912, 14
Housing, 53, 59–60
Hurling, 75
Hyde, Douglas, 107, 113, 163, 170, 171, 212
  Casadh an tSúgáin, 163
  Literary History of Ireland. A, 107–108, 170
  Love Songs of Connaught, 170
  Religious Songs of Connaught, 170

I
Ibsen, Henrik, 153
Ideals in Ireland, 155
Ighninidhe na hEireann, 30, 117
Infant mortality, 44, 72
Inniskillings Regiment, 104
Irish Catholic, The, 114
Irish Civil War, 205
Irish Cyclist, The, 77
Irish Daily Independent, The, 39
Irish Figaro, The, 27
Irish Free State, 205
Irish Guards Regiment, 22, 185
Irish Homestead, The, 166, 167, 202
Irish Independent, The, 202
Irish Ireland ideas, 30, 107, 109, 112–113, 155, 157, 170–171, 198–199, 202–204, 207–212
Irish labour movement, 9, 51
Irish Landowners' Convention, 132–133, 138
Irish language, revival of, 8, 107, 113, 159–160, 170–171, 210
Irish literary revival, 8, 150–151, 159–162
Irish Literary Theatre, 88, 154, 160–163
Irish newspapers, 14, 18, 39
Irish Parliamentary Party, 8, 15, 39–41, 89, 92–93, 96, 102, 105–107, 110, 140, 208
Irish People, The, 39, 105, 166
Irish Reform Association, 140, 145
Irish Republican Brotherhood, 105–106, 117
Irish Socialist Republican Party, 58, 117
Irish Statesman, The, 167
Irish Times, The, 18–19, 133, 163
Irish Tourist, The, 81, 85
Irish Transvaal Brigade, 103

Irish Transvaal Committee, 27, 98–99
Irish unionism, 9, 12, 19, 24, 88, 132–135, 208
Irish Unionist Alliance, 132
Irish Volunteers, 27, 128, 205
Irish Weekly Independent, The, 87, 163
Irish Wheelman, The, 77–78
Italy, 179, 193–194
Iveagh, Lord, 97

J
Japan, 187, 189
Johnston, Charles, 199, 201
Johnston, William, 69, 199, 202
Joyce, James, 13, 34, 80, 88, 93, 98, 100, 138, 147, 149, 151–54, 163, 169, 202–203, 207, 210–211
   Day of the Rabblement, The, 154
   Finnegan's Wake, 34
   A Portrait of the Artist as a Young Man, 93, 151, 153, 183, 203
   Stephen Hero, 151, 153
   Ulysses, 34, 60, 138, 152

K
Kavanagh, Hannah, 31, 35
Kerry, 96–97, 104, 131
Kettle, Thomas, 88
Keynes, John Maynard, 18
Kilkenny People, The, 37
Killarney, County Kerry, 57
Killiney Hill, 18, 124
Killybegs, County Donegal, 62
King Edward VII, 24
Kingstown, 18, 23, 24, 60
Kipling, Rudyard, 97, 131, 173, 180, 187
Kim, 173, 180
Kitchener, Lord, 96, 102, 131, 186
Kruger, Paul, 22, 98, 104, 195

L
Labour Movement, 193
Ladysmith, 103–104, 131
Land question, 66, 68–69, 106, 127–128, 132–133, 139–140, 208–209
Land reform legislation, 8, 66, 68–69, 132, 135, 209
Lansdowne, Lord, 125
Larkin, Jim, 40

Leader, The, 15, 49, 74, 84, 112–113, 150, 155, 165, 202
Lecky, W.E.H., 119, 138
Leeson Street Bridge, Dublin, 24, 26
Lenin, 194
Lever, Charles, 148
Liberal Party, 91, 125–126
Liberal Unionism, 141
Life expectancy, 44, 192
Limerick, 53, 73
Listowel, County Kerry, 7
Literacy, 112, 148
Literary Ideals in Ireland, 155
Living conditions, 51–60, 209
Lloyd George, David, 97
Local Government Act of 1898, 8, 93, 96, 118–119, 132–133, 135, 143, 204
Local Government Board, 37, 73, 129
Logue, Cardinal, 27, 69, 104, 115, 160
Londonderry, Marquis of, 134
London, Jack, 73
Lord Jim (Conrad), 180
Lough Derg, County Donegal, 95
Lynch, Arthur, 139
Lynd, Robert, 53, 55

M
MacBride, Major John, 26, 28, 32, 40
MacDonagh, Michael, 198, 202
MacDonald, Ramsey, 144
MacDonnell, Anthony, 140
'MacLeod, Fiona', 168
MacNeill, Eoin, 109
Mafeking, 104, 132
Mahaffy, John Pentland, 108
Mallon, John, 28
Mannix, Archbishop Daniel, 115
Marconi, Gugliemo, 190
Markievicz, Countess Constance, 88, 117
Marriage, 46
Martyn, Edward, 160–162
   Heather Field, The, 160
   Maeve, 161–162
Maynooth, 115
McAleese, President Mary, 205
McCarthy, Justin, 92
McKinley, President James, 186–187, 191

Middle class life, 58–59
Millennium, 13, 212
Milligan, Alice, 162
Moore, George, 108, 148, 150–153, 158, 161–164, 166–167, 172, 203, 212
   Bending of the Bough, The, 161–162
   Hail and Farewell, 151–152
   Lake, The, 152, 172
   Untilled Field, The, 152
Moore, Colonel Maurice, 152
Moran, D.P., 84–85, 101, 109–110, 112–113, 116, 137, 155, 158, 165, 202, 204
Mortality rates, 72
Motoring, 79–81
Muir, Ramsay, 179
Murphy, William Martin, 40

N
Nationalism, 12, 107, 180, 183
New Ireland Review, 112, 155, 162, 168, 170, 202
New Tipperary, 61
New Zealand, 102, 204
Nineteenth Century, The, 180, 198
Nobel Peace Prize, 183, 187

O
O'Brien, William, 12, 15, 23, 37–40, 61, 68, 93, 105–107, 139–140, 154, 208
O'Casey, Sean, 58–59, 73, 101, 148, 169, 212
O'Connell Bridge, Dublin, 3
O'Connell, Daniel, 15, 87, 199, 206
O'Connell Street, Dublin, 27
O'Connor, Frank, 93
O'Donnell, John, 40–41
O'Grady, James Standish, 109, 155, 167, 170
O'Leary, John, 116, 159
Olympic Games, 77, 183
Optimism, 189–191
O'Rahilly, Alfred, 26
O'Shea, Katherine, 92

P
Parnell, Anna, 23, 26
Parnell, Charles Stewart, 5, 7, 9, 13–15, 26, 32, 87, 91–93, 101, 124, 195

Parnell, John, 23, 26, 40–41, 119
Paul-Dubois, Louis, 53
Pawnbrokers, 58
Pearse, Patrick, 13, 110, 160, 170, 208
Penal Laws, 13
Phoenix Park, Dublin, 21, 28
Pile, Thomas Devereux, 22, 26
Pioneer Total Abstinence Association, 11, 115
Plunkett, Horace, 9, 40–41, 44, 64, 79, 110, 123, 135–139, 141, 144–145, 165, 203–204, 208, 212
Pope Leo XIII, 9, 113
Popular literature, 115 –117, 148
Popular theatre, 157–158
Population decline, 46, 49
Port Magee, County Kerry, 47
Port Rush, County Antrim, 83
Power, Tyrone, 158
Princip, Gavrilo, 176

Q
Queenstown, 49
Queen Victoria, 18, 104, 131, 194
    Royal Jubilees of 1887 and 1897, 19, 165
    visit to Ireland in April 1900, 18–30, 84, 45, 152, 165
        Nationalist reaction to visit, 22–24, 30
        Unionist reaction to visit, 24, 29

R
Rathmines, 27, 49
Railways, 60, 84
Rebellion of 1798, 89, 91, 165,
Recess Committee, 135
Redmond, John, 13, 22–23, 39, 93, 110, 139, 208
Reed, Andrew, 101
Revisionist view of Irish history, 13
Rhodes, Cecil, 180
Roberts, Lord Frederick, 26, 103, 131, 185, 206, 212
Rolleston, T.W., 101–102
Rooney, William, 30, 116
Roosevelt, Theodore, 187
Royal Dublin Fusiliers, 88, 101, 104, 180, 188, 212
Royal Irish Constabulary (RIC), 30, 59, 67, 77, 129

Royal yacht, Victoria and Albert, 18, 23
Rugby football, 74–75
Rural deprivation, 48, 51–55, 66
Russell, George (AE), 53, 69, 112–113, 150, 166–170
    Feast of Age, The, 167
    Ideals in Ireland: priest or hero?, 166
Russell, Lord, 195
Russell, T.W., 44, 60, 68–69, 119, 139, 141, 143–145, 208
Russia, 49, 178, 186–187, 189, 193–194

S
St Patrick's Day, 2, 22–23, 64, 103
St Stephen's Green, Dublin, 79, 88, 212
Salisbury, Marquis of, 19, 102, 119, 125
Sarajevo, 176
Saunderson, Colonel Edward, 103, 144
Schools, 49–50, 53–54, 110
Seasonal migration, 51–52
Sea transport, 84
Second World War, 205–206
Shamrock, wearing of, 22–23
Shaw, George Bernard, 97, 148
    Fabianism and the Empire, 97
Sheehan, Canon Patrick, 9, 171–172
    Luke Delmerge, 171
    My New Curate, 9, 171, 172
Shipbuilding, 64
Sinn Féin, 15, 106, 116, 162, 204–205
Sipido, Jean-Baptiste, 24, 194
Skeffington, Francis, 183
South Mayo by-election, 26, 40–41
Soviet Union, 14
Spanish-American War, 5
Spencer, Lord, 194
Sport, 74–79
Stalin, 193
Stoker, Bram, 1, 32
    Dracula, 1
Strachey, Lytton, 29
Suffragism, 118–119
Sullivan, A.M., 148
Sutherland, Hugh, 52
Synge, John Millington, 30, 116, 160, 162, 163, 169, 212

Playboy of the Western World, The, 30, 116, 160

T
Taxation, 104–105, 135
Temperance, 11, 36, 60, 115
Templetown, Lord, 133
Tennis, 77
Times, The, 19
Titanic, 50
Tone, Theobald Wolfe, 22, 88, 165
Tourism, 81–85
Tramore, County Waterford, 82
Tramways, 60
Treasury of Irish Poetry, A, 169
Trinity College, Dublin, 4, 19, 31, 103–104, 129, 134, 170
Turkey, 117–178
Turner, William, 190–191
Tynan, Katharine, 127, 167

U
Ulster, 12, 68, 96, 131, 208
Ulster Tenants' Defence Association, 144
Ulster Unionism, 134, 138, 141–144
Ulster Unionist Council, 145
Ulster Volunteers, 14
United Irish League, 15, 37–41, 44, 55, 61, 66, 69–91, 93, 101, 105–107, 114, 120, 126, 129
United Irishman, The, 27, 30, 103, 116, 155, 158, 202
United States of America, 5, 50, 85, 92, 196–187, 191
Universal Exhibition, Paris, 77, 80, 194–195
University question, 107, 114, 120, 127, 132, 143
Urban poverty, 45, 55, 58–60, 69

V
Verne, Jules, 2

W
Wages, 58–59
Walsh, Archbishop of Dublin, 27
War of Independence, 8, 149
Waterford, 65, 84, 101
Waterford County Council, 26
Weekly, Freeman, The 37, 50
Westmeath County Council, 37
Westport, 53

INDEX

White, General George, 103
Wilde, Oscar, 172
Wilson Hunter, William, 186
Wiggin, Kate Douglas, 52, 84
Wilhelm, II, German Emperor, 5, 18, 144, 177–179
Workers Republic, The, 202
Workhouses, 35, 59, 69–70, 118
Working conditions, 192
Wyndham, George, 54, 69, 97, 123, 127, 40–141, 145, 204

Y
Yeats, Jack B, 157
Yeats, William Butler, 1, 13, 15, 17, 23, 28, 32, 88–89, 100, 112, 116, 138, 147–148, 150, 152, 154–155, 157–169, 171, 199, 203, 211–212
Countess Cathleen, The, 116, 153, 160
Green Helmet and other poems, The, 164
In the Seven Woods, 164
Kathleen ni Houlihan, 165

Responsibilities, 164
Shadowy, Waters, The, 155, 157, 164–165
Wild Swans at Coole, The, 165
Wind among the Reeds, The, 163

Z
Zeppelin, Ferdinand von, 190
Zola, Émile, 191